INFERENCE AND STATISTICS IN SPSS

A Course for Business and Social Science

By Gwilym Pryce

GeeBeeJey Publishing

Published by GeeBeeJey Publishing

Email: g@geebeejey.co.uk
Website: www.geebeejey.co.uk

First edition published in Glasgow, Scotland, 2005

Printed in Scotland by Summit Media and Print:

Summit Media and Print
Units 15 + 16 Fleming Court
Clydebank Business Park
Clydebank
West Dunbartonshire
G81 2DR
Tel:0141 952 0008
Fax:0141 952 4632

ISBN 0-9551433-0-6

Contents:

Acknowledgements

My thanks to students and tutors, past and present, for their comments on earlier versions of this text. I would also like to express particular gratitude to my wife Dinah for her help with various stages of production. Thanks also to my son Ben for his patience with a rather preoccupied father during the creation of this book.

To Ben,
my Champion of the World

1 Introduction and Basic Concepts

Aim
The aim of this chapter is to clarify the structure and purpose of the book, and to review some of the basic concepts that underpin future chapters.

Objectives
By the end of this chapter you should be able to understand the difference between a variable and a constant, be able to distinguish between categorical and continuous variables and the various types of categorical variables; and understand the main ways of summarising data using tables, graphs and descriptive statistics. In addition, you should have made your first steps towards understanding the structure of SPSS and be able to perform basic data inputting, graphing and statistical procedures in SPSS.

Plan

1.1 Why Study Statistics?

Why do social scientists (I include business and management students under this heading) need to learn about statistics? This may be a topic on which you have strong views and on which nothing I say will dissuade you. You may share the view expressed (somewhat tongue in cheek) by the former Chief Economist of Scottish Homes that 'you should never work with children, animals or data'. You may have a deep-seated fear of numbers and mathematical symbols ('the stigma of sigma'[1]). You anticipate purgatory as you embark on re-living your traumatic childhood experience of classroom mathematics. Perhaps you are doing this course because it is a compulsory component of your degree or because your employer insists that you need to acquire certain skills. I may not be able to fully convince you that the benefits of studying statistics outweigh the costs, but it will considerably increase your chances of success, and alleviate some of the agony of learning the subject, if you will at least consider the following arguments:

A theory, unless verified empirically, remains a conjecture

> Even the purest theorists acknowledge the need to substantiate the assumptions and conclusions of their ideas. True, data are often inadequate to provide irrefutable proof, but the reasonable approach is to weigh up the evidence that *is* available and consider which theory, on balance, is most likely to correspond to reality. There is a caveat to be learnt here, though, for both the theorist and the empiricist: that a little agnosticism (and not a little scepticism) is usually a good thing when seeking to verify social and behavioural theories.

---

[1] *Ibid.*

Need for evidenced-based practice & policy

Policy and business decisions have to (and will) be made, irrespective of the quality of data. An informed decision is clearly better than an uninformed one, but the reality is that governments and company directors often make major strategic decisions on the basis of very little evidence. It is the role of statistically-aware social scientists and business analysts to inform the decision-making process both by making the most of the data that are available and by advising on what data are needed. This role is crucial to achieving the objective that now underpins most government funded research; that of achieving *evidenced-based policy.*

Greater availability of data and processing power

Economic and social data have dramatically increased in both quality and quantity over the past century and continue to do so, aided partly by the geometric expansion in computer processing power (with associated declining costs in data collection and processing), by greater financial resources invested into data collection (due to the post war prosperity of developed countries), and by continued development and dissemination of statistical theory and application. It would be foolish not to make use of these remarkable resources.

Information is complex and needs summarising

Too much data results in noise. Growth in human intelligence has spectacularly failed to keep pace with the growth in information! In order to harness this burgeoning resource, rather than be overwhelmed by it, we need techniques that will help us to categorise and summarise information, and draw the most appropriate conclusions from the mass of evidence available. That is the goal and purpose of statistics.

1.1.1 Why do we Need so Many Statistical Techniques?

'If I know how to calculate an average, I have all the statistical knowledge a social scientist needs'. This view was not uncommon among social scientists until remarkably recently, driven partly by a prevalent insecurity amongst the profession with respect to their own numerical literacy and partly by a misconception regarding the purpose of complex statistical techniques.

The *mean*, also called the *average*, is computed as the sum of values divided by the number of values. It can tell you a lot about a *variable.* (A variable is simply a list of numbers that describe some attribute or phenomena). It tells you the typical value of the entity you are trying to measure and is a good summary statistic. But suppose the variable you want to measure is the gender of victims of sexual abuse or the country of origin of computer viruses. (Such variables are called *categorical* variables, which allocate an observation to a particular category; as opposed to *continuous* variables, which measure phenomena along a continuum). What use is the average there? A more meaningful measure, of course, would be simply the *proportion* of observations in each category.

But suppose your data on sexual abuse or computer viruses are merely a *sample* of observations? Indeed, it is very unlikely that you would be able to observe data on **all** sexual abuse cases that have ever happened or **all** computer viruses that have ever been circulated. If you don't have information on what statisticians call the *population* or *universe* of observations, how do you know what you can reasonably infer from your sample?

Intuition will tell you that your sample may not be as good as having information on all cases, but it does tell you something. It seems highly improbable that if only 10% of your *sample* of sexual abuse victims are male, that the proportion in the *population* of sexual abuse cases will be 80% male, or even 50% for that matter. A little application of the laws of probability will allow you to make some statement about the likelihood that the proportion of males in the population of sexual abuse victims is, say, greater than 20% (this would be called a *hypothesis test*); or to obtain an estimate of the likely range of values of the proportion in the population. For example, you might want to be able to say that you are 95% sure that the proportion of sexual abuse victims that are male lies between 5.5% and 15.5% – this sort of statement is called a *confidence interval.*

Suppose again that the sample you have is only very small (say, less than 30 observations) which means that the usual law of probability used to calculate hypothesis tests and confidence intervals starts to break down (the law in question is called the *Central Limit Theorem* (CLT) which says that even if the variable in question does not have a *normal* – i.e. bell-shaped – distribution, the means from repeated samples will, provided the sample sizes are large). What are you to do? All is not lost. You just need to employ a slightly more complex piece of statistical machinery called the *t-distribution* which tells you how to correct your estimates when your sample is small.

But it turns out that even the t-distribution has its limits. You can only use it when your (small) sample has a normal distribution. So you actually need another set of statistical tools called *non-parametric* techniques, so-called because they make no assumption about the *parameters* – or essential qualities – of the distribution of your variable.

Finally, suppose you don't just want to say something about the proportion or mean of a single variable, but to look for evidence of a relationship between **two or more** variables. This sounds simple enough, but the appropriate statistical techniques are actually quite complex and depend again on the nature of your data. If your data are continuous, you can use what is called *regression analysis* which allows you to draw the line of best fit between two variables. You can use this technique if the variable you want to explain (the *dependent variable*) is continuous even if the *explanatory variables* (the variables that explain or determine your dependent variable) are categorical. Rather less flexible, but still very popular, is *analysis of variance* (ANOVA) which allows you to see how the mean of your dependent variable changes across the categories of another variable. If both your dependent variable and your explanatory variable are categorical, you need to use *two-way tables* and *Chi-square tests*.

A picture is beginning to emerge of why we need so many, and such complicated, statistical tests. The complexity is driven by the range of things we want to do with our data and also the nature of data itself. The crucial thing to remember is that you must find the appropriate statistical technique for your data. If your data are continuous, based on the population (the latter quality is highly unlikely) and you are only interested in one variable, then the mean might just be all you need.

Even so, you'll probably want to say something about the *variation* in your data. For example, your average body temperature may be recorded as normal even though you have placed your head in a hot oven and your feet in the freezer! A course in statistics will hopefully help you to be rather more careful. Sometimes a simple question requires very complex methods to find an answer. What you must avoid is using a technique the assumptions of which are violated by your data (that's when you end up with nothing but 'lies, damn lies and statistics'[2]).

1.1.2 *Why do we Need Mathematics?*

Statistics can be represented in a non-mathematical way, which we shall attempt here as far as possible, but some understanding and application of basic mathematics will help you. First, spoken language can be ambiguous and varies in interpretation and application across countries and cultures. Mathematical notation, on the other hand, is unambiguous, concise and understood across all major cultures and languages. It is the true *lingua franca* of the modern age. Indeed, it's worth bearing in mind that if you can express your research and ideas in mathematical notation you will be more likely to reach an international audience. It is also the language used by many of the statistical texts you may have need to refer to over the course of your research career, and is increasingly used by social science journals. So some investment in learning the language of mathematics at this stage is worthwhile. Second, it is difficult to accurately and succinctly describe complex formulae in words. Even though computers will do our calculations for us, it is often useful and sometimes essential to be able to check our results by hand. This means that while you won't be required to prove or manipulate mathematical formulae in this text, you will need to know how to read and apply them.

[2] 'There are three kinds of lies: lies, damned lies, and statistics' – attributed to Benjamin Disraeli (1804-81) by Mark Twain. The statistician's retort is that it is indeed possible to lie with statistics but that it's easier to lie without them...

1.1.3 Overview of the Book

I believe the approach used in this text to be unique. To my knowledge, it offers the only primer in classical statistics that is truly integrated into SPSS. A number of texts teach SPSS and a myriad teach statistics. However, because SPSS does not have built-in procedures for the more basic classical statistical tests (no shortage of advanced ones!) most courses teach theory and practice in a disjointed way. A particular problem is that SPSS does not easily allow you to run a statistical test when you only have access to summary data. For example, if you are reading a published report or journal article and you want to estimate the *confidence interval* for the mean of a variable, which may be crucial to the conclusions of that publication, it is unlikely that the canned procedures in SPSS will be able to assist because you do not have the original data used by the author to calculate the mean. But you need only the mean, standard deviation and sample size to calculate a confidence interval, so it would be useful to have an automated procedure with the flexibility to take advantage of such summary information.

A third problem relates to the way SPSS calculates certain statistics: the built-in method may not be the most appropriate for your data and it is not always easy to tell unless you have spent considerable time trawling through the manuals. Nevertheless, SPSS offers one of the most user-friendly menu systems of any advanced statistical program, and has an unrivalled interface for inputting and viewing raw data. So there is much to be gained from adding some basic commands to SPSS using its macro programming language to allow users to run statistical tests using only summary data. With these commands added, SPSS becomes a more complete and versatile package, offering the social science researcher pretty much everything he or she needs to do basic statistical analysis either on his/her own data, or on the published results of other authors. **The macros and installation instructions are available from the Downloads page of www.geebeejey.co.uk where you will find copies of the files and installation instructions. Printouts of these files are also included as appendices at the end of this text.**

1.1.4 Aim

The goal of this text is to lead the reader through both the basics of statistical inference and the basics of SPSS. I try to assume no previous knowledge of either. It should be emphasised that the ethos of the book is to provide you with skills for applied statistical research and not just for passing statistics exams. As such, there is little emphasis on learning formulae, and a lot of emphasis on understanding results and on choosing the right statistical procedure for the right problem (crucial to good research).

On the SPSS side, this text deviates from almost every other introductory guide to the software in that it endeavours to teach the basics of SPSS syntax, rather than relying entirely on the Windows click-and-point interface. This makes learning apparently more difficult and long-winded at first, but there are dividends to be reaped in the long run:

1. *A succinct and secure record*

   Using the Windows interface alone leaves the researcher with no simple record of how he/she derived or customised variables. It is possible to tell SPSS to record every action you make, but this can result in huge volumes of information that are impossible to decipher – you need a record of only the commands which contributed to your final results, not all the permutations along the way. Relying on 'point-and-click' routines poses a great risk. What if a data file, which may have taken months to construct, becomes corrupted? How will you work out the source of errors that are not identified until the final stage of research? Syntax files allow the researcher to keep a very precise and succinct record of his/her work and this provides much needed security. The final data set and output files can very quickly be derived from the original data set if you have a well-maintained syntax file. And since SPSS syntax files are basically simple text files, they take up very little disk space. This means that several years of research can be stored in less than a megabyte, and multiple backups can be kept at virtually zero storage cost. The trivial file size also makes it very easy to create backups that are stored remotely – the best way to safeguard against data loss due to fire or theft. You simply email your syntax file to your home computer or to colleagues located elsewhere.

2. *Transparency and Reproducibility*

   If the funder of a research report, the reviewer of a journal article or the external examiner of a thesis asks for details of how a variable was calculated or a statistic computed, how will the author be able to reply with any certainty? Reproducibility – the ability of other researchers to recreate your results – is a fundamental tenet of good science.

3. *Efficiency*

   With a bit of practice at writing and editing syntax files you will soon find that the majority of tasks can be accomplished much more rapidly and precisely using syntax, particularly when you have to reproduce a similar procedure or transformation many times over. This is because you can copy and paste syntax, and then edit only the part of the command that changes. Even opening and saving a data file can be done many times more quickly using syntax, particularly if you are using the same data set over and over again. This is because simply finding the right file in a complex file structure (inevitable on a large project) can take several minutes, whereas highlighting and running a line of syntax takes a few seconds.

4. *Paste and Learn*

   One of the unique features of SPSS is that it allows you to *paste* into a syntax file the commands that underlie the point-and-click procedure you have just completed. This means that you can start writing and using syntax right from the outset – even with virtually no knowledge of SPSS. It is also a great way to learn syntax: rather than looking up the syntax for a procedure in the manuals, you can just work out the point-and-click routine and then click Paste.

5. *Accessing Extra Resources and Expanding SPSS*

   There is a fantastic array of free SPSS resources available via the Web and SPSS user groups, much of it in the form of syntax files. Sites such as www.spsstools.net offer new routines, automated tasks, and thousands of extra facilities that greatly expand the versatility of the standard SPSS package. Learning the basics of SPSS syntax will make many of these resources accessible to you and may prove to be the first steps towards creating a few of your own.

1.1.5 Summary of the Macro Commands

Much of the material in this book is structured around the calculation, application and theoretical basis of the syntax commands (which have been specifically written for this text) listed in the following table. While we will usually present SPSS Windows point-and-click equivalents where they are available (as we have already noted, the standard set of SPSS routines is rather limited when it comes to dealing with summary data, for example) and spend considerable time exploring the intuition behind the tests, along with other material, it is worth casting an eye over these commands and their definition at this point since they conveniently summarise the learning objectives of this book. Once you can execute and understand these commands you have reached the finish line.

These commands can be accessed once you have installed the relevant files onto your computer. As noted earlier, these files and installation instructions are available from the Downloads page of www.geebeejey.co.uk and are included as an appendix at the end of this text.

Summary of Macro Syntax Commands

Confidence Intervals (CI)		Hypothesis tests	
Macro command	Definition	Macro Command	Definition
CI_L1M	Large sample CI for one mean	**H_L1M**	Large sample significance test on one mean
CI_S1M	Small sample CI for one mean	**H_S1M**	Small sample significance test on one mean
CI_S2MP	Small independent samples CI for difference between 2 means (pooled variance)	**H_S2MP**	Small independent samples significance test for equality of 2 means (pooled variance)
CI_S2MD	Small independent samples CI for difference between 2 means (different variances)	**H_S2MD**	Small independent samples significance test for equality of 2 means (different variances)
CI_L1P	Large sample CI for one proportion (presents output for both Traditional and Wilson methods of calculation)	**H_L1P**	Large sample significance test on one proportion
CI_L2P	Large sample CI for comparing two proportions (presents output for both Traditional and Wilson methods of calculation)	**H_L2P**	Large samples significance test on two proportions
		H_S2VF	Simple small sample F-test on equality of two variances (see also Levene's test in the SPSS help menu for more sophisticated test of homogenous variances).
N_L1M	Sample size for desired margin or error for the mean		

In addition, we shall introduce two methods of examining relationships between variables:

- Chi Square Two-way Tables (Chapter 7)
- Regression Analysis (Chapter 7)

These terms and tests will, of course, seem fairly meaningless to you now, but are presented here to provide an overview of the structure of the course and will hopefully serve as a useful reference tool later on. The structure is presented graphically in the following figure. I would recommend that you take a good look at this map before you proceed, to remind yourself of where you are and where you are going.

Aerial View of Introductory Statistics

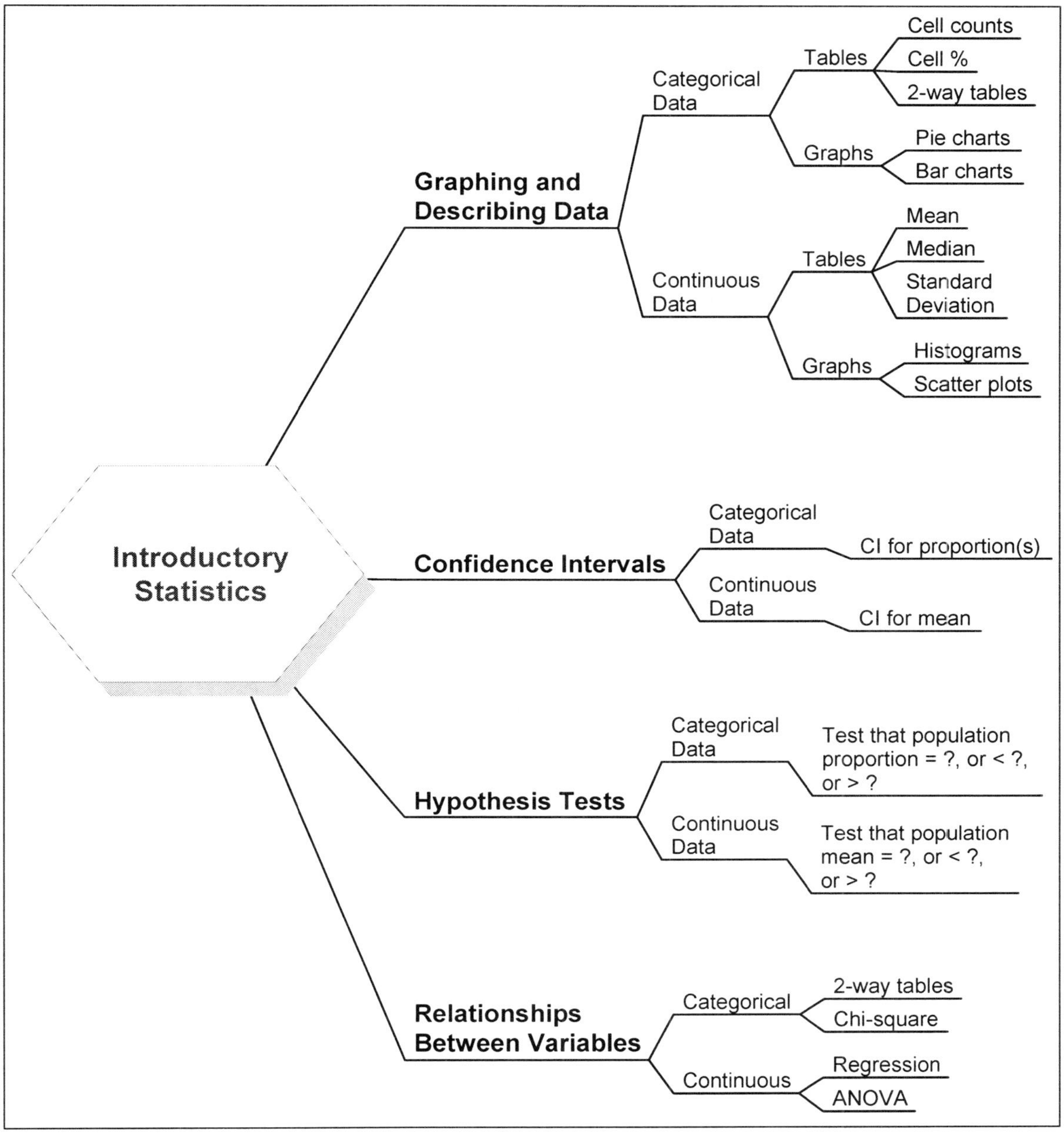

Summary of the basic structure of SPSS

SPSS uses three basic types of files: *data files* (these store information as a table – variables are stored as columns of numbers or text), *output files* (these are where SPSS sends the results of statistical tests and procedures, as well as graphs and tables), and *syntax files* (these are simple text documents in which you enter commands to tell SPSS what to do, and which you can create and edit). While it is possible to use SPSS without opening or creating syntax files, by using your mouse to point-and-click at the various menu options, it is a very good idea to learn how to use this facility, so we shall cover the basic syntax operations associated with most of the SPSS functions covered in this book. One of the very useful features of the SPSS point-and-click system is that it allows you to Paste an operation as a command into the syntax file (it pastes at the end of the open syntax file, or opens a new one if no syntax file is currently open).

This is a great way to learn SPSS's syntax language since you can easily find the procedure you are looking for using the menu system and then click the Paste button to write the syntax for this procedure to your syntax file. Sometimes the pasted syntax is unnecessarily complex (i.e. there are simpler ways to write the syntax) but this doesn't really matter. You can then edit the syntax from within the syntax file. This can save you a lot of time in the long run. For example, rather than having to go through many repetitions of the same point-and-click routine, you can paste the syntax into a syntax file, copy it as many times as you wish within that syntax file, make whatever changes you need to (such as changing the variable name), then select the syntax and run the whole procedure in one go. Also, once you have saved the syntax file, you can open it up and run the whole procedure again in a matter of seconds on a different file, rather than having to repeat the whole point-and-click process all over again. Don't worry if this sounds confusing at this stage – all will become clear in due course!

Exercise 1.1 The Motivation and Structure of the Basic Statistics

Review what you've read so far by answering the following questions:

1. Why do you think even a theoretician should have a basic grounding in statistics?

2. Discuss what you think is meant by the term 'evidenced-based policy'. Try entering these words into a Web search engine with a view to finding an official definition and also to get some idea of the prevalence of the term in policy related research.

3. How do the greater availability of computing processing power and the burgeoning complexity and volume of information at all levels of social inquiry point to a greater role for statistics?

4. Explain, using a series of examples from social research, why knowledge of how to calculate a mean will not suffice. Use examples that are comparable with those given in the text but from different topics of research.

5. Try to memorise the commands and definitions listed in the above table. You won't understand the meaning of these terms at this stage, so it's purely a memory exercise. Learning them off-by-heart will, however, greatly increase your efficiency when you come to use them, and, more importantly, will help you appreciate the structure of the material you intend to learn.

   As you memorise the table, keep asking yourself what you think the terms mean – this will create 'pegs' in your thinking on which your brain will add information as you proceed through the course. Indeed, it would be a good idea at this stage to flick through the subsequent chapters to find the meaning of terms you don't understand – this will help you familiarise yourself with the rest of the book.

6. Try to memorise the mind-map presented in the figure above. Re-draw the map, adding in details from the table of macro definitions to the branches on confidence intervals and hypothesis tests.

7. Open up SPSS. Depending on how your computer has been set up, you can do this by clicking on the SPSS icon on the Windows Desktop or click on the Start button in the bottom left corner of the screen, select All Programs, then click on SPSS for Windows.

   If your version of SPSS comes up with a mini-window asking, 'What would you like to do?', click the Cancel button in the bottom left corner of this window. Now click on the Help menu (top right corner in the SPSS window) and click on Tutorial. There are many tutorials to choose from. Try working through the first three or four in the list to get a feel for how SPSS operates.

1.2 Basic Concepts

One of the things you will notice from even a cursory examination of the *Aerial View of Introductory Statistics* presented in the figure above is that the crucial factor that determines the appropriate method for your analysis is whether the data you are looking at is continuous or categorical. This is true whether you are seeking to describe data, derive confidence intervals for estimates, perform hypothesis tests or analyse the relationship between variables. First of all, though, you need to understand what a variable is. Although we have briefly touched on the meaning of these basic concepts, it is worth considering them more carefully to ensure they are clear in our minds before we proceed to more demanding topics.

1.2.1 What is a Variable?

A *variable* is a measurement or quantity that can take on more than one value, for example:

- size of planet: varies from planet to planet
- weight: varies from person to person
- gender: varies from person to person
- fear of crime: varies from person to person
- income: varies from household to household

Sometimes we define and describe variables in terms of *individuals*:

Individuals = basic units of a dataset which we observe or experiment on in a controlled way. Individuals are not necessary persons – they could be schools, organisations, countries, groups, policies, or objects such as cars or safety pins. Sometimes called *observations* or *cases*, they form the rows in our SPSS data file.

We can now define variables as follows:

Variables = information that can vary across the individuals we observe. For example: age, height, gender, income, exam scores, whether a particular government has signed a Nuclear Test Ban Treaty (in the first five in this list, the individuals being referred to are persons; in the last item, the individuals being referred to are countries).

1.2.2 What is a Constant?

A measurement or quantity that has only one value for all the objects described in our data. It is sometimes also called a *scalar* or *parameter*. Examples are given below:

- speed of light in a vacuum: constant for all light transmissions
- ratio of diameter to circumference: constant for all circles
- average increase in life expectancy: approximately constant at 1 year per annum since the year 1900.

Note that often it is a constant that we are attempting to estimate. For example, we often use statistics to arrive at an estimate of a parameter that summarises the variable or relationship of interest:

- *mean*: typical value of a variable = measure of central tendency
- *standard deviation*: measures the variability of a variable = measure of spread
- *correlation coefficient*: measures the correlation between two variables
- *slope coefficients*: how much y increases when x increases.

So, although age might vary from individual to individual, the *mean age* of the population (at a particular point in time) is constant – that is, there is only one possible value.

1.2.3 What are the Different Types of Variables

Numeric variables are those that contain only numbers which can be used in mathematical calculations. *String* variables are not numeric (or not entirely so), and hence cannot be used in calculations, but can often be recoded using numerical values and hence transformed into a numerical variable that can then be used in mathematical computations. So, for example, if we have a variable in our data set that says which country a respondent is from, that variable is likely to be coded as a string variable. But we can easily convert this string variable into a series of numerical codes that transforms our string variable into a numerical variable. The example below shows you how to create your own dataset in SPSS and then recode a string variable as a numerical one.

Example 1.2.3(a) Creating your own data set

1. Open SPSS (we shall assume that you are using SPSS version 12, but other recent versions of SPSS will suffice for the point-and-click instructions; the syntax instructions will apply to almost any version of SPSS – yet another advantage of learning SPSS syntax!). Depending on how your computer has been set up, you can do this by clicking on the SPSS icon on the Windows Desktop or click on the Start button in the bottom left corner of the screen, select All Programs, then click on SPSS for Windows. If your version of SPSS comes up with a mini-window asking, 'What would you like to do?', click the Cancel button in the bottom left of this window. You will now be presented with a screen of empty cells called the *Data View* window. You will notice that in the bottom left corner of this window there are two tabs, one labelled **Data View** and the other labelled **Variable View**.

2. Click on the **Variable View** tab and enter the word 'country' in the first cell of the column headed *Name*. You are about to create a string variable for the country of origin of data on health variables such as proportion of smokers. By typing 'country' in the Name column, you have just told SPSS the name of your first variable.

3. You now need to tell SPSS what type of variable it is (whether it is a string variable or a numeric variable, for example). Click on the ... button in the column headed **type** and select the **String** option, then click OK.

4. You now need to create a label for this variable. This will help remind you in future what the exact meaning of this variable is. We don't have much to say about our first variable, so simply enter 'Nation state' in the label column for this variable, and hit Enter.

5. You need to tell SPSS the maximum number of characters your data for this variable will take. If it is going to be a string variable, which it is, you will need to leave plenty of room for a long string of text. So, click on the cell headed **Width**, enter 20 and hit Enter. This will allow you to enter names of countries of up to 20 characters (i.e. letters and spaces) in length.

6. Create a second variable called 'smokers' (a numerical variable) and label it 'Proportion of the adult population who smoke'.

7. You now need to enter some data for your two variables. Before you do this, it's a good idea to save your file. First create a folder called 'STATISTICS' in your C:\ drive (to do this, you need to click on the Start button in the bottom left corner of your screen, open My Computer or Windows Explorer, click on the C:\ drive, select File, New, and Folder, and enter 'STATISTICS' as the folder name).

8. Now return to SPSS by clicking on File; Save As, choosing the folder where you want to save the file; and then entering **CountryHealth.sav** as the file name. Click on OK to complete the operation. Now click the Data View button at the bottom of the window. You will see that you still have a blank data sheet, but the first two columns are headed 'country' and 'smokers'. Click on the first blank cell under the **country** heading, and type, 'Argentina' and hit Enter. In the second row of the **country** column, enter 'Brazil'. In the third row, enter 'Chile'. Now click on the first cell of the 'smokers' column and enter 30.7 and hit Enter. Enter 40.2 for the smoking rate for Brazil and 15.1 for Chile.

9. You now have a data set of two columns and three rows. It is important to understand that in the Data View window, SPSS always reads columns as variables, and the rows as the values of those variables for each individual in your data. In fact, in your own mind, it's a good idea to think of variables as a column of numbers or names. The country variable is a string variable since it is a column of country names entered using letters of the alphabet rather than numerical codes. The smokers variable is a numerical variable since it contains a list of numbers. Save the changes to your data by clicking on File and Save.

10. Now close SPSS by clicking on File, and selecting Exit. You don't have to do this to go onto the next step, but it's a good idea to learn how to close and open data files. If you want to close the data file without exiting SPSS altogether, just click on File and select New, then Data.

Example 1.2.3(b) How to Recode Variables

Open SPSS using the Start menu or Desktop icon for SPSS. Click on File, and select Open, and Data. Select the folder where you saved your file, and click on CountryHealth.sav, then click the Open button.

Having opened the file successfully using the menu system, now try doing it using a syntax file (we shall assume that the file was saved in the C:\STATISTICS\ folder):

<u>*Opening a data file from within a syntax file:*</u>

1. Open SPSS

2. Click File, New, Syntax

3. Type the following in the first line of the syntax window:

   GET FILE='C:\STATISTICS\CountryHealth.sav' .

   NB: If you're feeling lazy, you can get SPSS to paste this syntax for you: just go to the file menu, select Open Data, choose the file you want, and then click the Paste button rather than the Open button.

4. Then highlight this line of text using the mouse (hold down the left mouse button and drag across the text), and press Ctrl+R (or click on the little arrow button in the syntax window, the one to the right of the button with an icon of binoculars on it).

5. Now save this syntax file by clicking on File, Save As. Call the file 'Chapter2' and click Save. We shall add more to this file as we go along.

Now suppose you want to recode your country variable using numerical codes. We shall do this by creating a new variable called 'countrycode' and entering the following values for Argentina, Brazil and Chile: 1, 2, and 3 respectively. There are many ways to do this. You could achieve it manually by editing the Data View and Variable View windows as explained above. Alternatively you could use the **Recode** option in the **Transform** menu (see menu bar at the top of the screen):

<u>*Using the Recode Variable facility*</u>

1. Click on Transform, and select Recode, Into Different Variables...

2. Then click on '**country**' in the list of variables box on the left (depending on how your version of SPSS is set up, the variables may be listed by your label description, in which case it will say '**Nation state**' for the country variable).

3. Then click on the ▶ button to copy the country variable into the adjacent box, which will now say '**country -> ?**'.

4. You need to tell SPSS the new variable name, so in the Output Variable Name box on the right, type 'countrycode' (in earlier versions of SPSS you may have to choose a shorter name).

5. In the Label box, type 'Numeric code for Country' and click the Change button.

6. Then click the Old and New Values button. A new window will pop-up.

7. In the Old Value box, type 'Argentina', and in the New Value box on the right, type '1'. Then click Add.

8. Click on the Old Value box again, and type in 'Brazil', and enter '2' in the New Value box, and again click Add. Repeat for 'Chile', coding it as '3'.

9. When you are done, click Continue, and then click Paste.

10. Now go to your syntax file by selecting Window from the menu bar and clicking on the name of your syntax file (which in this case should be 'Chapter 2'). The last 5 lines of that file should now read:

```
RECODE
  country
  ('Argentina'=1) ('Brazil'=2) ('Chile'=3) INTO countrycode .
VARIABLE LABELS countrycode 'Numeric code for Country'.
EXECUTE .
```

You will see that the point-and-click operation you have just attempted is achieved using two commands: the RECODE command and the VARIABLE LABELS command. You know when a command has come to an end because SPSS reads the full-stop[3] as the end of a command. This means that you can spread a single command over several lines if you choose, as indeed is the

[3] Or 'period' if you are more familiar with the American labels for grammatical terms.

case here: the RECODE command, as used above, is spread over three lines, but we could actually fit it onto one if we preferred:

```
RECODE country ('Argentina'=1) ('Brazil'=2) ('Chile'=3) INTO countrycode .
```

Many commands won't run, however, without the EXECUTE command being included at the end (the commands for opening and saving data files are exceptions to this rule, as are many other commands that do not alter the data). If you have more than one command you want to run, you can either include EXECUTE after each individual command, or simply at the end of the block of commands as we have done here.

11. Highlight these five lines with your mouse and click the ▶ button to run them. Go to the SPSS Data Editor view (by clicking on Window, and selecting the name of your dataset, which at the moment should be 'CountryHealth') where you will see a new variable called **countrycode** with the desired numerical codes.

12. Go back to your syntax file and create a new variable called 'Continent' which, as the name suggests, records the Continent to which each country in the data belongs. You can do this by copying and pasting[4] the five lines of RECODE syntax used above. Before you do this, however, hit the Enter key a couple times after the end of your first set of RECODE syntax and enter a sub-heading entitled '*Create the Continent Variable*'. It is important to include headings and notes of explanation in your syntax file, otherwise when you return to it in a few months' time, it will seem very confusing. Keeping an orderly syntax file is helped by the use of the '*' character, since SPSS will ignore any line that begins with this character (as long as the previous line ended with a full stop) so start your sub-heading with this character. Also, use a row of dashes above and below this subheading (again initiated with the '*' character) to highlight the heading. Now paste your five lines of RECODE syntax after this sub-heading, and edit it so that:

    - the new variable is called 'Continent' instead of 'countrycode' (you don't want to overwrite your countrycode variable!)
    - the new variable Continent has 'South America' listed for Argentina, Brazil and Chile.
    - Because your new variable is a string variable, you need to tell SPSS before you create it. So before your new recode syntax you should type,

      ```
      STRING Continent (A15) .
      ```

      The 'A15' in brackets tells SPSS that this variable is to have an alphanumeric format (can include numbers and/or letters) with up to 15 characters. If you plan to include entries with more than 15 characters for your new variable (unlikely since in this particular example) then select a higher number.
    - At the end of this syntax, add a row of dashes, then hit the Enter key on your keyboard a couple of times to create a couple of black lines and type the following:

      ```
      SAVE OUTFILE='C:\STATISTICS\CountryHealth1.sav' .
      ```
    - Also, add headings to your earlier syntax to make it look clearer and save the syntax file by clicking on File, and Save.

Your syntax file should now look something like this:

```
*--------------------------------------------------------------------------------.
*Open dataset:
*--------------------------------------------------------------------------------.
GET FILE='C:\CountryHealth.sav'.
*--------------------------------------------------------------------------------.
*Create a Numerical Code for Country:
*--------------------------------------------------------------------------------.
RECODE country
('Argentina'=1) ('Brazil'=2) ('Chile'=3) INTO countrycode .
VARIABLE LABELS countrycode 'Numeric code for Country'.
EXECUTE .
*--------------------------------------------------------------------------------.
*Create the Continent Variable:
*--------------------------------------------------------------------------------.
STRING Continent (A15) .
RECODE country
('Argentina'='South America') ('Brazil'='South America') ('Chile'='South America') INTO Continent.
```

[4] To copy and paste, highlight the desired text, right-click on the selected text, choose Copy, then move the cursor to where you want the text to go, right-click and choose Paste

```
VARIABLE LABELS Continent 'Continent to which each country belongs'.
EXECUTE .
*-------------------------------------------------------------------------------------.
*Save dataset:
*-------------------------------------------------------------------------------------.
SAVE OUTFILE='C:\CountryHealth1.sav' .
```

If you have edited correctly, you should be able to highlight the whole file and click the ▶ button to run the entire sequence. Try this. If you get error messages coming up in the Output window[5] go back and check your syntax file for mistakes.

Categorical vs Continuous Variables

You have just created a numerical variable for country, but note that the values you have chosen have no inherent meaning. Also, the increment between values means nothing – we have incremented by a value of one each time, with 1 as our starting point (for Argentina). But we could have chosen to start at 898454 for Argentina, and increment in 100s or 1000s or whatever. Such variables, whether described using strings or numerical codes, are called *categorical* variables because they essentially allocate an observation to a particular category. They are variables that have values which fall into two or more discrete categories. *Continuous* variables (also called *scale* or *quantitative* variables), on the other hand, are those whose data values are numeric, and increase along a continuum such as age or income. Scale variables must be numeric.

One way of thinking of the difference between categorical and continuous variables is to think of the difference between a conventional light switch and a dimmer switch. The latter allows the brightness of light to vary along a continuum from total darkness to full brightness, whereas the former switches between the two extremes. Similarly, you can choose to measure many socio-economic phenomena using either method (you should always choose continuous measurement if possible since this can always be converted to categorical measurement if needs be by recoding the data, whereas converting categorical data into continuous data are not usually possible).

For example, if you wanted to do a survey of education achievement amongst shop-floor workers, you could either ask them whether or not they have qualifications (this would give you a binary categorical variable, coded as '1' or '0' for example to denote 'yes' or 'no'), or you could ask them how long they have spent in education (a truly continuous measurement would be one that measures this in fractions of a second, but such precision is rarely needed or possible in social science, so 'years in education' is likely to give you a sufficiently smooth continuum for you to treat it as a continuous variable).

It is worth pointing out at this stage that there are two types of categorical variables: *Ordinal* categorical variables and *Nominal* categorical variables. Your country and countrycode variables (which are essentially the same) are examples of the latter because there is no intrinsic ordering to the categories:

Ordinal variables: Data values represent categories with some intrinsic order

e.g.1: low, medium, high
e.g. 2: strongly agree, agree, disagree, strongly disagree.

Ordinal variables can be either string (alphanumeric) or numeric values that represent distinct categories (e.g., 1=low, 2=medium, 3=high). Values fall within discrete but ordered categories – i.e. the sequence of categories itself has meaning

e.g. education categories:

1 = primary
2 = secondary
3 = college

[5] depending on how your version of SPSS has been installed, the Output window will only appear if you make a mistake or if you have produced a table or graph; alternatively, you can set up SPSS to show commands you have entered in the Output window – go to the Data Editor window and select **Edit**, choose **Options**, select **Viewer**, under **Item**, select **Log** and then click the '**Display commands in the log**' option, then click **OK**.

4 = university undergraduate
5 = university postgraduate Masters
6 = university postgraduate PhD

e.g. 1= very poor, 2= poor, 3=good, 4=very good

Nominal variables: Data values represent categories with no intrinsic order. The sequence of categories is arbitrary and so ordering has no meaning in and of itself:

e.g. country of origin: Wales, Scotland, Germany…
e.g. make of car: Ford, Audi
e.g. job category
e.g. company division

Nominal variables can be either string (alphanumeric) or numeric values that represent distinct categories (e.g., 1=Male, 2=Female).

Types of Variable

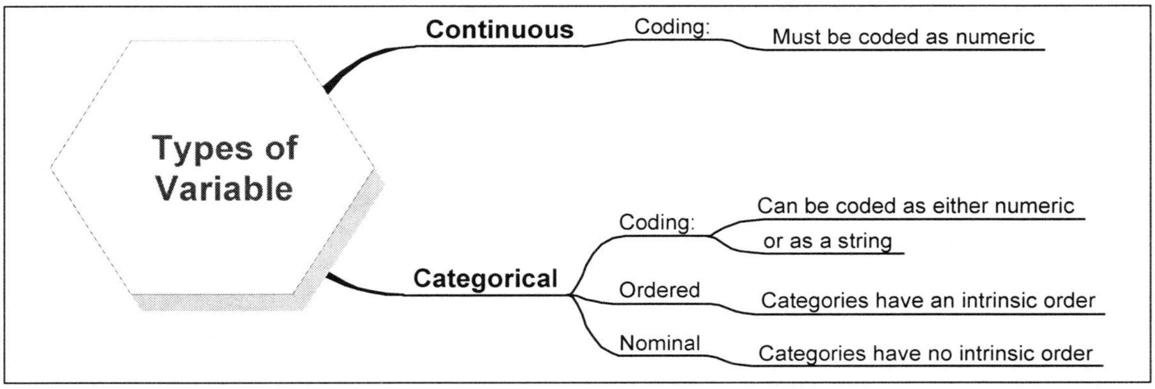

This figure summarises the types of variable we have considered and how they should be coded. Understanding the difference between continuous and categorical variables is fundamental to the material that follows in subsequent chapters (because it determines which statistical procedure you need to adopt) so it's worth spending some time making sure that this topic is clear in your mind.

Exercise 1.2 Understanding Variable Types; Creating and Recoding Data

1. If you have not already done so, carefully work through the examples above of creating and recoding variables.
2. Once you have done this, close any existing data file you have open (make sure you have saved your work first) and enter the following table of information as a new dataset called '**mortgagedata**':

month	mortgage	period	interest	rmethod	price	new	Dwellage	dwelltyp	region
1	10500	25	10.2	2	11000	2	5	4	6
1	30400	25	10.3	3	33333	2	0	3	5
1	15900	20	10.4	1	16000	1	1	5	3
1	43000	22	10.05	1	44000	2	3	3	6
1	190000	25	10.8	1	250000	2	4	1	6
1	20000	25	10.9	2	24300	1	2	4	6
1	36000	30	11.1	2	41000	2	1	3	5
1	16000	20	10.4	3	16020	2	2	4	6
1	64550	25	10.9	1	65000	0	2	3	1

Where:

month = month in which the mortgage was taken out;
mortgage = amount borrowed;
period = duration of mortgage in years;
interest = interest rate charged on the mortgage;
rmethod = method of repayment where 1 = normal repayment, 2 = endowment, and 3 = other;
price = purchase price;

new	=	whether old or new where 0 if not known, 1 if new, and 2 if second-hand;
dwellage	=	age category of dwelling= 0 if not known, 1 if pre-1919, 2 if 1919-1939, 3 if 1940-1960,4 if 1961-1980, and 5 if post-1980;
dwelltyp	=	type of dwelling
	=	1 if bungalow, 2 if detached house, 3 if semi-detached house, 4 if terraced house, 5 if flat or maisonette in converted house, 6 if purpose-built flat or maisonette, 7 if other type;
region	=	government region
	=	1 if Northern, 2 if Yorks. & Humberside, 3 if East Midlands, 4 if West Midlands, 5 if London, 6 if South East.

Make sure you label and fully code the variables using the information given above. Note that to enter value labels (to give meaning to the numerical codes for the rmethod variable, for example), go to **Variable View** and select the appropriate cell under the 'Values' column and click the three dots button [...]. A window will then pop-up which will allow you to enter the value given to a particular category and associated labels. Click [**Add**] to move onto the next category, and click [**OK**] when you are done. Remember to save your data before you proceed.

3. Consider the following questions about the data you have entered:

   (a) Which of the columns of data represent variables and which are constants?

   (b) Which of the variables represent categorical variables and which are scale/quantitative/continuous variables?

   (c) Which of the categorical variables are nominal and which are ordinal?

4. Create a new categorical variable out of the selling price variable and call it 'priceband'. It should have four bands: less than £30,000; £30,000 to £39,999; £40,000 to £69,999; and £70,000+. To recode as bands, go to [Transform], [Recode], [Into Different Variables], enter name and label, click [Change], then click [Old and New Values], select the appropriate Range option (either '? Through' or 'Lowest through ?' or '? through highest'), and proceed as before.

   When you're done, click [Continue], and paste the syntax for this into your Chapter 2 syntax file under the new subheading, 'Exercise 1.2.4'. Also include the syntax for opening the mortgagedata file you have created before the priceband syntax. Once you have made the transformations to your data, include the appropriate syntax in your syntax file for saving the data under a new name: **mortgagedata1** (make sure you run the syntax for saving the file, don't just type it!).

5. What sort of variable is your priceband variable?

<u>Answers to Exercise 1.2:</u>

3. (a) All are variables except 'month' which is constant at 1 for all individuals in the data.

   (b) mortgage, period, interest and price are all continuous (or approximately so: e.g. houses rarely sell for fractions of a penny!); the rest are all categorical variables.

   (c) this depends rather on your theoretical view of each variable. For example, method of repayment might be considered at first sight to be a nominal variable, unless you regard the different categories as reflecting some underlying continuous variable such as risk. If repayment mortgages are less risky than other types then there is some order to the categories. So your view of whether a categorical variable is ordered or not depends on how you intend to use the data. The most obvious ordered variables are **new** and **dwellage** (both can be ordered by age since construction).

4. The syntax you have added to your syntax file should look something like this:

```
*-------------------------------------------------------------------------------------.
*Exercise 1.2.4.
*-------------------------------------------------------------------------------------.
GET FILE='C:\STATISTICS\mortgagedata.sav'.
RECODE price
(Lowest thru 29999=1) (30000 thru 39999=2) (40000 thru 69999=3) (70000 thru Highest=4) INTO priceband .
VARIABLE LABELS priceband 'Selling price band of property'.
EXECUTE .
SAVE OUTFILE='C:\STATISTICS\mortgagedata1.sav' .
```

6. It is an ordered categorical variable.

1.3 Summarising Data

Small data sets can be presented in their entirety by listing each and every observation in a table. If our data only has 10 observations and 3 variables, we can easily list all the information we have on a single page. But even then we might want to know what is the typical value of a variable. The real challenge, though, comes when we want to absorb the information stored in large data sets. Summaries of the data are essential if our limited brains are to grasp anything about the information stored in such files. Lots of information can be confusing, particularly if it is numerical. Most of us need headline figures or stylised facts to be able to draw any meaningful conclusions about the information we are presented with. For those of us who think pictorially, graphical representation of information is even more helpful. How we summarise data will vary according to whether the data are continuous or categorical.

1.3.1 Summarising Categorical Data Using Tables

Categorical data can be summarised in table form by stating the proportion and/or number of cases that fall within a particular category. The following table shows the total Income Support Claimants that claim help with mortgage costs (excluding the unemployed) and the breakdown of this total across four possible categories: aged over 60 (35%), lone parent (25%), disabled (33%) and other (6%).

Income Support Take-up

Income Support claimants with housing costs by statistical group: May 1999

	Total (All Claimants with Mortgage Interest)	Aged 60 or over		Lone Parents		Disabled		Other	
	000s	000s	%	000s	%	000s	%	000s	%
1999	263	93	35	67	25	88	33	15	6

DSS Quarterly Statistical Enquiry

Categories can be listed either in columns or rows (respecting the order of categories if the variable is ordinal) and can be merged if the number of categories is large. For example, if the variable records country of origin, this could be collapsed into continents if there are many countries listed. Three things to remember when constructing tables:

- A table should give a clear message: it should tell a story. Never include a table in a dissertation, report or paper unless it is fully described in the text and is worth describing.
- Too much information in a table defeats its purpose: the *raison d'être* of summary tables is to reduce data anxiety, not exacerbate it.
- Always give the source of the information recorded in the table.

We shall now use the mortgage data to demonstrate how to create tables in SPSS. SPSS has a very powerful suite of tables it can produce, so we shall only be able to give a taster here (once you've created a basic table, it's fairly easy to experiment making use of the very detailed help system built into SPSS).

Example 1.3.1 How to Create a Table of Proportions in SPSS

1. Open up your **mortgage1.sav** dataset (see Exercise 1.2).

2. We want to add more observations to the data. Rather than typing in more hypothetical data we are going to cheat by copying and pasting our existing 9 cases. Simply go to the Data Editor, Data View window, use your mouse to select all the data cells of all 9 cases (from row 1 of **month** through to row 9 of **priceband**), then right-click on your mouse, select Copy and then place the cursor in cell 10 of the **month** column, and paste. You should now have 18 observations (i.e. 18 complete rows of data). Save the data as '**mortgagedata2**'.

3. In your syntax file, introduce a new heading: '*Example 1.3.1: How to Create a Table of Proportions in SPSS*'. Then type,

```
GET FILE='C:\STATISTICS\mortgagedata2.sav'.
FREQUENCIES VARIABLES=priceband .
```

Select both lines of syntax and run (press Ctrl+R on your keyboard or click the ▶ button). The following table should appear in the output window:

Simple Frequency Table

Selling price band of property

		Frequency	Percent	Valid Percent	Cumulative Percent
Valid	1.00	8	44.4	44.4	44.4
	2.00	2	11.1	11.1	55.6
	3.00	6	33.3	33.3	88.9
	4.00	2	11.1	11.1	100.0
	Total	18	100.0	100.0	

This first column of the output table simply lists the categories of the variable you are using. The second column of the table tells you how many observations are in each category and that you have a total of 18 observations.

The third column tells you what percentage of your observations are in each price band: 44.4% of which are in price band 1, 11.1% are in price band 2, 33.3% are in price band 3 and 11.1% are in price band 4.

The valid percent column tells you the same as column 3 but excludes missing values from the total (we have no missing values in this case and so the two columns are the same).

The cumulative percent column adds the percentages in each category as it progresses (so we know, for example, that 88.9% of properties are in priceband 3 or below).

This sort of table only works with categorical data. If we run it on continuous data, SPSS will try to tell us how many observations take on each and every value of the variable. If we have a large dataset, a continuous variable may have thousands of different values, and so this table could go on for many hundreds of pages and be of no practical use. Indeed, this is why researchers sometimes convert continuous variables (like **price**) into categorical variables (like **priceband**) to make it easier to summarise the data (though as we shall see, there are other ways of summarising continuous variables).

Note that you can achieve the same table using point-and-click: select Analyze, Descriptive Statistics, and Frequencies from the menu bar at the top of the screen. Select **priceband** from the list of all variables in your data, click the ▶ button to paste into Variables box, make sure the Display frequency tables box is ticked, and then click OK (or the Paste button if you want to paste it to your syntax file).

4. One of the problems with the simple frequency table presented above is that it does not tell us the meaning of the 4 price bands – only the numerical codes are listed. This is because we have not labelled the values for our **priceband** variable. You can do this by editing the Values column in the Variable View window, or you can use the following syntax:

```
VALUE LABELS priceband 1 'less than £30,000' 2 '£30,000 to £39,999' 3 '£40,000 to
£69,999' 4 '£70,000+'.
```

If you now re-run the frequency table syntax,

```
FREQUENCIES VARIABLES=priceband .
```

you will find that the table includes the labels associated with each category of priceband:

Simple Frequency Table with Category Labels

Selling price band of property

		Frequency	Percent	Valid Percent	Cumulative Percent
Valid	less than £30,000	8	44.4	44.4	44.4
	£30,000 to £39,999	2	11.1	11.1	55.6
	£40,000 to £69,999	6	33.3	33.3	88.9
	£70,000+	2	11.1	11.1	100.0
	Total	18	100.0	100.0	

Source: author's own data.

To copy this table into a word processing document such as Word, right-click on the table in the SPSS output window, and click Copy Objects. This will copy the table as a graphics image and is the best way to avoid changes to format when you past it into a Word document. If you want to copy it into a spreadsheet such as one created in Excel, right-click on the table in SPSS and select Copy. When you paste the table into Excel, you will find that the cell structure of the table is preserved. You should always include the source of the data as a footnote. If you have created or collected the data yourself, you can simply reference it as, 'author's own data' or something similar.

Remember to save any changes to your syntax and data files (save your data as '**mortgagedata3.sav**'). You might also want to save your output file (though this can be easily recreated by re-running your syntax file). Go to the output file displayed in SPSS Viewer, click File, Save As, and save it as '**Chapter2output**'.

1.3.2 Summarising Categorical Data Using Graphs

An alternative to using tables is to represent your data graphically. Graphs allow us to visualise the distribution of data across different values or categories. They can be used to tell us how many (or what proportion) of cases fall within certain categories or ranges of values.

Pie Charts

If all the categories sum to a meaningful total, then you can use a pie chart. Pie charts emphasise the differences in proportions between categories. They are useful for representing a single snapshot, but not very good for showing trends in the data over time (you would need to present a separate pie chart for each year, for example). Graphs should follow the same rules as those listed above for tables in terms of simplicity, source and purpose. Any tables or graphs you present in a research report or journal article should be fully explained in the text.

Example 1.3.2(a) Creating a Pie Chart of Categorical Data

1. Open **mortgagedata3.sav**
2. Select Graphs, Pie Charts from the menu bar;
3. From the pop-up window, select 'Summaries for groups of cases' and click **Define**.
4. From the list of variables, choose priceband, paste it into the 'Define Slices by' box;
5. Under the 'Slices Represent' option, choose '% of cases';
6. Click Paste to add the following command to your Chapter 2 syntax file assuming it is still open (if you click OK, the graph command will run without the syntax being pasted to your syntax file):

```
GRAPH /PIE=PCT BY priceband .
```

This will create a circular graph where each pie slice shows proportionally the number of cases in each category defined by the BY variable.

7. Select this line of syntax and press Ctrl+R to run. The following pie chart should appear in your output file, which you can copy and paste as an image into a word processing file using the Copy Objects option in the right-mouse-click menu:

8. If you want to add a title, simply use the /TITLE option in the syntax:

   GRAPH /PIE=PCT BY priceband /TITLE= 'Selling Price Bands'.

   or click on the Titles button in the Pie Chart window. Further options are available if you double click on the graph as displayed in the Output window. For example if you double click on the graph, then double click on the colour boxes in the legend you can change the colour. Once you have finished editing, you must close the graph window by going to File, and selecting Close. In the copy of the graph below we have changed the colours to greyscale shades to make it more readable in black-and-white printouts. Once in a word processing document you can rescale the image by clicking once on it, then dragging the corners of the box that appears.

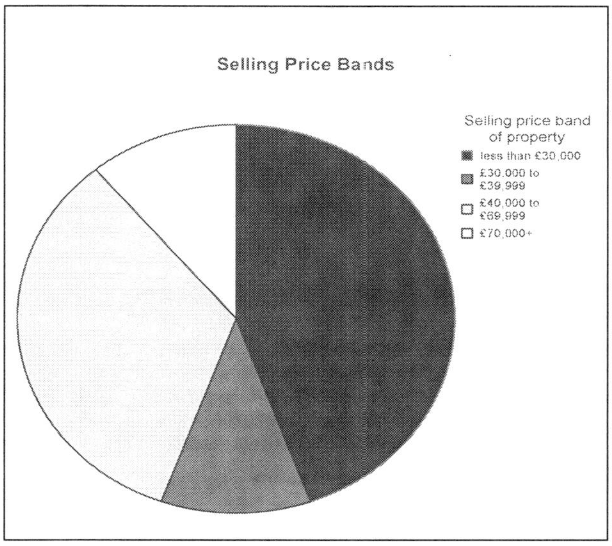

Bar Charts and Line Graphs

Bar charts can be used to show either % or counts but are again not very good for showing trends in more than one category. If you have several variables or categories that you want to trace over time, it is best to use a line graph.

Example 1.3.2(b) How to Create a Bar Chart in SPSS.

1. Open **mortgagedata3.sav**

2. Select **Graphs**, **Bar...** from the menu bar.

3. From the pop-up window, select '**Simple**' and choose '**Summaries for groups of cases**'; then click **Define**.

4. From the list of variables, choose **priceband**, paste it into the 'Category Axis' box;

5. Under the 'Bars Represent' option, choose '% of cases'.

6. Click the Titles button, and type 'Selling Price Bands' and click **Continue**.

7. Click **Paste** to add the following command to your Chapter 2 syntax file – assuming it is still open (if you click **OK**, the graph command will run without the syntax being pasted to your syntax file):

   GRAPH /BAR(SIMPLE)=PCT BY priceband /TITLE= 'Selling Price Bands'.

If you run this syntax (select and press Ctrl+R) it will create a circular graph where each bar shows the number of cases in each category (given as a %).

Example 1.3.2(c) How to Create a Simple Line Chart in SPSS.

Some software packages (such as Excel) allow you to trace the path of bars over time by allowing you to construct a 3D bar chart, but such charts should be used with caution since the perspective used can distort the interpretation of the data and results can be obscured altogether if large bars are in front of shorter bars. Line graphs are usually the best way to present trends in many variables over time, but in both bar and line graphs, be aware of how scaling will affect how people interpret the graph.

PBand1	PBand2	PBand3	PBand4	Year
44.40	11.10	33.30	11.10	1990.00
33.50	10.20	36.10	20.20	1991.00
28.90	9.60	39.80	21.70	1992.00
22.10	8.90	40.30	28.70	1993.00
21.40	8.10	43.30	27.20	1994.00

1. Open a new data sheet in SPSS and enter the above data, where PBand1 to PBand4 are price bands based on the same intervals as in the previous example. Save the file as '**price bands over time.sav**'.
2. Click Graphs, Line... and from the pop-up window select **Simple** and **Values of Individual Cases**. Then click Define.
3. Select **priceband1** from the variable list and click ▶ to paste the variable into the 'Line Represents:' box.
4. From the 'Category Labels:' options, choose '**Variable**' and then select **year** from your variable list and use ▶ to paste the variable into the category labels box.
5. Click on Titles... to add = 'Price Band 1 Proportions Over Time' as the title and 'Source: Pryce (2005) House Price Data' as the footnote.
6. Click Continue, Paste and the following syntax should appear at the end of your syntax file:

```
GRAPH /LINE(SIMPLE)=VALUE( pband1 ) BY year
/TITLE= 'Price Band 1 Proportions Over Time'
/FOOTNOTE= 'Source: Pryce (2005) House Price Data'.
```

Highlight and run this syntax to obtain your graph. You can then edit the graph in the SPSS Output Window by double clicking on it. For example, try double clicking on the graph, then double click on the line, select a new colour by clicking one of the coloured boxes, click Apply. Change the line weight to 2 and Style to dashed. Then click the Interpolation Line tab, and select Spline (a method of smoothing the data) Click Apply. Unless you have further edits you want to perform on the graph (you can change the format of the axes, headings, and labels by simply double clicking on them), click Close, then to close the Chart Editor altogether, click File, Close (or click the ☒ button in the top right corner of the Chart Editor window). You should end up with a chart that looks something like the one presented in (a).

(a)

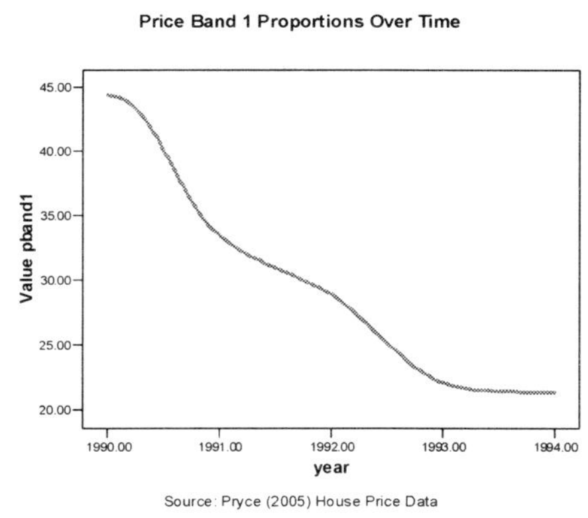

(b)

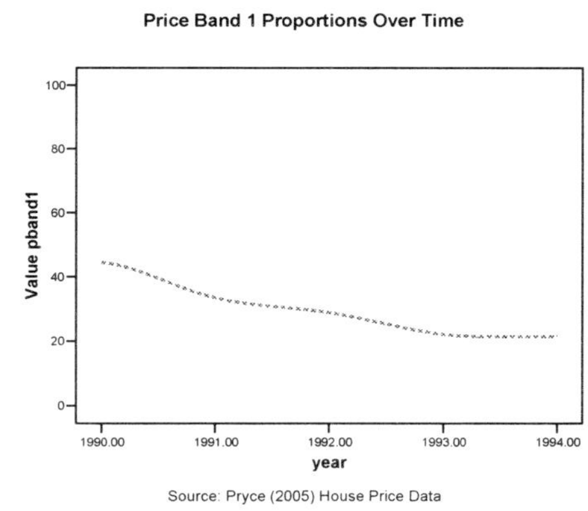

Note that by changing the scale on the vertical axis you can change the story the graph appears to tell. For example, if we open up the Chart Editor again and double click on the vertical axis, select the Scale tab and change the minimum and maximum to 0 and 100 respectively, we will end up with graph (b) above. Although the two line graphs represent the same data, because of different scaling of the y-axis, the proportion of house sales in the lowest price bracket appears to decline much more rapidly in the first compared with the second.

You should be aware that SPSS allows you to save the format of a graph not as syntax but as a 'chart template'. While in the Chart Editor, click on File, Save Chart Template and select your desired options and template name. If you want to apply this template to a graph in future, open up the chart editor for the new graph, click File and select Apply Chart Template.

Once you have finished editing the graph, you can then copy the graph into another windows program by right-clicking on it in the Output window, and selecting Copy Objects.

Note that you can easily run the graph on different variables without having to go through the tedious point-and-click sequence. Just copy and paste the syntax you have created, and change the variable names and titles listed in the syntax. The following syntax was created in a matter of seconds using this method and, once activated, will run single line graphs for the other price bands in sequence:

```
GRAPH /LINE(SIMPLE)=VALUE( pband2 ) BY year
      /TITLE= 'Price Band 2 Proportions Over Time'
      /FOOTNOTE= 'Source: Pryce (2005) House Price Data'.

GRAPH /LINE(SIMPLE)=VALUE( pband3 ) BY year
      /TITLE= 'Price Band 3 Proportions Over Time'
      /FOOTNOTE= 'Source: Pryce (2005) House Price Data'.

GRAPH /LINE(SIMPLE)=VALUE( pband4 ) BY year
      /TITLE= 'Price Band 4 Proportions Over Time'
      /FOOTNOTE= 'Source: Pryce (2005) House Price Data'.
```

Example 1.3.2(d) How to Create a Multiple Line Chart in SPSS.

1. Open your **price bands over time.sav** data.

2. Click Graphs, Line..., and from the pop-up window select **Multiple** and **Values of Individual Cases**. Then click Define.

3. Select **priceband1**, **priceband2**, **priceband3** and **priceband4** from the variable list and click ▶ to paste the variables into the 'Line Represents:' box.

4. From the 'Category Labels:' options, choose '**Variable**' and then select **year** from your variable list and use ▶ to paste the variable into the category labels box.

5. Click on Titles... to add = 'Price Band Proportions Over Time' as the title and 'Source: Pryce (2005) House Price Data' as the footnote.

6. Click Continue, Paste and the following syntax should appear at the end of your syntax file:

```
GRAPH /LINE(MULTIPLE)= VALUE( pband1 pband2 pband3 pband4 ) BY year
 /TITLE= 'Price Band Proportions Over Time'
 /FOOTNOTE= 'Source: Pryce (2005) House Price Data'.
```

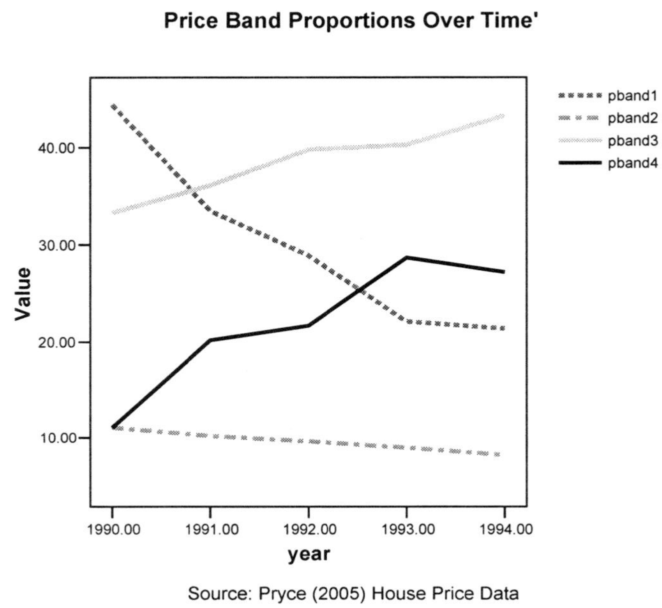

1.3.3 Summarising Continuous Data

Tables of data are not much use unless you have only a few values. Scale or continuous (sometimes also called quantitative data) are usually a measurement of size or quantity and so it is not meaningful to report a percent or a count unless you intend to break the variable into categories, and then it ceases to be continuous data and becomes categorical data.

Suppose for example that you have 129,000 observations on income. How would you tabulate this? The first thing we need to think about in order to answer this is what it is we are interested in when describing the income data. We might want to know, for example, whether or not income is evenly spread or whether wealth is highly concentrated amongst a few etc. These are questions about the variable's *distribution*. We can represent the whole data set with one picture called a histogram which simply measures the frequency (either as a count or a proportion) of values in categories of equal width.

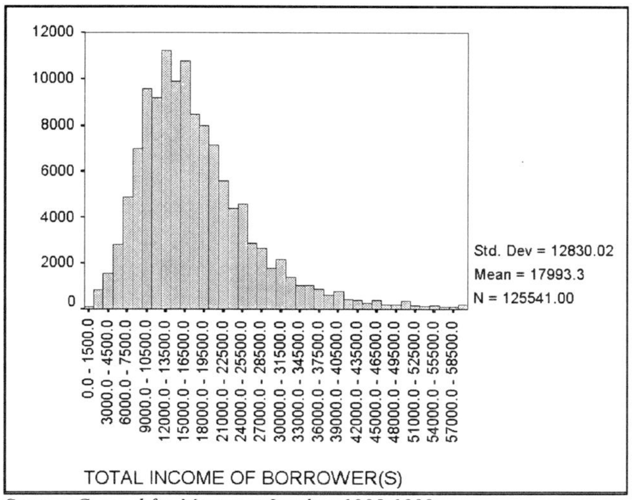

Source: Council for Mortgage Lenders 1995-1998

Looking at the histogram of income above, we would say that the distribution of income has a *positive skew* because it has a long upper-tail which pulls up the mean (more on this later...). Histograms like this can easily be produced in SPSS by selecting Graphs, Histogram from the menu at the top of the screen in the data window. There is a certain skill however in making sure the histogram is easy to read.

For example, consider the following four histograms of the loan to value ratio (LTV) derived from mortgage transaction records. From the first it is difficult to tell what the distribution of LTVs really looks like – the bars of the histogram are all bunched up on the left of the graph. You can see that, by varying the width of each category (sometimes called 'bins') and by limiting the range of values of the data to be graphed, it is possible to derive a more useful graph. You can edit the graph in this way either by double clicking on the graph, or by right-clicking on the graph, selecting SPSS Chart Object, and select Open. If you then double click on histogram options you can then alter the number/width of intervals and also the range of data to be graphed.

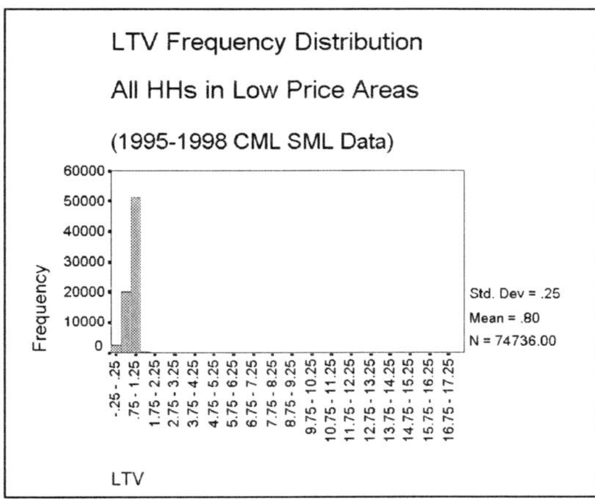

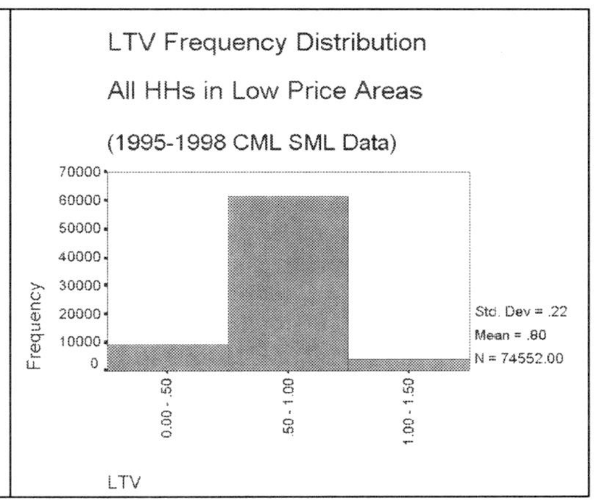

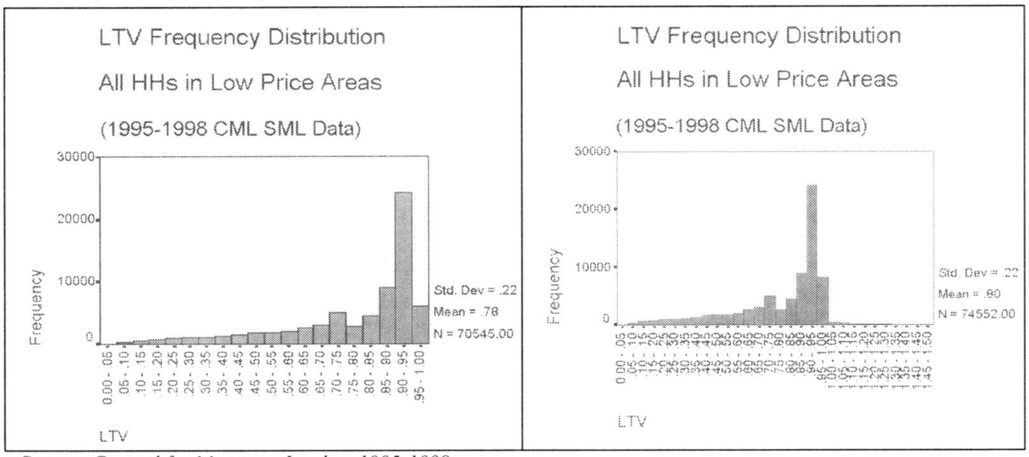

Source: Council for Mortgage Lenders 1995-1998

Example 1.3.3 How to Create a Histogram in SPSS.

1. Open the **householddata.sav** file – available from: www.geebeejey.co.uk .

2. Click Graphs, Histogram..., and select the variable for which you want to plot a histogram. Click ▶ to paste the variable into the *Variable:* box. Then click Titles and type, 'Histogram of House Purchase Price' as the heading and 'Source: Hypothetical House Price Data' as a footnote.

3. Click Continue and Paste and run the syntax by highlighting it and clicking ▶:

```
GRAPH
 /HISTOGRAM=Dprice
 /TITLE= 'Histogram of House Purchase Price '
 /FOOTNOTE= 'Source: Hypothetical House Price Data'.
```

4. From the Output window, open the Chart Editor by double clicking on the histogram that appears.

5. In Chart Editor, double click on the horizontal axis to bring up the Properties window and select the Histogram Options tab. Change the Interval width to 40,000. Click Apply and Close. Note how the graph has changed.

6. Now double click again on the horizontal axis and select the Scale tab, and change the maximum value for the horizontal axis to 200,000. Click Apply and Close.

7. Change the interval width back to 20,000 (double click on the horizontal axis to bring up the Properties window and select the Histogram Options tab) and note the changes. You should end up with the following graph:

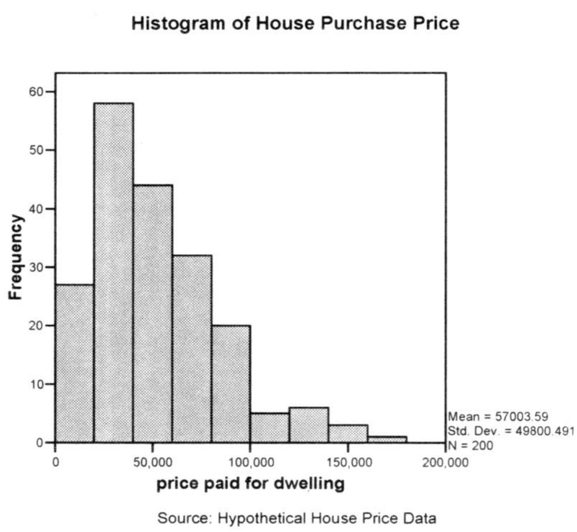

8. Go back into the Chart Editor, click File, Save Chart Template, select the options you want, click Continue and save the file template as **histogramtemplate.sgt**.

9. Try applying the template to a new histogram. For example, copy and paste the histogram syntax you have written and change the variable name to

```
GRAPH
 /HISTOGRAM=Bincbasic
 /TITLE= 'Histogram of Basic Income'
 /FOOTNOTE= 'Source: Hypothetical Basic Income Data'.
```

Double click on the new histogram, click File and select Apply Template. Choose the template file you have just saved. The look of the final Basic Income histogram will depend on the options you selected when you saved the original template file.

1.4 Summarising Continuous Relationships using Scatter Plots

Scatter plots are useful ways to visually inspect relationships between variables. A scatter plot is created simply by plotting the values of one variable against that of another. Usually we have some idea of which of the two variables causes the other. We generally call this variable the ***explanatory variable*** (sometimes also called the ***independent variable*** or ***covariate***). This is conventionally denoted as the x variable and is plotted along the horizontal axis. The variable we are trying to explain – the ***dependent variable*** is usually plotted on the vertical axis and is denoted as the y variable.

Often, we start out with a hypothesis that x determines y and then examine our data on the two variables to see if there is indeed a relationship. A scatter plot will help us do this. If the dots appear to cluster along a line or curve that is not completely horizontal or vertical, then there is possibly evidence of a relationship. Note however that the scatter plot cannot confirm or deny our assumption regarding the direction of causation. We have to use theory and common sense to ascertain whether this is the most reasonable way to conceive of the relationship we are measuring.

Example 1.4.1 How to Create a Scatter Plot in SPSS.

Suppose you are attempting to investigate the factors that determine an employee's commitment to the firm he/she works for. You have recorded information on a variety of firms and entered the data into an SPSS file entitled **employee.sav** (available from www.geebeejeey.co.uk). To ascertain whether there is evidence of a relationship between **commitment** (your index of how committed an employee is to his/her employer) and **emp_duration** (the number of years each employee has worked for a firm) you decide to graph a scatter plot.

1. Open the **employee.sav** data. Click Graphs, Scatter..., Simple and Define.

2. Then select the variable you want to plot on the horizontal axis (the x variable = the explanatory variable) and the variable you want to plot on the vertical axis (the y variable = the dependent variable). Let's assume that **commitment** is determined by how long a person has worked for a firm, **emp_duration**. Your hypothesis is that the longer a person has worked for a firm, the greater their commitment to that firm. So select **commitment** as your y variable and **emp_duration** as your x variable. Click ▶ to paste the variables into their appropriate boxes. Then click Titles and type, 'Scatter Plot of Employee Commitment & Duration of Employment' as the heading and 'Source: Hypothetical Data employee.sav' as a footnote.

3. Click Continue and Paste and run the syntax by highlighting it and clicking ▶:

```
GRAPH /SCATTERPLOT(BIVAR)=emp_duration WITH commitment
 /TITLE= 'Scatter Plot of Employee Commitment & Duration of Employment'
 /FOOTNOTE= 'Source: Hypothetical Data employee.sav '.
```

4. Now add a line of best fit: from the Output window, open the Chart Editor by double clicking on the histogram that appears, right-clicking on the data points, and selecting Add Fit Line at total from the drop-down list. Select Linear, Apply and click Close.

5. Close file editor and return to the output window. Note how the graph has changed: it now has a straight line going through it.

The line is upward sloping which suggests that employee commitment is positively correlated with the number of years worked in the firm (i.e. the longer an employee has worked in an organisation, the more committed he/she tends to be). But which way does the direction of causation go?... Do you think that it is possible that commitment actually drives the length of time a person stays with the same firm?

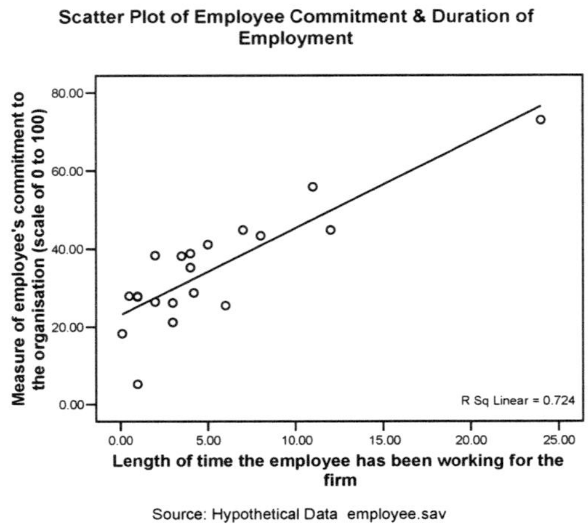

1.5 Review of Basic Concepts and Mathematical Notation

Before proceeding any further, some readers will find it useful to remind themselves of some basic mathematical concepts and notation:

1. Integers, Fractions, Percentages and Decimals
2. Adding Variables
3. Multiplying Variables
4. Multiplying a Variable by Itself
5. Exponents and Logs
6. Subscripts
7. Summation Sign: the Mean, Median, Standard Deviation, Trimmed Mean

1.5.1 Integers, Fractions, Percentages and Decimals

An Integer is a whole number:

e.g. 2, or 7, or 503

A fraction is the ratio of two numbers or variables. That is, it is one number or variable (called the numerator) divided by another (called the denominator). For example, the ratio of one to three, called a third, is written as,

$^1/_3$

More generally, we could write a fraction as,

$^x/_y$

A proper fraction is one were the numerator is less than the denominator, such as a half,

$^1/_2$

An improper fraction is a fraction where the numerator is greater than the denominator and can be expressed as a mixed number. For example,

$^4/_3 = 1\,^1/_3$

A decimal fraction has as its denominator a number which is a power of 10. For example, one 100th can be written as one over 10 squared, or $1/10^2$). Other examples of decimal fractions include,

- $^3/_{10}$
- $^4/_{100}$
- $^5/_{1000}$

Using the decimal point notation means that the denominator can be omitted for the sake of brevity. One place to the right of the decimal point means dividing by 10^1. That is, denominator = $10^1 = 10$. Another example is three tenths,

$^3/_{10} = 0.3$

Moving a figure two places to the right of the decimal point can be achieved by dividing by 10^2. That is, the denominator = $10^2 = 100$. Similarly, four hundredths can be written as either a fraction or a decimal,

$^4/_{100} = 0.04$

To move three places to the right of the decimal point means dividing by 10^3 (i.e. denominator = 10^3 = 1000). Five thousandths can be written as follows:

$^5/_{1000} = 0.005$

Percent is a way of representing a number as a fraction of 100. For example,

- 45 percent = 45% = $^{45}/_{100}$ = 0.45
- 125 percent = 125% = $^{125}/_{100}$ = 1.25

Decimals can be written as percentages by multiplying by 100. For example,

- 0.3 = 30%
- 0.04 = 4%
- 0.005 = 0.5%.

1.5.2 Using Integers, Fractions and Decimals in SPSS

It is possible to achieve all of the following computations using SPSS's point-and-click facilities (just click on Transform, Compute, type the name of your new variable in the Target Variable box, and then create the expression you need by pasting variables from the list into the Numerical Expression box and making use of the Functions box and keypad). However, it is much quicker in the long run to learn how to write the syntax, so the following examples will present the syntax rather than the point-and-click routines.

Example 1.5.2(a) Creating an Integer from a Fraction.

Suppose you want to round up the number of years a person has been employed to the nearest year:

1. Open up the **employees.sav** data.
2. Click Transform, Compute, and type **emp_dur_integer** in the Target Variable box.
3. Then scroll down the list of Functions, and select RND(numexpr) and click the ▲ button to paste it into the Numerical Expression box.
4. Now select **emp_duration** from the variable list and paste it into the parentheses of the **RND(?)** function in the Numerical Expression box by clicking ▶.
5. Now click the Type and Label button, choose numerical (rather than string) and enter the following as the label 'Years in employment rounded to the nearest year.' and click Continue.
6. Then click Paste. The following syntax should appear at the end of your Chapter2 syntax file (assuming that you have kept this syntax file open throughout and not started any new syntax files – SPSS allows you to have more than one syntax file open at one time). Run this syntax and return to the Data Editor window to inspect your new variable. You will see that the new **emp_dur_integer** variable has rounded up the **emp_duration** variable to the nearest whole number, as planned.

```
COMPUTE emp_dur_Integer = RND(emp_duration) .
VARIABLE LABELS emp_dur_Integer 'Years in employment rounded to the nearest year.' .
EXECUTE .
```

7. Save your data as **employees1.sav**.

Example 1.5.2(b) Creating the Ratio of Two Variables.

Suppose you want to create the ratio of employee commitment to years in employment. This is computed by simply dividing **commitment** by **emp_duration**. SPSS uses '/' as its *divide by* sign.

1. Open up the **employees.sav** data.
2. Click Transform, Compute, and type **commit_dur_ratio** in the Target Variable box.
3. Now select **commitment** from the variable list and paste it into the Numerical Expression box by clicking ▶.
4. Type '/' (or click the / button on the virtual keypad below the Numerical Expression Box).
5. Select **emp_duration** from the variable list and paste it into the Numerical Expression box by clicking ▶. Make sure the **emp_duration** variable is pasted after the '/' sign.

6. Click on Type & Label... and enter 'Ratio of Commitment to no. of yrs in employment' as the label and click Continue.
7. Click Paste and the following syntax should appear at the end of your syntax file. Run the syntax and inspect your new variable in the Data Editor window.

```
COMPUTE commit_dur_ratio = commitment / emp_duration .
VARIABLE LABELS commit_dur_ratio 'Ratio of Commitment to no. of yrs in empnt.' .
EXECUTE .
```

8. Save your amended data as **employees1.sav**.
9. Suppose you hypothesise that the ratio of commitment to number of years in employment falls with the size of firm. Do a scatter plot to investigate this by running the following syntax:

```
GRAPH /SCATTERPLOT(BIVAR)=size WITH commit_dur_ratio
 /TITLE= 'Scatter Plot of Commitment: Years in Employment against Firm Size'
 /FOOTNOTE= 'Source: Hypothetical Employee Data: employee.sav'.
```

10. The data should be downward sloping in the scatter plot. Add a line of best fit by double clicking on the graph to enter Chart Editor, right-clicking on the data points, and selecting Add Fit Line at total from the drop-down list. Select Linear, Apply and click Close. You will see that the line is downward sloping, which suggests that commitment does indeed decline with size of firm. You will also notice that SPSS automatically displays the R Sqaure measure as in the graph below. This is a measure of the *goodness of fit* of the line and ranges between zero and one. It actually measures the proportion of the variation of the variable on the vertical axis that is explained by the variable plotted on the horizontal axis, so the higher the value the better the fit (see Chatper 7 for more information on R Square and lines of best fit). SPSS does not always put the R Square label in a convenient place. You can move it easily enough in the Chart Editor window – just click once on the "R Sq Linear ..." text and drag the highlighted box to where you need it. If you want to delete the R Sq label altogether (or anything else on the graph, for that matter) simply right-click on it, and select Delete.

1.5.3 Adding and Multiplying Variables

The process of **adding** two variables, x and y is denoted by,

$$x + y$$

and involves adding the value of x to the value of y that belongs to the same observation (i.e. on the same row in the data window of SPSS).

The **multiplying** of two variables, x and y is denoted by,

$$xy$$

and involves multiplying the value of x by the value of y that belongs to the same observation (i.e. on the same row in the data window of SPSS).

Sometimes you need to multiply a variable by itself. This is called the '**square**' of a variable and is denoted by:

x^2

If we plot y against x^2 we have what is called a **quadratic function**. You may have noticed when you added the line of best fit to your scatter plots in the above examples that SPSS gave you the option to use a quadratic line rather than a linear line. Go back to these scatter plots and double click on them to open up Chart Editor, click on the data points and try adding the quadratic line of best fit to see what it looks like.

Example 1.5.3(a) Adding Variables in SPSS

1. Open the **employees1.sav** data file.

    GET 'C:\STATISTICS\employees1.sav'.

2. Now add the number of employees variable to the number of directors to obtain **totalpeople**, the total number of people associated with each firm, and label the variable using the VARIABLE LABELS command:

```
COMPUTE totalpeople = size + directors.
VARIABLE LABELS totalpeople 'Total no. people associated with the firm' .
EXECUTE .
```

3. Save the file **as employees2.sav**.

    SAVE OUTFILE='C:\STATISTICS\employees2.sav' .

Example 1.5.3(b) Multiplying Variables in SPSS

1. Open the **employees2.sav** data file.

    GET 'C:\STATISTICS\employees2.sav'.

2. Suppose you want to obtain a measure of the total salary bill of each firm in your sample. Suppose further that you were unable to collect data on the salary of the individual employees you interviewed but you were able to collect data on the average salary paid to employees in each firm (**avesalary**). By multiplying average salary by the total number of employees, you can obtain an approximate measure of the total salary bill which we shall call **totsalary_estimate**. Label the variable using the VARIABLE LABELS command:

```
COMPUTE totalsalary_estimate = size * avesalary.
VARIABLE LABELS totalpeople 'Estimate of the total salary bill of the firm = size * avesalary ' .
EXECUTE .
```

3. Save the file as **employees2.sav**.

    SAVE OUTFILE='C:\STATISTICS\employees2.sav' .

    This will overwrite your existing file of this name.

Example 1.5.3(c) Multiplying a Variable by Itself in SPSS

1. Open the **employees2.sav** data file.

    GET 'C:\STATISTICS\employees2.sav'.

2. Suppose you think that the linear best fit line in the scatter plot of the ratio of commitment to employment duration and firm size does not fit the data well. The true relationship, you think, looks non-linear – i.e. curved. By 'stretching out' the firm size variable (i.e. making the higher values even larger relative to the smaller values of the variable) you might be able to make the relationship more linear and hence allow the linear best fit line to more closely represent the data. One way of 'stretching-out' a variable is to multiply it by itself – i.e. squaring it. We can do this one of two ways. We can either compute size * size; or we can use the SPSS syntax for raising a variable to a power: '**'. So *x*-squared would be written as '*x***2' which is exactly equivalent to writing '*x* * *x*'. And *x*-cubed can be written as '*x***3' which is the same as typing '*x***x***x*'. To verify this, run both versions to create size_sq and size_sq1 respectively:

```
COMPUTE size_sq = size**2.
VARIABLE LABELS size_sq 'Size squared = size**2' .
EXECUTE .
```

```
COMPUTE size_sq1 = size*size.
VARIABLE LABELS size_sq 'Size squared = size*size' .
EXECUTE .
```

Now compare the values for each case in the Data Editor. The size_sq column of data should be exactly the same as the size_sq1 column.

3. Now see if your transformation results in the scatter plot being more linear – i.e. the line of best fit more closely representing the scatter of data points. Run the following syntax,

```
GRAPH /SCATTERPLOT(BIVAR)=size_sq WITH commit_dur_ratio
 /TITLE= 'Scatter Plot of Commitment: Years in Employment against Firm Size Squared'
 /FOOTNOTE= 'Source: Hypothetical Employee Data: employees3.sav'.
```

and add a line of best fit by entering Chart Editor, right-clicking on the data points, and selecting Add Fit Line at total from the drop-down list. Select Linear, Apply and click Close. You will see that the line is still downward sloping, but fits the data even less well than before. It seems that we don't need to stretch our size variable but rather compress it (bring the higher values closer to the smaller values). Perhaps what we should do is take the square-root which does the opposite of squaring...

4. Take the square root of size using the following syntax:

```
COMPUTE size_sqrt = SQRT(size).
VARIABLE LABELS size_sqrt 'Square-root of Size = SQRT(size)' .
EXECUTE .
```

5. And re-run the histogram using size_sqrt as the explanatory variable:

```
GRAPH /SCATTERPLOT(BIVAR)=size_sqrt WITH commit_dur_ratio
 /TITLE= 'Scatter Plot of Commitment: Years in Employment against Square Root of Firm Size'
 /FOOTNOTE= 'Source: Hypothetical Employee Data: employees3.sav'.
```

If you add a linear line of best fit, you will see that there is some improvement, but not much. This is because the variable on the vertical axis also looks as though it needs compressing. You could also try taking the square root of the ratio variable and plotting this against the square-root of size. But all this is becoming a bit long winded. There is a much easier way: just use logarithmic scaling. As we shall see below, taking logs is another way of compressing a variable. The reason logs are easier to use than square-roots is that logarithmic scaling is built-in as a standard option in the Graph Editor window. Just click on the vertical axis, select the Scale tab, and select Logarithmic scaling, click Apply and Close. You will see a dramatic improvement in the line of best fit. But we are running ahead of ourselves...

6. Save the file as **employees3.sav:**

```
SAVE OUTFILE='C:\STATISTICS\employees3.sav' .
```

And remember to save your syntax file (in the syntax window, click **File**, **Save**).

1.5.4 Exponents and Logs

'Taking the exponent' of a variable or constant means raising it to the power of a constant or variable. For example, 4 (a constant) raised to the power of a variable x is written as,

$$4^x$$

and results in a new variable with each value equal to 4 raised to the power of each corresponding value of x. A particularly important exponent is the number 2.71828 (called simply 'e' or the 'natural exponent') raised to a particular power,

$$2.71828^x \equiv \exp[x] \equiv e^x$$

where '≡' means 'always equivalent to'. So the natural exponent of x is simply e raised to the power of x. It is equally possible to raise a variable raised to the power of another variable and this is written as,

$$y^x \ .$$

Another commonly applied transformation employs the number 10 rather than 2.71828 as the basis of the exponentiation. That is, we might want to raise 10 to the power of our variable:

$$10^x .$$

What about *logs*? All you need to know for the purposes of basic statistics is that taking logs compresses a variable – pulling the larger values down towards the smaller values. Taking the log of a variable is the reverse of taking the exponent. In fact, if you have taken the natural exponent of a variable and you then take the natural log (known as 'log to the base e') it returns the variable to its original values. Similarly, if you take the natural log and then take the natural exponent, you end up where you started. Statisticians usually use logs simply as a means of rescaling a variable so that it is easier to read when plotted on a graph or so that it is easier to measure its relationship with another variable. Again, the most common types of logs other than those based on e, are those that are based on the number 10. In fact, the base 10 logarithmic transformation is the default setting in SPSS for log scaling the axes of graphs. But for our purposes, base 10 logs and natural logs achieve the same result (they compress variables) and so we won't worry about how to compute them (SPSS does that for us).

Example 1.5.4(a) Using Exponents in SPSS

1. Open the **employees3.sav** data file.

```
GET 'C:\STATISTICS\employees3.sav'.
```

2. Another way of 'stretching out' a variable (i.e. making the high values larger relative to the low values) is to take the natural exponent. That is, raise 2.71828 to the power of your variable. You could try this for the size variable by either typing **2.71828**size**, or by taking advantage of SPSS's EXP function and typing **EXP(size)**, which is more precise[6]. There is a problem, however. Taking an exponent is a much more extreme 'stretching-out' method than squaring it, so some of the larger values of size, when exponentiated, will be beyond the number of digits SPSS can cope with! An easy way round this is to rescale the variable first. For example, we could measure the number of employees in hundreds by dividing the size variable by 100 first. We can tell SPSS to divide by 100 first by putting size/100 in parentheses (whenever you put something in parentheses it means that this component of the calculation must be computed first):

```
COMPUTE size_exp = 2.71828**(size/100).
VARIABLE LABELS size_exp 'Natural exponent of size/1000 = 2.71828**(size/100)' .
EXECUTE .

COMPUTE size_exp1 = EXP(size/100).
VARIABLE LABELS size_exp1 ' Natural exponent of size/1000 = EXP(size/100)' .
EXECUTE .
```

If you compare these two new variables in your Data Editor window, you will see that both ways of computing the exponent are equivalent. You will also see, if you run a scatter plot against the ratio variable, that stretching-out the size variable using exponents has only worsened the line of best fit as a summary of the relationship between the variables. As noted earlier, what we need to do is compress the variables on both axes. Which leads us to our next exercise: taking logs. But before you move on, make sure you save your revised data:

```
SAVE OUTFILE='C:\STATISTICS\employees4.sav' .
```

Also remember to save your syntax file. It is probably a good idea to make backups of your syntax file – because they are text-only documents, they take up very little space on your hard drive so there's no reason not to make multiple copies. You might simply want to regularly save your syntax file as **Chapter 2 backup1.sps** and then save it as the original name so you don't get confused.

Example 1.5.4(b) Using Logs in SPSS

Suppose you have decided that you want to 'compress' both the size variable and the ratio variable (i.e. ratio of commitment to duration of employment). You are going to achieve this by taking the natural logs of both files (note that you can only do this if all the values of both variables are greater than zero – otherwise SPSS will produce missing values for the cases with zero or negative numbers). Your plan is to obtain a scatter-plot of the natural log of size against the natural log of our ratio variable and compare the outcome with the base-10 logarithmic scaling included as standard in SPSS. Finally, we shall take the exponents of both our logged variables to show that this will indeed return us to our original values.

1. Open the **employees4.sav** data file.

```
GET 'C:\STATISTICS\employees4.sav'.
```

2. Compute the base-e logarithm (i.e. natural log) of **size** and the base-e logarithm of commit_dur_ratio using the 'LN' command:

---

[6] It is more precise because SPSS will use an estimate of e with more than five decimal places.

```
COMPUTE size_ln = ln (size).
VARIABLE LABELS size_ln 'Natural log of size' .
EXECUTE .

COMPUTE commit_dur_ratio_ln = ln (commit_dur_ratio).
VARIABLE LABELS commit_dur_ratio _ln 'Natural log of commit_dur_ratio ' .
EXECUTE .
```

3. Look at the column of figures for **size_ln** in the Data Editor and compare the values with those of **size**. You will see that the values of **size** have been compressed, particularly the larger values. This is also true of the **commit_dur_ratio_ln** variable.

4. Run a scatter plot of **size_ln** against **commit_dur_ratio_ln**:

```
GRAPH
 /SCATTERPLOT(BIVAR)=size_ln WITH commit_dur_ratio_ln
 /TITLE= 'Scatter Plot of ln(Commitment/Years in Employment) against ln(Firm Size)'
 /FOOTNOTE= 'Source: Hypothetical Employee Data: employees4.sav'.
```

5. Add a linear line of best fit by opening the Chart Editor, right-clicking on the data points, and choosing Add Fit Line at Total. Select Linear, Apply and Close. Move the R Sq label to where you want it on the graph (by clicking once on the R Sq label and then dragging the highlighted box with your mouse). You can alter the font and text in the axis labels and titles by clicking on them, then selecting the desired font and/or editing the text.

6. Now compare this to the scatter plot of **size** against **commit_dur_ratio** using the SPSS's built-in base-10 logarithmic scale: run the following syntax,

```
GRAPH
 /SCATTERPLOT(BIVAR)=size WITH commit_dur_ratio
 /TITLE= 'Scatter Plot of Commitment/Years in Employment against Firm Size'
 /FOOTNOTE= 'Source: Hypothetical Employee Data: employees4.sav'.
```

   Now change the scaling of both axes to base-10 logs (double-click on the axis in question, select the Scale tab, then select Logarithmic scaling base 10, click Apply and Close – notice how the R Sq changed when you adopted log scaling). Now add a line of best fit and compare with your base-e log scatter plot. You will see that although the axis scales are different, the line fits both sets of data equally well (the R Sq figure measures the *goodness of fit*: the larger the number, the better the fit – there is very little difference in the R Sq values for the two plots below).

7. Save your data:

```
SAVE OUTFILE='C:\STATISTICS\employees5.sav' .
```

Scatter Plots: Comparison of Base e and Base 10 Scaling

(a) Natural Log Scale	(b) Base 10 Log Scale
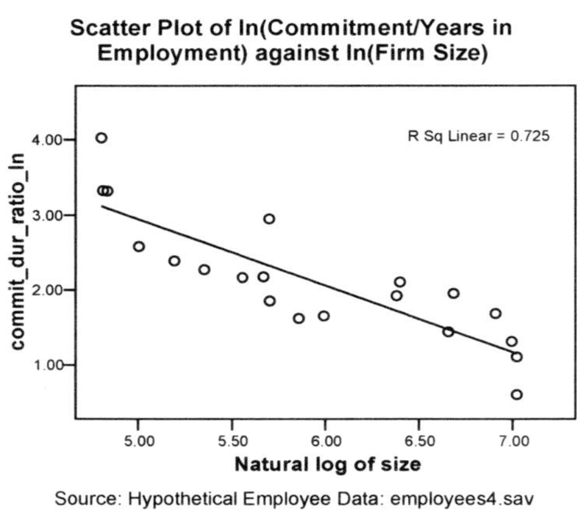	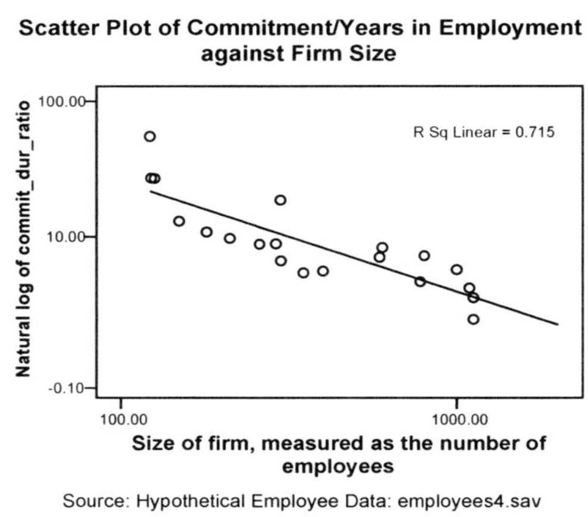

1.5.5 Subscripts

Somewhat confusingly, x (lower case) is sometimes used to denote a particular value of a variable X (upper case). If you want to refer to any six observations (numbers) of X without specifying which particular values you mean, you can use numbered subscripts such as x_1, x_2, x_3, x_4, x_5, x_6. This can be abbreviated further as:

$$x_i = x_1, \ldots, x_n \text{ where } n = 6.$$

On other occasions, x_1, x_2, x_3 etc. are used to describe separate variables observed in a sample, where the upper case counterparts X_1, X_2, X_3 etc. refer to the same variables in the population as a whole. So you have to look at the context before deciding which an author is referring to. Crucially, though, you should appreciate that subscripts are not complicated things to understand. They are simply a form of shorthand for describing a list of observations or variables without having to be too specific (i.e. without having to refer to the actual values of a particular variable or the actual names of specific real variables).

1.5.6 Summation

Perhaps the most common use of the summation sign is in the formula for the sample mean:

Sample Mean:
We have already said that the mean is simply the sum of values divided by the number of values:

mean of six numbers: 1,3, 8, 7, 5, 3 = (1 + 3 + 8 + 7 + 5 + 3) / 6 = 4.5

We can write this more succinctly, and more generally, by giving labels to each of the components of this calculation. First, abbreviate the sample mean using $\overline{x}$ (sometimes written as *x*bar). Second, abbreviate the process for summing the list of numbers in your sample using the Greek symbol for capital S, called capital sigma and written: Σ. Now use our subscript notation to succinctly write our six numbers as $x_i = x_1, \ldots, x_n$ where $n = 6$. We can now write the formula for the sample mean as:

$$\text{sample mean} = \text{average} = \frac{1+3+8+7+5+3}{6}$$

$$= \frac{\sum x_i}{6} \text{ where, } x_i = 1,3,8,7,5,3$$

$$\overline{x} = \frac{\sum x_i}{n}$$

A good tip to help you cope with formulae is to simply read them out loud (or under your breath, depending on how daft you want to look). Read them component by component, starting from the top and reading left to right, working your way across and then down (read any expression in brackets on a particular row first). So the above formula would read as: 'the sample mean, *x*bar, equals the sum of the observations on variable X divided by n, the number of observations in the sample'.

Example 1.5.6 Computing the Sample Mean in SPSS

1. Suppose we want to compute the average number of employees who worked in the firms you sampled. The simplest way to compute the mean of a variable is to use the Descriptives function obtained by running the following syntax:

```
DESCRIPTIVES VARIABLES=size
/STATISTICS=MEAN .
```

2. Alternatively, you can click on Analyze, Descriptive Statistics, Descriptives, select **size** from the list and paste it into the Variable(s) box by clicking the ▶ button, click on Options to choose which summary statistics you want to include, click Continue, Paste, then highlight the pasted syntax and click ▶. Both methods will produce the following table which tells us that the average firm size, measured as the number of employees, is 495, based on a sample of 20.

Descriptive Statistics

	N	Mean
Size of firm, measured as the number of employees	20	495.3000
Valid N (listwise)	20	

The question you should immediately ask yourself is the extent to which your sample mean is a good estimate of the population mean. In other words, how close will the average size of all firms in the UK be to your 495 figure? Even if your sample is truly random (i.e. each firm in the population has an equal chance of being included in your sample), you might have randomly selected an unusual group of firms. This is called **sampling variation**. Later in the book we will explore ways of deriving *confidence intervals* for the population mean which will tell us the range of values the population mean is likely to take given your sample mean of 495 and the properties of your sample.

Population mean

Often the constant (or '*parameter*') we are most interested in estimating is the population mean. We can rarely calculate it directly since we rarely have a full set of observations on the population. However, we often need to refer to it, even though it is essentially a hypothetical concept in many cases. Anyhow, the custom is to refer to it by the lower case Greek symbol for 'm' which is called 'mu' and written: μ. As you'd expect, μ is calculated as the sum of all the values of the variable X, divided by the total number of observations in the population (denoted by N):

$$\mu = \frac{\sum X_i}{N}$$

Variance

Another common use of the summation sign is to calculate the variance. This is essentially a measure that attempts to gauge the average deviation from the mean. It is calculated as simply the sum of all squared deviations from the mean divided by the number of observations and, as such, it is the 'average squared deviation from the average'. It is usually denoted by lowercase sigma raised to the power of two:

$$s^2 = \frac{(x_1 - \bar{x})^2 + (x_2 - \bar{x})^2 + \ldots + (x_n - \bar{x})^2}{n-1}$$

$$\boxed{s^2 = \frac{1}{n-1}\sum (x_i - \bar{x})^2}$$

A reasonable question to ask at this point is why square the deviations before taking their average? Why not simply take the average mean deviation? The answer is that the sum of deviations from mean will always equal zero. Positive deviations cancel out negative deviations, but if we square the deviations first, they all become positive, and the 'cancelling out' problem is removed.

Standard Deviation

The problem with the variance is that its value is not in the same scale as that of the original variable (its scale is the square of the original scale, which is not particularly useful). This problem is overcome by taking the square root of the variance, a process which gives us the *standard deviation*:

$$\text{Standard Deviation} = s = \sqrt{\frac{1}{n-1}\sum(x_i - \bar{x})^2}$$

To see how this is calculated in practice, consider the following table seeking to measure the variability of the price per night of 3-star London hotel rooms. There are ten observations with a mean of £71.01. If we simply sum the deviations from the mean (penultimate column) we find that they sum to zero as predicted above. However, if we square these deviations (i.e. times them by themselves) before summing them, we find that the result – the sum of squared deviations – has a positive value of £621.99. If we divide this sum by the sample size we get the variance, £69.11, which is effectively the average squared deviation from the mean. A more useful measure is obtained by taking the square root of this figure to give us the standard deviation of hotel prices = £8.31. This tells us that the average deviation from the mean is just over £8, just over ten percent of the mean.

Observation	Price per night of 3 star London hotels			
	x_i	$\bar{x}$	$x_i - \bar{x}$	$(x_i - \bar{x})^2$
1	£ 67.20	£ 71.01	-£ 3.81	£ 14.50
2	£ 70.49	£ 71.01	-£ 0.52	£ 0.27
3	£ 78.26	£ 71.01	£ 7.25	£ 52.59
4	£ 65.80	£ 71.01	-£ 5.21	£ 27.12
5	£ 70.56	£ 71.01	-£ 0.45	£ 0.20
6	£ 83.23	£ 71.01	£ 12.22	£ 149.38
7	£ 80.01	£ 71.01	£ 9.00	£ 81.04
8	£ 66.99	£ 71.01	-£ 4.02	£ 16.14
9	£ 73.15	£ 71.01	£ 2.14	£ 4.59
10	£ 54.39	£ 71.01	-£ 16.62	£ 276.16
		Sum:	£ 0.00	£ 621.99
		Sum / (n-1)	0	£ 69.11 (Variance)
		√ (sum / (n-1))		8.31 (Standard Deviation)

Example 1.5.6 Computing the Sample Standard Deviation and Variance in SPSS

1. Suppose we want to compute the standard deviation of employees who worked in the firms you sampled (i.e. the average deviation of firm size from the mean). Again, the simplest way to compute the standard deviation of a variable is to use the Descriptives function obtained by running the following syntax:

   DESCRIPTIVES VARIABLES=size
   /STATISTICS= **STDDEV**.

2. If you want to calculate the *variance* as well, simply add this to the list of statistics you ask SPSS to compute:

   DESCRIPTIVES VARIABLES=size
   /STATISTICS= STDDEV **VARIANCE**.

   This will yield the following table:

   Descriptive Statistics

	N	Std. Deviation	Variance
Size of firm, measured as the number of emnployees	20	362.79298	131618.7
Valid N (listwise)	20		

   which tells us that the average deviation from the mean firm size is 363 employees. Again your immediate reaction should be to ask how this compares to the standard deviation in the population. Perhaps you have chosen a sample with a lot more variation (or a lot less) in size of firm than in the population of all firms.

3. Alternatively, you can click on Analyze, Descriptive Statistics, Descriptives, select **size** from the list and paste it into the Variable(s) box by clicking the ▶ button, click on Options to choose which summary statistics you want to include, click Continue, and Paste.

Coefficient of variation

Because the standard deviation is measured in the same units as the original variable, it cannot be used to compare variables that are measured in different units. One method of comparing the spread of such variables is to divide the standard deviation of each variable by its mean. This is called the *Coefficient of Variation*:

$$\textit{Coefficient of Variation} = \frac{\sigma}{|\mu|}$$

Where σ is the standard deviation, and $|\mu|$ is the absolute value (i.e. ignoring the sign) of the mean. If we were computing this for the population, the denominator would obviously be the absolute value of *x*bar. The greater the coefficient of variation, the greater the spread of the variable. In the above example, this comes to 0.117 which can alternatively be expressed as a percent, as in fact we did intuitively above. Essentially, what the coefficient of variation tells us, therefore, is that the standard deviation is 11.7% of the mean. Suppose we were comparing it to the variability of square footage for each hotel room, which for sake of argument is measured (using the coefficient of variation) to be 45.2%, then we would conclude that price per room varies more than area per room.

There is no simple way of computing the coefficient of variation in SPSS and, in a way, there's no need to have a special function to derive it since it is so simple to calculate once you have the mean and standard deviation.

Trimmed Mean

Another useful measure that makes use of the summation sign is the trimmed mean which equals simply mean of the observations between the third and the first quartiles. The first quartile is the value of X below which a quarter (25%) of the data fall. The third quartile is the value of value of X below which three quarters (75%) of the data fall. Incidentally, the *second quartile* is another name for the **median** which is value of X below which a half (25%) of the data fall.

The trimmed mean is useful because unlike the mean it is a 'resistant measure' – unaffected by very large or very small values of the variable we are trying to summarise. Outliers and extreme observations do not affect this alternative measure of the mean (the median is similarly described as a resistant measure).

1.5.7 Guide: Obtaining a Summary of File Info

Before we conclude this chapter, it is worth learning how to summarise the whole data set you have constructed. You have worked on a number of datasets in this chapter, some you constructed from scratch, others you have significantly added to. A useful facility in SPSS is the *Display Data File Information* function, which pastes to your output file a list of all your variable names, formats, labels, and value labels. It is easy to derive and a useful way of checking whether you have coded all your variables correctly. It is also a very helpful way to introduce yourself to a new dataset, particularly if it is a large file with many hundreds of variables.

Example 1.5.7 How to Obtain a Summary of File Information

1. Open up the **employees5.sav** dataset:

   ```
   GET 'C:\STATISTICS\employees5.sav'.
   ```

2. Click on File, Display Data File Information, Working File, or simply run the following syntax,

   ```
   DISPLAY DICTIONARY.
   ```

   If you have a very long list of variables, you may find that you cannot see all of them listed in the file information that has been pasted to your output file. This is because, in recent versions at least, SPSS pastes the file information as a text box. To see all of the text, double click in the text box, and you will then be able to scroll down the text to view any element. Once you're in the text box, you can select and copy elements of the text (using Ctrl+C, or right-clicking on the highlighted text and choosing "Copy" from the list) to a word processor. If you want to select all the file information, simply press Ctrl+A once you have double clicked on the text box, and then copy.

N.B. In earlier versions of SPSS the menu route for obtaining file information was different. If you have an earlier version of SPSS try clicking, Utilities on the menu bar at the top of the screen, and then selecting File Info. Or simply run the DISPLAY DICTIONARY syntax since the syntax has remained unchanged. Actually, this raises an important additional reason for learning and using syntax. Each time a new version of SPSS comes out, there are changes to the menu system, but the syntax commands usually remain unaltered.

1.6 Enhancing our Overview

Before we proceed, it is worth enhancing our overview of the course now that we understand some of the basic concepts of data analysis, such as the difference between a *sample* and the *population*, the nature of *continuous* as opposed to *categorical* variables, and the meaning of means and proportions. The two 'mind-maps' below set out the tree of decisions along which we merrily proceed when we want to decide on the appropriate *confidence interval* or *hypothesis test*. For example, if you want to know the appropriate formula to use for your confidence interval, you must first identify whether your data are categorical or continuous. Then you must decipher whether you are dealing with a single sample or whether you want to compare two or more populations. Sometimes the size of your sample will determine the method you need to apply, as will the question of normality (i.e. how bell-shaped is your data distribution?).

These two diagrams show us, therefore, that to be able to run and understand hypothesis tests and confidence intervals on sample data we need to:

- understand the difference between a population and a sample
- know the difference between continuous and categorical variables
- know the meaning and calculation of the mean (since the mean is used extensively in inference)
- know the meaning and calculation of the standard deviation (also used extensively in inference)
- know the meaning and calculation of a proportion (used extensively in inference on categorical variables
- understand the implications of sample size
- understand the theory of inference that underpins the use of t-and *z*-distributions both of which are used for confidence intervals and hypothesis tests.
- understand how to run an F-test since the F-distribution is used to test for differences in variation of variables.

As such, the two diagrams summarise the knowledge we need to acquire in order to perform introductory statistics.

Enhanced Overview of Confidence Interval Estimation

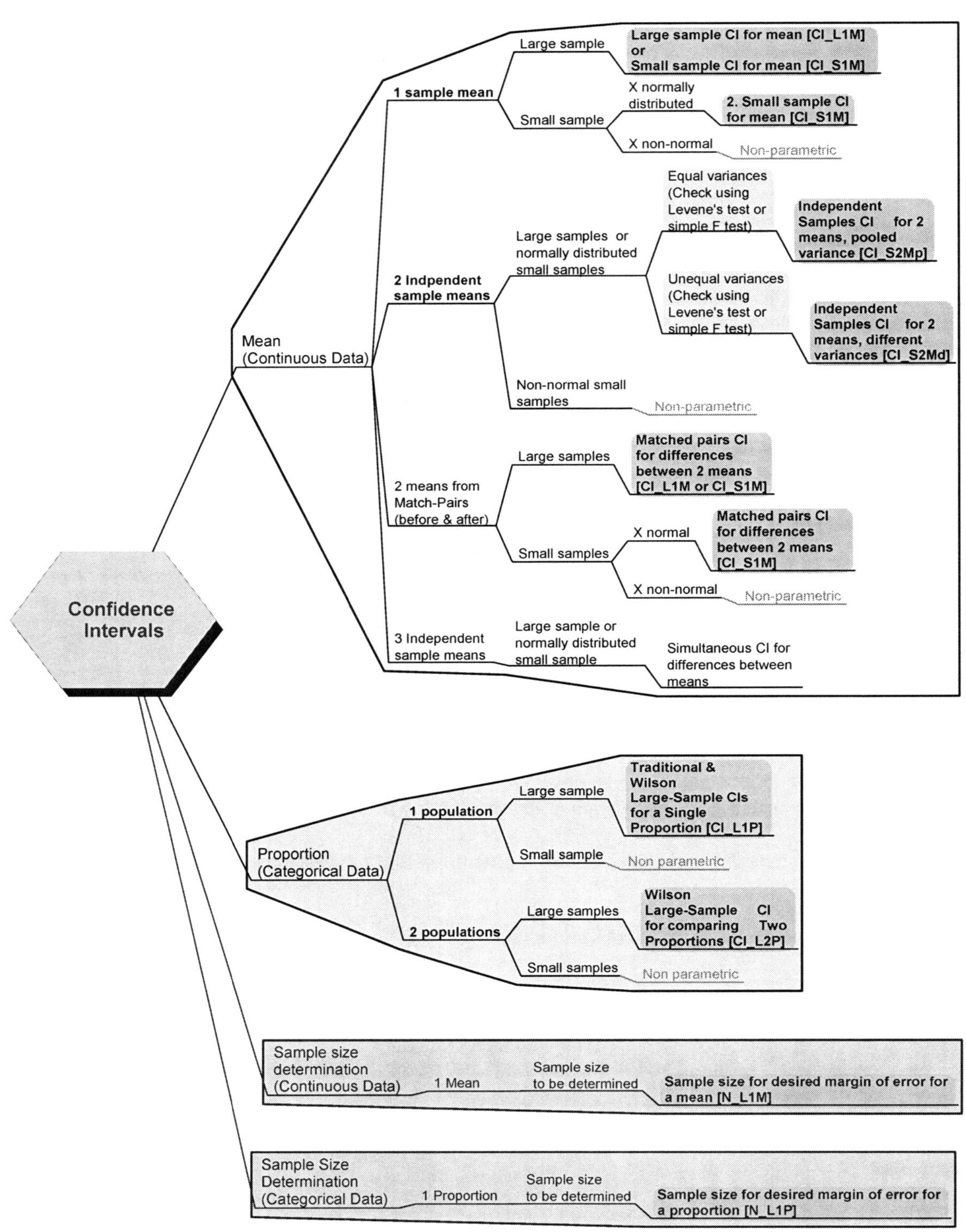

Enhanced Overview of Hypothesis Tests

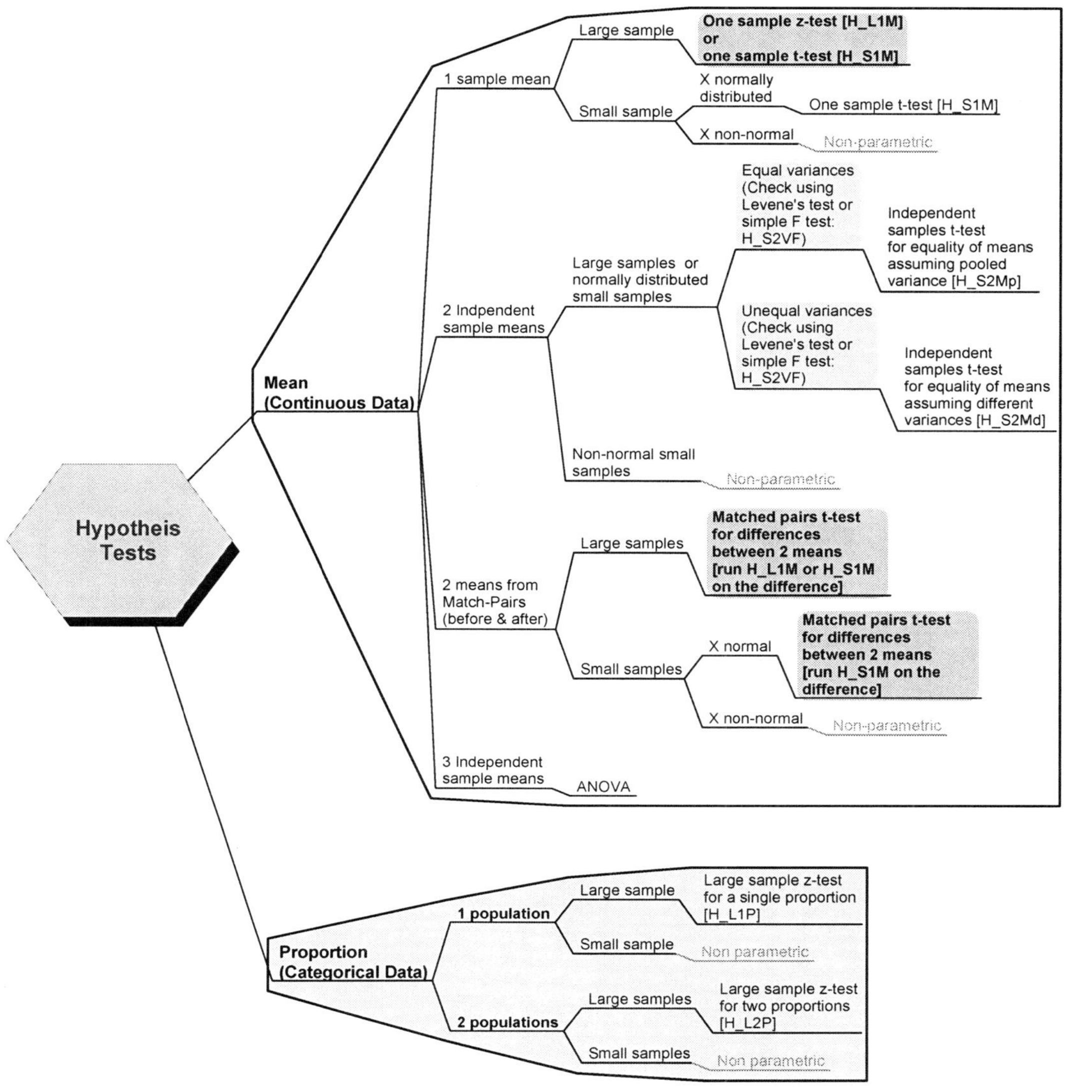

1.7 Further Study

Indicate whether the following variables are quantitative or qualitative. If they are qualitative (i.e. categorical), identify whether they are nominal or ordinal. If they are ordinal, describe briefly what the ordering is.

a) Rainfall in mm (measured in litres if you live in Glasgow…)

b) Responses to the following statement, 'Keeping inflation low is more important than higher wages', are recorded as *strongly agree*, *agree*, *undecided*, or *strongly disagree*.

c) The number of unemployed men in Glasgow

d) A person's country of origin

e) How educated a person is

f) Method of contraception.

2 Probability and Statistical Inference

Aim:
The aim of this chapter is to introduce the concepts of probability and statistical inference.

Objectives:
By the end of this lecture students should be able to understand the principles that allow us to make inferences about the population from samples. These include the meaning of randomness and the basic laws of probability, the properties of density curves, the Central Limit Theorem and Student's t-Distribution.

Further Reading:
Moore, D.S. and McCabe, G.P. (2003) *Introduction to the Practice of Statistics* 4th Ed. (San Francisco: Freeman), Ch. 4 and 5 and section 7.1.
Gonick, L. and Smith, W. (1993) *Cartoon Guide to Statistics*, Harper Collins, New York, Ch. 3-6.

Plan:

2.1 Introduction

Where do social scientists get their data? Researchers in the disciplines of natural science can observe planets, construct experiments, analyse minerals, peer down microscopes. Such methods are rarely transferable to social research. Our approaches are inevitably somewhat "softer". We are usually resigned to conducting surveys or accessing administrative records (such as mortgage transactions data or unemployment counts). Nevertheless, our data shares a common feature with the data used by all researchers: it is almost always drawn from a *sample* rather than the *population*. The *population* refers to all possible observations on a particular variable. It might be all the individuals that we would like to interview, or it might be the sum total of stars in the Universe. Whatever the variable of interest, we can rarely gain access to all occurrences of that variable, so we attempt to identify and extract an appropriate sample.

For example, suppose you would like to measure the degree of employee loyalty among UK employees. You cannot realistically interview all UK employees. That would take too long and cost too much. You may, however, have the time and funds to contact 1,000 employees. The million Euro question is, to what extent are results based on your sample typical of the population? This is the subject of this chapter. In fact, it is the preoccupation of the rest of the book.

The formal name for our dilemma is the problem of *inference*. That is, what and how can we infer from a sample to the population? The first step in answering this question is to understand how difficult the problem of inference is. Because it is really a question about probability, our first port of call will be to consider the basic laws of probability. One of the goals here will be to establish just how poor humans are at "guesstimating" the right answer to problems of probability and hence the need to establish a robust systematic method for generalising results from a sample to the population.

It turns out that the solution to the problem of inference rests with the *CLT*. No, the CLT is not a sandwich but a mathematical discovery given the unassuming title of the *Central Limit Theorem*. It is a brilliant and beautiful theorem, without which we would be severely hampered in our ability to draw reliable and meaningful conclusions about the population. So it is crucial that we understand the concepts that underpin it and its limitations. We shall therefore devote a good chunk of this chapter to the workings of the CLT and what happens when its assumptions break down. One key assumption is that the sample size is large. When our sample does not live up to the requirement of this assumption, we may be able to draw upon another important mathematical discovery: *Student's t distribution* – the final major topic in this chapter.

2.2 The Long Run Average

A lecturer stands in front of a class of 70 students and predicts that there is at least one birthday in the class that week. His prediction turns out to be correct. How did he do this?

Well, one way would have been to observe that there is always a 1 in 52 chance that it is a stranger's birthday in any given week (he is assuming that birthdays in general are evenly spread across the year – this is of course a fallacious assumption but one we shall make for the purposes of our example). If there are 70 strangers in a room then the expected number of birthdays in that week is given by seventy divided by fifty two:

Expected number of birthdays = $70 \times {}^{1}/_{52} = 1.346$.

What does this figure mean? Does it mean that every class of 70 has exactly 1.346 birthdays every week? No, it is impossible to have 1.346 birthdays in any given class. It means simply that, in the *long run* (that is, when we have considered many lecture classes of size 70) the average number of people with birthdays will be 1.346.

The following table records the number of birthdays in different weekly classes of seventy students. The final column lists the *running average*, which is the average recorded each week based on all classes up to that point. You will notice that in the first three classes there were no birthdays, and so the lecturer's prediction would have been incorrect in those lessons. Then, like buses, 4 birthdays come at once in the fourth week, followed by 5 in the following week

Date	Class Size	Number of Birthdays in class	Running Average Number of Birthdays (= sum of all birthdays ÷ no. classes up to that point)	
14th Oct '02	70	0	0÷1 =	0.00
21st Oct '02	70	0	(0+0)÷2 =	0.00
28th Oct '02	70	0	(0+0+0)÷3 =	0.00
4th Nov '02	70	4	(0+0+0+4)÷4 =	1.00
11th Nov '02	70	5	(0+0+0+4+5)÷5 =	1.80
18th Nov '02	70	1	(0+0+0+4+5+1)÷6 =	1.67
25th Nov '02	70	0	(0+0+0+4+5+1+0)÷7 =	1.43
2nd Dec '02	70	0	(0+0+0+4+5+1+0+0)÷8 =	1.25
9th Dec '02	70	0	(0+0+0+4+5+1+0+0+0)÷9 =	1.11
16th Dec '02	70	0	(0+0+0+4+5+1+0+0+0+0)÷10 =	1.00
23rd Dec '02	70	2	(0+0+0+4+5+1+0+0+0+0+2)÷11 =	1.09

If we consider enough classes, the running average will change less and less from week to week. This is because, if an average is based on several hundred numbers, a given change any one of those numbers will only have a small effect on the final calculation. Conversely, if the average is based on only a handful of numbers (as it is in the first few lessons), a given change in any one number will have a relatively big effect. So the average will *stabilise* as we consider more classes, but it will also *converge* to a particular number. That number is the *long run average*, or *expected value*.

Perhaps the most startling thing to note about this example is how long it can take for the long run average to emerge. The intervals in the following graph are every week, though there is only room to label the date every two years on the horizontal axis. In total, seventy years' of weekly classes are considered, a total of 3,640 different classes (70x52 = 3,640). Yet it is only after the 3,600th class or so that the running average converges closely to the expected value of 1.346. We have considered these classes sequentially, but we might equally conceive of asking the same question of 3,600 simultaneous classes of 70 students. The implication would, however, be the same. If we only consider a few classes of 70 students, the average number of birthdays might be quite different from the average computed on all possible classes of 70 students. We need to consider many classes before we get a reliable estimate of the long run average.

2.2.1 What About Categorical Variables?

The number of birthdays in a class is not a truly continuously variable because each *observed* value has to be an integer – that is, a whole number. The number of birthdays in each class is really a *count* variable. Nevertheless, for the purposes of the above example, our calculations were the same as they would be if we were considering a truly continuous variable (such as height, age or weight).

But what if the variable we want to consider is a categorical variable? How do our conclusions about the long run average translate when our variable has only two possible outcomes, for example? The answer is much the same. Consider the following example about a very patient man tossing a coin...

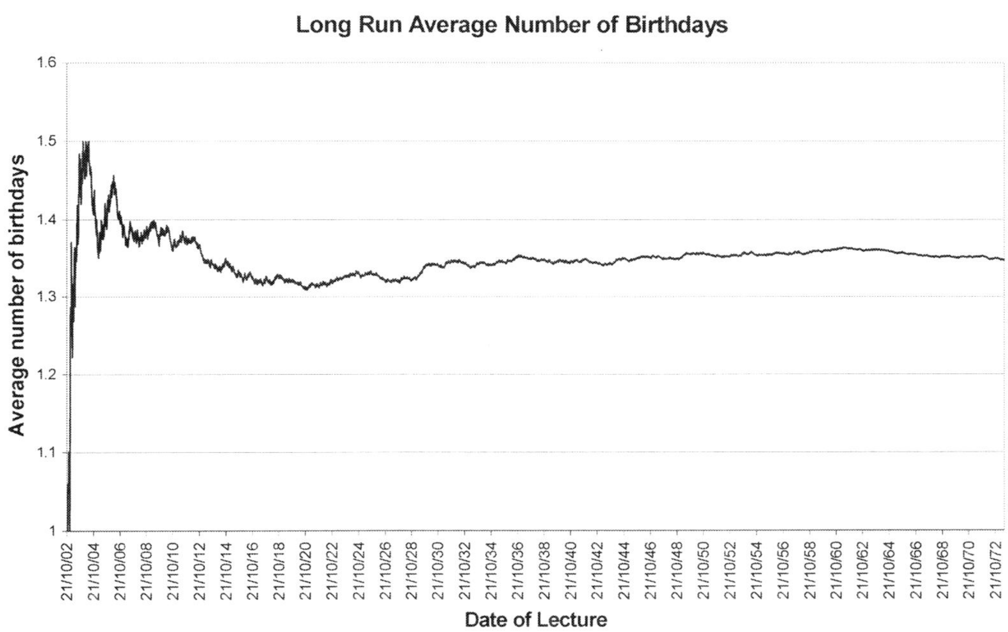

Example 2.2.1 Coin Tossing Experiment

Assuming a fair coin, what is the probability of throwing a head? The answer of course is ½ = 0.5 = 50%. But how do we arrive at this answer? The calculation of the probability of an event occurring is simple if we know the total number of possible outcomes and if each possible outcome is equally likely to occur. The toss of a fair coin has two equally likely outcomes – heads or tails – so the probability of either occurring is simply the number of specific outcomes we are considering divided by the number of all possible outcomes, which in this case, is one divided by two.

Does that mean that on repeated tosses the outcome will exactly alternate between H & T? Intuitively we would say no, but we might be surprised at how long it takes for the long run average of 0.5 to emerge, as the following example shows.

Consider a long-suffering researcher who tosses a fair coin and records a 1 if the outcome is heads, and records a 0 if the outcome is tails. He then tosses the coin again, and once more records 1 if heads, 0 if tails. He then calculates the running average which equals the sum of scores of ones and zeroes divided by the total number of tosses. He continues this process 500 times. The following table records the results from the first ten throws.

The results are surprising because even though we know that the coin is fair, after 10 throws the running average is 0.7. In other words, the coin comes up heads 70% of the time, which suggests that it is biased towards heads, even though it is not.

Toss	Score (= 1 if heads, 0 if tails)	Running average	
1	1	1÷1 =	1.000
2	1	(1+1)÷2 =	1.000
3	1	(1+1+1)÷3 =	1.000
4	0	(1+1+1+0)÷4 =	0.750
5	1	(1+1+1+0+1)÷5 =	0.800
6	1	(1+1+1+0+1+1)÷6 =	0.833
7	1	(1+1+1+0+1+1+1)÷7 =	0.857
8	0	(1+1+1+0+1+1+1+0)÷8 =	0.750
9	0	(1+1+1+0+1+1+1+0+0)÷9 =	0.667
10	1	(1+1+1+0+1+1+1+0+0+1)÷10 =	0.700

You could of course look at the coin-tossing experiment from another perspective. Suppose you don't actually know whether the coin is fair. The coin may have microscopic imbalances that you don't know about. As a result, heads may be slightly more likely than tails. Then again, it may not. The question you are faced with is this: "How many times must I toss the coin before I know for sure whether or not it is truly fair?" The short answer is that you would have to toss it an infinite number of times to be absolutely sure that the probability of heads exactly equals 0.5.

But suppose that you would be content with knowing with reasonable confidence whether the coin is almost fair with, say, a probability of heads no lower than 0.4 and no higher than 0.6. How many times would you have to toss the coin to reach a conclusion? What would happen if you based your conclusion on the first 10 tosses? Well, we can see from the table above that the running average is 0.7 so we would most likely reject the hypothesis that the coin is fair. So suppose you based you answer on the average proportion of heads after 40 throws. The running average after 40 throws is 0.65 (i.e. heads has been tossed 65% of the time), which means we would still reject the coin as biased, but the proportion of heads declines as we continue to throw the coin, coming very close to 50% after 500 throws:

Toss	Running Average
40	0.650
50	0.600
100	0.550
500	0.506

The figure below plots the running average for all 500 throws and demonstrates how conclusions based on a sample of 10 tosses, or 20 tosses, or even 40 coin-tosses, could be misleading. Unfortunately it means that we need to obtain large samples for our results to be generalised to the population. Which means a lot of extra cost and effort. Worse still, there are occasions where large samples are simply not attainable. One consolation you can take from the coin-flipping experiment, however, is that it is just the sort of tedious research that natural scientists devote their lives to and is a good reminder of why you decided to study *social* science in the first place...

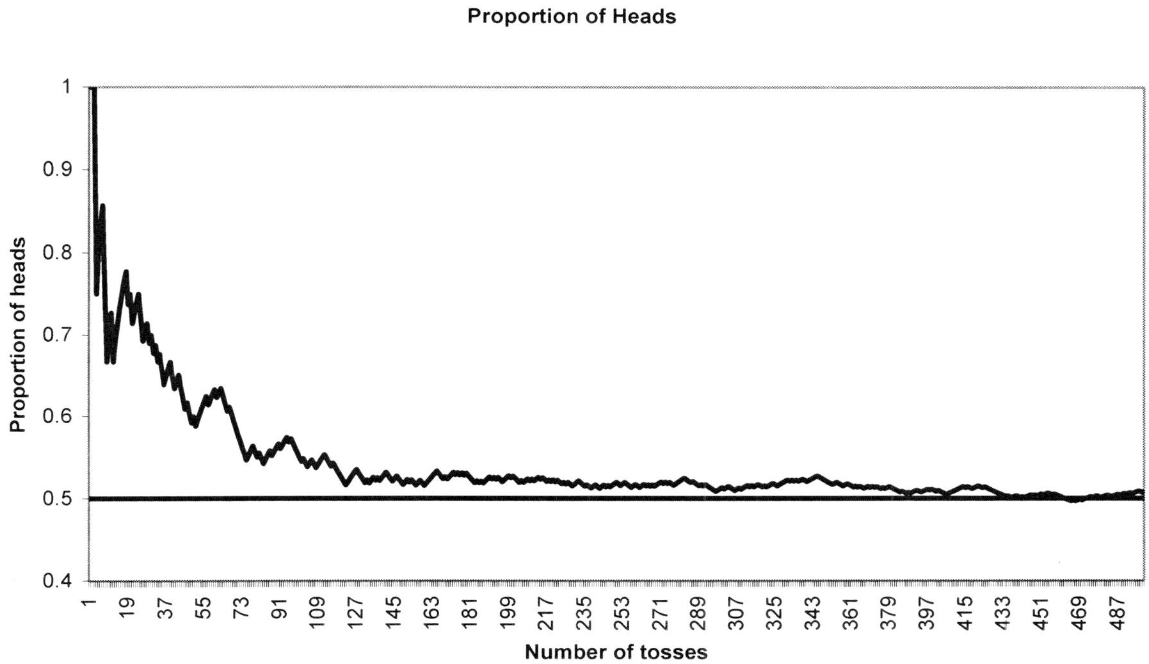

2.3 Randomness and the Laws of Probability

A phenomenon is said to be *random* if individual outcomes are uncertain. Randomness does not imply absence of regularity. Although we don't know the outcomes beforehand, there may nonetheless be a regular distribution of outcomes observed after the event, particularly when we consider a large number of repetitions of the event in question. So, for example, if you do not yet have children, although you may not at this stage know with any certainty the sex of your first child, you do know that there is a pattern to the gender-outcome of all babies born. Roughly half are born male and half are female.

We have established that the probability of any outcome of a random variable is the proportion of times the outcome would occur in a very large number of repetitions.

Probability = Long-run relative frequency = Proportion of times an event occurs in the long run

If we know for certain that each possible outcome is equally likely, and we know the range of possible outcomes, then we can compute the probability of each individual outcome (or combinations of outcomes) using logic and mathematics alone (i.e. we don't need to do an experiment or observe outcomes). This is because we know that the probability of an outcome equals the number of equally likely outcomes we are interested in divided by the total number of equally likely outcomes. For example,

Probability that a stranger's birthday is this week = 1/52
Probability that flipped fair coin is heads = 1/2
Probability of picking a red ball out of a bag that contains 2 red balls and 8 blue balls = 2/10 = 0.2 = 20% = "1 in 5 chance" = "5 to 1 against".

In social science research we are rarely able to calculate the probability of events occurring from theory – we usually have to estimate probabilities from data – but once these probabilities have been estimated they obey the same laws as probabilities computed from logic alone. This means that we can manipulate the probabilities we have estimated to compute other probabilities. This is important. The following five laws of probability not only allow us to solve basic probability problems but also provide the foundation for important statistical methods that allow us, for example, to determine whether there is a relationship between variables.

2.3.1 *The Law of Complements*

All probabilities always lie between 0 and 1. This means that we can easily calculate the probability of an event not occurring. This is called the *complement* of an event and is calculated as follows:

Pr(A does not occur) = 1 – Pr(A does occur) ,

where "Pr", or simply "P" is short for "probability". So if there is a 10% chance that someone from a working class background will go to university, we know that there is a 90% chance that they will not go to university. We calculated this as follows:

We know that: Pr(someone from a working class background goes to university) = 0.1
We know that: complement of an event = 1 – Pr(event)
We can therefore deduce that: Pr(someone from a working class background *does not* go to university) = 1 - Pr(someone from a working class background goes to university)
We compute 1- 0.1 = 0.9 and conclude that Pr(someone from a working class background *does not* go to university) = 0.9 = 90%.

2.3.2 *The Law of Disjoint Events*

Two events A and B are *disjoint* if they have no outcomes in common and so can never occur simultaneously (also called *mutually exclusive* events). For example, suppose we have one die and we want to know the probability of rolling a 4 or a 6. You know that, if the die is fair, the chance of rolling a 4 is 1/6. Similarly, the chance of rolling a 6 is also 1/6. Given that you can't roll both numbers at the same time, the chance of rolling either a 4 or a 6 is simply the sum of the two probabilities:

Probability of rolling a 4 or a 6 = 1/6 + 1/6 = 1/3.

More generally, when A and B are disjoint (mutually exclusive), the rule for calculating the probability of A or B is given by:

Pr(A or B) = Pr(A) + Pr(B)

Venn diagram of disjoint events:
The above problem can be depicted graphically using a Venn diagram. Each circle represents a particular event (or set of events). If the circles do not overlap, then it is not possible for the two events to occur simultaneously.

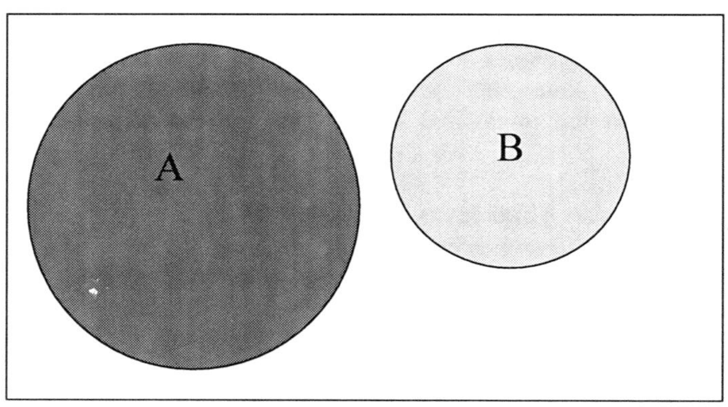

2.3.3 The Law of Complementary Events

Consider the implication of 2 events occurring together. Suppose that you now have a die and a coin and you want to compute the probability of throwing a 4 and/or heads (assuming both the die and coin are fair). We know that the probability of rolling 4 = 1/6. We also know that the probability of tossing heads = 1/2. So you might think that the correct way to calculate the probability of rolling 4 and/or heads is as follows:

$$Pr(4 \text{ and/or heads}) = 1/6 + 1/2 = 4/6$$

Or is it? You have, in fact, double-counted the probability of getting 4 and heads. This is perhaps best understood by looking at the Venn diagram below. If you simply add Pr(A) and Pr(B) you count the area of intersection twice, so this area needs to be deducted.

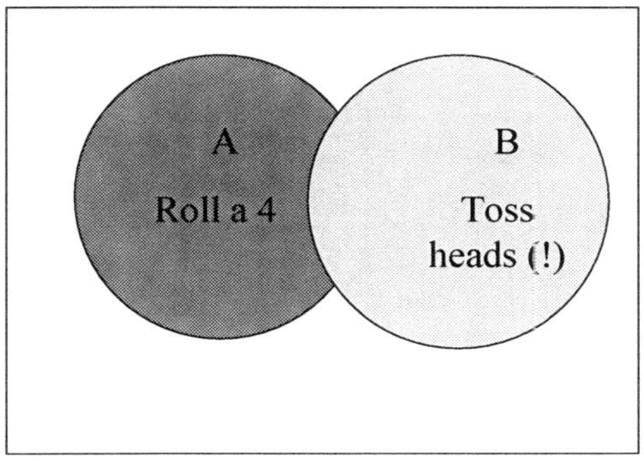

So we need to deduct this probability ($^1/_6 \times ½$) from our calculation. The true probability of rolling 4 and/or heads is computed as follows:

$$Pr(4 \text{ and/or heads}) = {}^1/_6 + ½ - ({}^1/_6 \times ½)$$
$$= {}^4/_6 - {}^1/_{12}$$
$$= {}^7/_{12}$$

<u>Example 2.3 The two sided die</u>

The need to deduct the probability of both events is perhaps more clearly illustrated in the following (rather convoluted) variation of our example. Suppose now that you only have a two sided die that allows you to only roll a one or a two, and a coin. Both are fair. You want to compute: Pr(1 and/or tails). We know that Pr(1) = ½ and Pr(heads) = ½. If we incorrectly simply add the probabilities to compute Pr(1 and/or tails) we get:

$$Pr(1 \text{ and/or heads}) = ½ + ½ = 1$$

This says that the probability of obtaining a 1 and/or a heads is exactly equal to one. In other words, we will obtain a 1 and/or heads with complete certainty, which is clearly incorrect since it is possible to throw a 2 and a tails. There are, in fact, four possible outcomes, three of which qualify as "1 or tails or both":

(1,H) (1,T) (2,H) (2,T)

Each of these four outcomes is equally likely, so the Pr(1 and/or heads) = ¾. By simply adding the Pr(1) = ½ and Pr(heads) = ½ we have double counted Pr(both) = Pr(1,H), where:

$$Pr(1,H) = ½ \times ½ = ¼$$

So the correct calculation would have been,

$$Pr(1 \text{ and/or heads}) = Pr(1) + Pr(heads) - Pr(1 \text{ and heads})$$
$$= ½ + ½ - ¼$$
$$= ¾ .$$

More generally, we can write,

P(A and/or B) = P(A) + P(B) - P(A and B)

If A and B are mutually exclusive, P(A and B) = zero, and the formula reduces to the formula we used for disjoint events.

Probability Notation:
We could write this same equation in a slightly different way by using the probability notation for unions and intersections:

$A \cup B$	= A union B	= A or B occur
$A \cap B$	= A intersection B	= A and B occur

So we can re-write the above as:

$$P(A \cup B) = P(A) + P(B) - P(A \cap B) = \tfrac{1}{2} + \tfrac{1}{2} - \tfrac{1}{4} = \tfrac{3}{4}$$

2.3.4 *The Law of Independent Events*

If knowing that one event occurs does not affect the outcome of another event, we say those two outcomes are **independent**. If A and B are independent, and we know the probability of each of them occurring, we can calculate the probability of them both occurring.

Continuing our two sided die example, find the probability of rolling a one and tossing heads. Intuitively you might think that you would need to multiply the probability of rolling a one by the probability of tossing heads, and you would be correct.

Pr(1 and heads) = $\tfrac{1}{2} \times \tfrac{1}{2} = \tfrac{1}{4}$

which leads us to the general rule for calculating the probability of two independent events both occurring:

$$\mathbf{Pr(A \cap B) = Pr(A) \times Pr(B)}$$

Another example would be calculating the probability of getting two heads after two flips of the same coin. Suppose:

A = outcome of 1st flip is a head
B = outcome of 2nd flip is a head

then we want to know the probability of $A \cap B$. Because A and B are independent and are not disjoint we know that $Pr(A \cap B) = Pr(A) \times Pr(B)$. Given that Pr(A) = 0.5 and Pr(B) = 0.5, we can say that

$$Pr(A \cap B) = 0.5 \times 0.5 = 0.25$$

2.3.5 *The Law of Contingent Events*

If the outcome of one event *does* affect the outcome of another event, then the two events are *not* independent and are said to be *contingent*. If events are contingent on each other then we can say that there is some kind of relationship between them. So testing for contingency is one way of testing for a relationship.

Example 2.3.5 Contingent probability of going to university:

Suppose there is a 70% chance that a child will go to university if its parents are middle class, but only a 10% chance if its parents are working class. Given that there is a 60% chance of a child's parents being working class, what are the chances that a child will be working class and go to University? What proportion of people at university will be from working class backgrounds?

The following tree diagram will help us understand the problem:

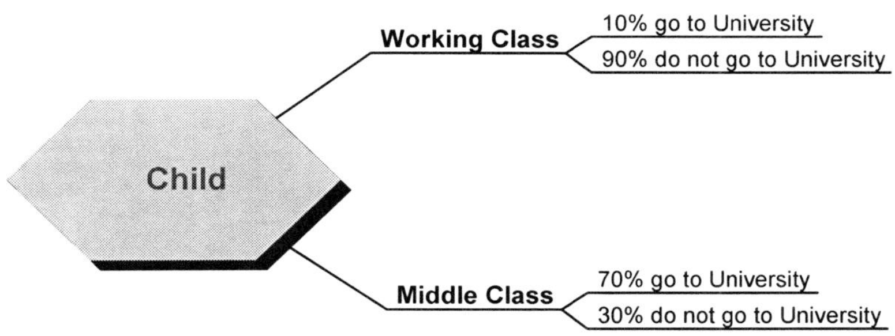

We can compute the probability of each of the final outcomes by multiplying the probabilities of each sequence of branches. So, for example, the probability of being middle class and not going to university is 40% × 30% = 12%. Similarly, the probability of being working class and going to university is 60% × 10% = 6%.

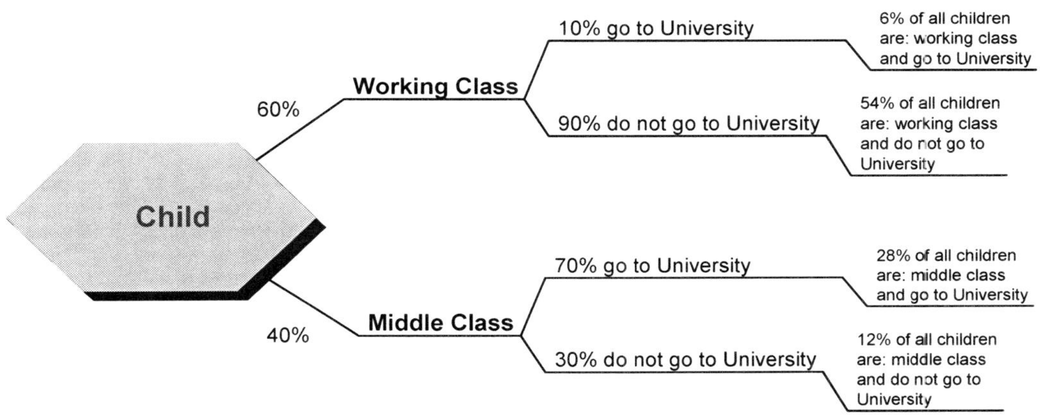

So, of all children, only 34% end up at university, 6% from working class homes plus 28% from middle class homes. This also means that six out of every 34 University students are from working class backgrounds, which means that 100x6÷34 = 17.65% of University students are working class.

Note how we computed the probability of a working class child going to university. We did not simply multiply the probability of being working class (0.6) by the probability of any child going to university (0.34). This is because the probability of going to university is contingent on class background. So our calculation was in fact as follows:

$$\begin{aligned} Pr(WC \cap Uni) &= Pr(WC) \times Pr(Uni \text{ given } WC) \\ &= 0.6 \times 0.1 \\ &= 0.06 \end{aligned}$$

This in fact follows the general rule of computing probabilities when events are not independent but contingent:

$$Pr(A \cap B) = Pr(A) \times Pr(B \text{ given } A)$$

2.3.6 Using Probability Rules to Test for Relationships

We have already noted that if A and B are independent, then the probability of events A and B simultaneously occurring is simply equal to the product of the two events occurring:

$$Pr(A \cap B) = Pr(A) \times Pr(B)$$

However, if A and B are not independent, in other words they are contingent, then the probability of them both occurring is equal to the probability of one event multiplied by the contingent probability of the other event (e.g. probability of B given that A has happened):

$$\Pr(A \cap B) = \Pr(A) \times \Pr(B \text{ given } A)$$

We can use the difference between these two rules to test whether events are independent. The basic rationale of this test is to ask whether the distribution of *observed* outcomes resembles the random distribution we would get if events were truly independent. In other words, if we assume independence and calculate the *expected* number of cases in each category of combined outcome, do these figures correspond fairly closely to the actual distribution of outcomes found in our data?

Example 2.3(c) Relationship Between Class and Higher Education

Suppose we are interested in whether there is a relationship between social class and access to higher education. One way of testing whether the two are connected is to look at the following categories in our data: working class, middle class, attend University, do not attend University. Suppose we have 300 observations in our data distributed across these categories as follows:

		A **Working Class**	B **Middle Class**
1	**Go to university**	18	84
2	**Do not go to university**	162	36

To test for independence we need to compare *expected* number of observations in each cell in the above table with the *observed* number of observations in each cell. Given that we already know the observed counts in each cell (given in the table above), the next step is to calculate e_i, the expected number of observations in category *i*. How do we do this? First of all we need to understand what it is we are actually trying to calculate. The "expected number of observations" is in fact the number of cases expected in cell *i* assuming that the variables are independent. The formula for e_i is derived by multiplying the probability of an observation falling into category *i* (assuming independence between class and education) by the total number of observations in our entire sample:

$$e_i = \textbf{expected number of cases in cell } i = \textbf{Pr(observation being in cell } i\textbf{)} \times n$$

where *n* is the total sample size = 300.

How do we calculate Pr(observation being in cell i)? We use the *independence* probability formula. For example, to compute the probability of an observation in our sample being in cell **A1** of our table, assuming independence, means using the following formula:

$$\Pr(WC \cap Uni) = \Pr(Uni) \times \Pr(WC)$$

Similarly, the probability of an observation in our sample being in cell **A2** is given by:

$$\Pr(WC \cap \textit{no } Uni) = \Pr(\textit{no } Uni) \times \Pr(WC)$$

The probability of an observation in our sample being in cell **B1** is given by:

$$\Pr(MC \cap Uni) = \Pr(Uni) \times \Pr(MC)$$

The probability of an observation in our sample being in cell **B2** is given by:

$$\Pr(MC \cap \textit{no } Uni) = \Pr(\textit{no } Uni) \times \Pr(MC)$$

But how do we work out Pr(Uni), Pr(WC), Pr(*no* Uni), and Pr(MC) – the probabilities needed to calculate the above equations? The answer is simple. Because we are assuming for the sake of argument that class and education are independent, we can estimate these probabilities by dividing the total observations in our sample by the total number in the headline category. So, for example, Pr(Uni) assuming independence is given by:

$$\begin{aligned}\Pr(Uni) &= \text{Total no. observations that go to university} \div n \\ &= (18 + 84) / 300 = \underline{0.34}\end{aligned}$$

So the expected number of observations in cell A1 will be given by:

$$\Pr(WC \cap Uni) = \Pr(Uni) \times \Pr(WC)$$

The full workings of computing expected cell counts, e_i, for each cell are given in the table below:

		A **Working Class**	B **Middle Class**
1	**Go to university**	e_{A1} = Pr(Uni) × Pr(WC) × *n* = (no. at Uni ÷ *n*) × (no. WC ÷ *n*) × *n* = (102 / 300) × (180 /300) × 300 = 0.34 × 0.6 x 300 = **61.2**	e_{B1} = Pr(Uni) × Pr(MC) × *n* = (no. at Uni ÷ *n*) × (no. MC ÷ *n*) × *n* = (102 / 300) × (120 /300) × 300 = 0.34 × 0.4 × 300 = **40.8**
2	**Do not go to university**	e_{A2} = Pr(no Uni) × Pr(WC) × *n* = (no. not at Uni ÷ *n*) × (no. WC ÷ *n*) × *n* = (198 / 300) × (180 /300) × 300 = 0.66 × 0.6 × 300 = **118.8**	e_{B2} = Pr(no Uni) × Pr(MC) × *n* = (no. not at Uni ÷ *n*) × (no. MC ÷ *n*) × *n* = (198 / 300) × (120 /300) × 300 = 0.66 × 0.4 × 300 = **79.2**

We can now compare our observed counts for each cell with the expected counts based on an assumption of independence:

			A **Working Class**	B **Middle Class**
1	**Go to university**	*Observed:* *Expected:*	18 61.2	84 40.8
2	**Do not go to university**	*Observed:* *Expected:*	162 118.8	36 79.2

If you have the original data, you can very easily obtain this type of table in SPSS: click on Analyse, Descriptive Statistics, Crosstabs, Cells, and choose Expected count.

If the expected and observed cell counts are similar, then we can reasonably conclude that the two variables – education and class – are independent. This is because our observed cell counts would be what we would expect if the variables are truly independent.

However, the differences between observed and expected cell counts is fairly stark in the above table. If class and education were indeed independent we would expect three times as many people from working class backgrounds to go to university than we observe in our sample. This means that it is very unlikely that class and education are independent. We have established that there is a relationship between the two variables, but we cannot say from the data alone which variable causes the other. This is where social science theory (rather than statistical theory) is crucial. Because class background precedes going to university it is very unlikely indeed that attending university determines class background (even if you wanted to, you could not change your class background after graduating from university – that is determined long before you go to university). So in this case, the direction of causation is pretty clear.

The hypothetical data we have used here show very large differences between expected and observed cell counts. However, sometimes the differences are much smaller and our conclusions more ambiguous. We would like, therefore, to state what the *probability* is that the two variables are independent. This is the subject of our penultimate chapter: *Relationships between Categorical Variables* where we shall return to this example and attempt to derive the probability that there is a relationship between class and education.

But we are rushing ahead of ourselves. Before we think about relationships between variables, we need to return to the much more basic question of how to interpret the simple descriptive results we have computed for single variables in our sample – such as the mean of a variable or the proportion of cases that fall into a particular category. We would like to infer from our sample to the population as a whole. Rather like the conclusion we have reached here – that ideally we would like to be able make some probability statement about the existence of a *relationship* – our goal will be to make probability statements about *simple descriptive measures* such as the mean or proportion of a variable in the population.

Exercise 2.3.1 Understanding Randomness and Probability

Review what you've read so far by answering the following questions:

1. What do statisticians mean when they talk about the 'long run average' or 'expected value'?

2. Toss a coin a hundred times keeping a record of outcomes (mark "1" for heads, and "0" for tails) and compute the running average. If the coin is fair, what value would you expect the long run average score to be? What is the average score after 10 tosses? What is the average score after 30 tosses? Do you think that your coin is a 'fair' coin? How many repetitions of an event do you need before the true 'long run average' emerges? What do you think are the implications for sample size?

3. Define the terms 'random' and 'probability'. How are these concepts related?

4. What is the *complement* of an event? The probability of a working class male over 60 having a heart attack before the year is out equals 0.4. Calculate the complement of this event.

5. What do we mean if we say that two events are *disjoint*?

6. What do we mean if we say that two events are *independent*? Explain the difference between the formula for computing the intersection of two events when those events are independent, and the formula for when those events are not independent. How does this difference help us derive a method that tests for the existence of a relationship between two variables?

2.4 Introduction to Inference

For a course in applied statistics, the theory of inference can appear a rather abstract diversion. It is tempting just to use SPSS without properly learning statistical theory first, and many social scientists learn SPSS this way. SPSS is, without question, a very powerful statistical package. But rather like the aircraft carrier referred to in the following quote from a Royal Navy recruitment poster, its facilities are only as good as the knowledge and skills of the user,

> 13 decks stuffed with 21st century attack and command technology.
> Without highly skilled engineers they may as well be stuffed with sage and onion.

Some of the principles explored below (particularly with regard to sampling distributions) underpin the most important elements of statistics. So it's worth devoting particular care to ensuring that you fully grasp the material covered in the remainder of this chapter.

2.4.1 Review of Measures of Central Tendency and Dispersion

Before we start looking at the principles of sampling distributions, we need to remind ourselves of the relevant material from the previous chapter:

Measures of Central Tendency

We looked at a number of measures of the *typical value* – or *central tendency* – of a variable, including the mode (the most frequently occurring value), median (the middle value when the variable is sorted by size of value), and mean (sum of observations divided by the number of observations). For our present purposes, the most important measure is the mean, which has the following formula:

$$\bar{x} = \frac{\sum x_i}{n}$$

where $\bar{x}$ is the sample mean, n is the number of observations on variable x in our sample, and x_i denotes particular observations ranging from 1 to n.

Measures of Spread

We have looked at a number of measures of *spread*, including the range (difference between the maximum and minimum value of a variable), the variance (the average squared deviation from the mean) and the standard deviation (the average deviation from the mean). The most relevant for our present purposes is the sample standard deviation, s, which is defined as follows:

$$s = \sqrt{\frac{1}{n-1}\sum (x_i - \bar{x})^2}$$

The mean and standard deviation are important because they define the shape of the *normal distribution*, also known as the *bell-curve*. The meaning and relevance of the normal distribution to the problem of inference will become clear as we proceed.

2.4.2 Density curves

You will recall from chapter 1 that one of the most useful ways to summarise a continuous variable is to plot a histogram. A histogram graphs the frequency of observations that lie within particular intervals of our variable. Provided our database has no shortage of observations, and assuming that the variable in question has a fairly regular distribution, the narrower we set those intervals, the smoother the ceiling of the histogram will be. Conceivably, if we make the intervals infinitesimally small, the histogram will take on a perfectly smooth shape, as illustrated in the graphs below.

A density curve is essentially the smooth ceiling of a histogram as drawn in the third graph. Density curves are in effect 'idealised' histograms, drawn by fitting a precise mathematical curve to the stepped surface of the histogram.

But they are more than that. Unlike a standard histogram, which plots frequency on the vertical axis, density curves use a standardised scale that ensures that the total area under the curve exactly equals one. The vertical axis on a density curve is therefore a measure of *relative* frequency, rather than the actual frequency. So the curve drawn in the third graph below is not a true density curve.

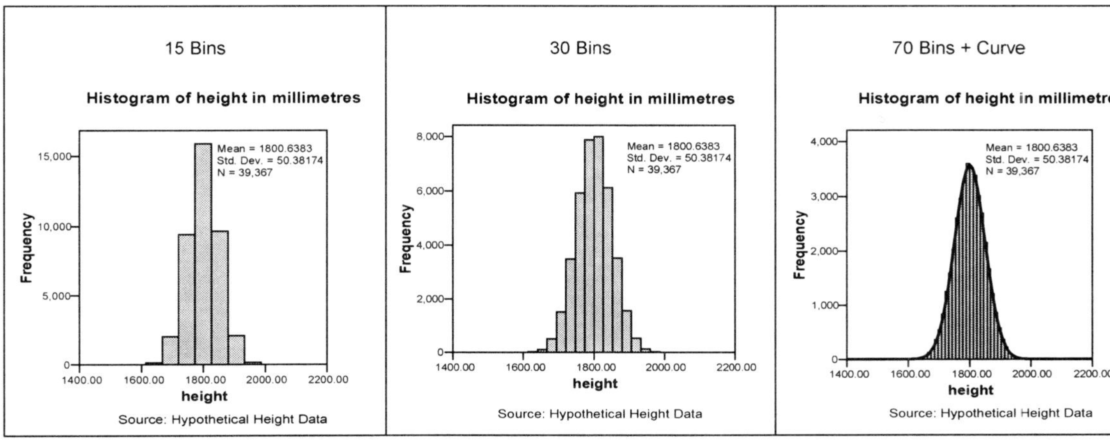

To achieve true a density curve plot we would have to re-scale our histogram so that the height of the bars is such that the sum of the areas of each bar equals 1. The result is plotted in the left figure below. The curve approximating the ceiling of the histogram, plotted in the second graph below, is now a true density curve. This curve is drawn to ensure that the area under it exactly equals one.

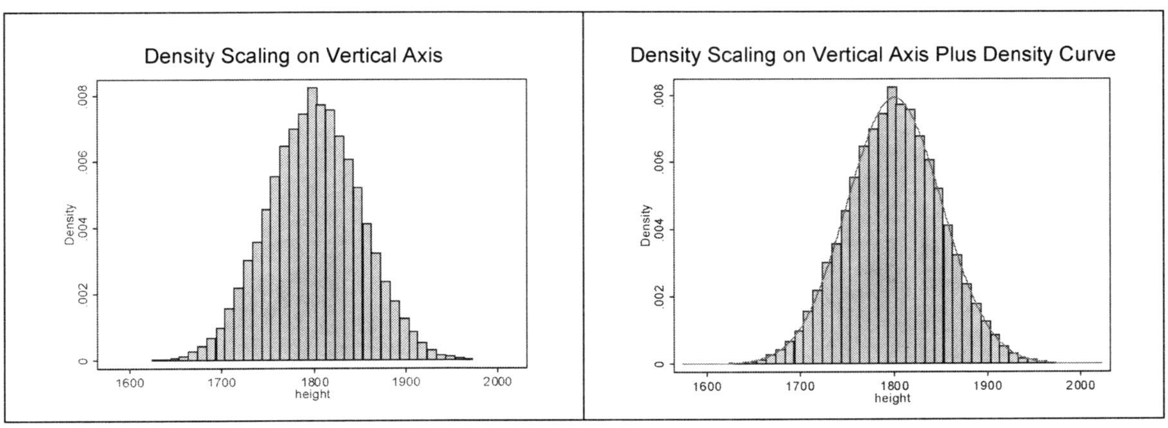

It just so happens that the height variable plotted above has a *normal* distribution (characterised by a symmetrical bell shape), but for other variables alternative shaped distributions might emerge as we narrow the intervals and plot the density curve.

House prices usually have a distribution with a positive skew, as demonstrated in the figure below. Nevertheless, the area under the density curve is still equal to one, and this is an important property because it allows us to treat vertical segments of the area under the density curve as *probabilities*.

For example, the area under the density curve to the right of 150,000 tells us the proportion of houses that sell for over £150,000. Suppose this area equals 0.11 (which is in fact a good approximation), then we know that 11% of houses sell for over £150,000.

The fact that the total area under the curve equals one, also allows us to calculate the size of other areas under the curve. For example, if we know the area to the right of £150,000 = 0.11, then we know that the area to the left of £150,000 = 1 – 0.11 = 0.89. In other words, 89% of properties sell for less than or equal to £150,000.

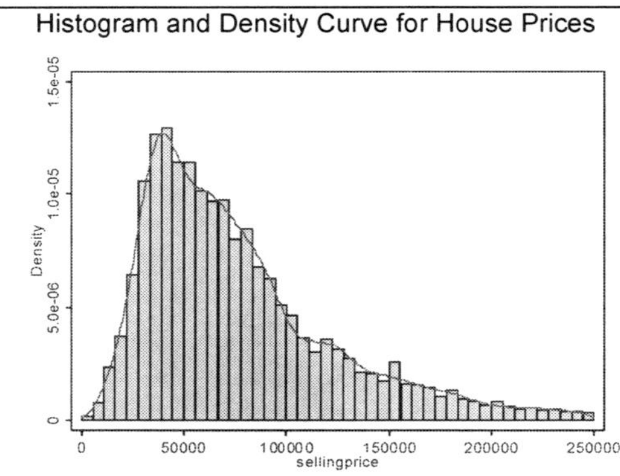

Source: GSPC Data

Further calculations are possible if the density curve is symmetrical, as is the case with the normal distribution. For example we know that, if the density curve is symmetrical, then:

- Mean = median
- 50% of sample < mean
- 50% of sample > mean

Suppose we know that the mean height = 1,801mm. Because the distribution of heights is symmetrical, this implies that the median also = 1,801mm. This implies that 50% of people are taller than 1,801mm and 50% are shorter than 1,801mm. It also means that if we know the proportion of people above say 1,901mm, then we will be able to work out the proportion of people below 1,701.

If a distribution is symmetrical, obviously its tails will also be symmetrical. So the area to the left of a height defined as 100mm *less than* the mean will exactly equal the area to the right of a height defined as 100mm *greater than* the mean. And if we know the area to the right of a point and the area to the left of another, we can work out the area between the two points (= 1 minus the sum of the two tail areas).

Exercise 2.2: Understanding and Calculating Areas under a Density Curve:

In the symmetrical bell-shaped distribution below, what is the probability of being less than 6ft tall?

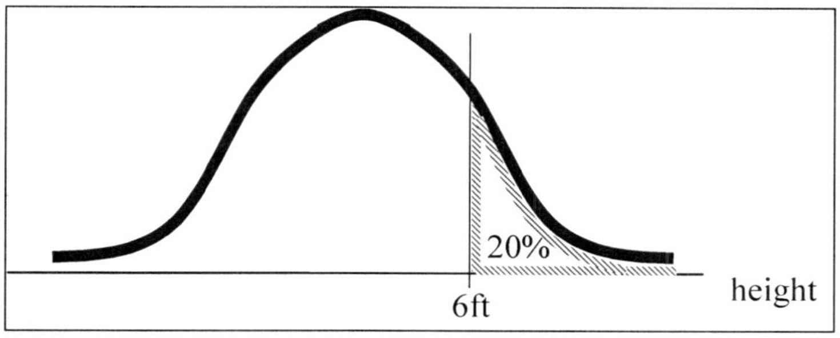

In the following symmetrical distribution, if 60% of the sample falls between *a* and *b*, what % is greater than b? (Assume that a and b are equally spaced from the centre of the distribution). What's the probability of randomly choosing an observation greater than b?

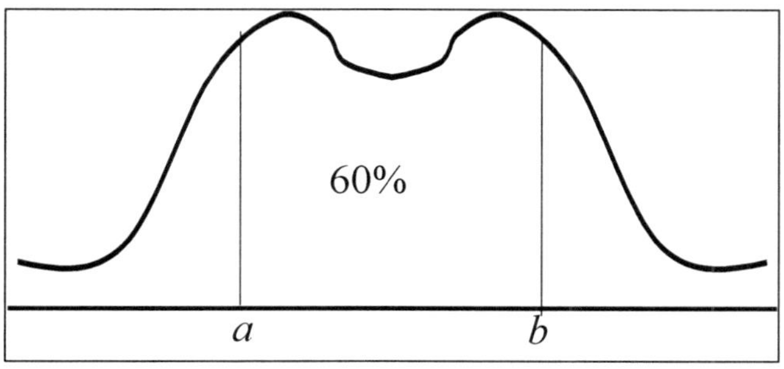

2.5 Normal Curve and the *z*-Distribution

We have already intimated that a particularly important symmetrical density curve is the *normal distribution.* There are in fact an infinite number of different normal distributions, but all are linked by certain common properties:

- all normal distributions vary only by mean and standard deviation, so in effect they are all scaled versions of each other;

- areas within a given number of standard deviations either side of the mean will be the same in all normal distributions. In particular 68% of the data will fall within one standard deviation either side of the mean; 95% of the data will fall within two standard deviations either side of the mean.

A baseline normal distribution has been invented called the *standard normal curve* which has zero mean and one standard deviation. This distribution is more succinctly known as the *z*-distribution. Points on all other normal distributions can be translated into points on the standard normal distribution by **subtracting the mean** from each value and **dividing the result by the standard deviation**. This can be thought of as a conversion formula that allows us to standardise any observation from any normal distribution by showing where it fits on the standard normal curve.

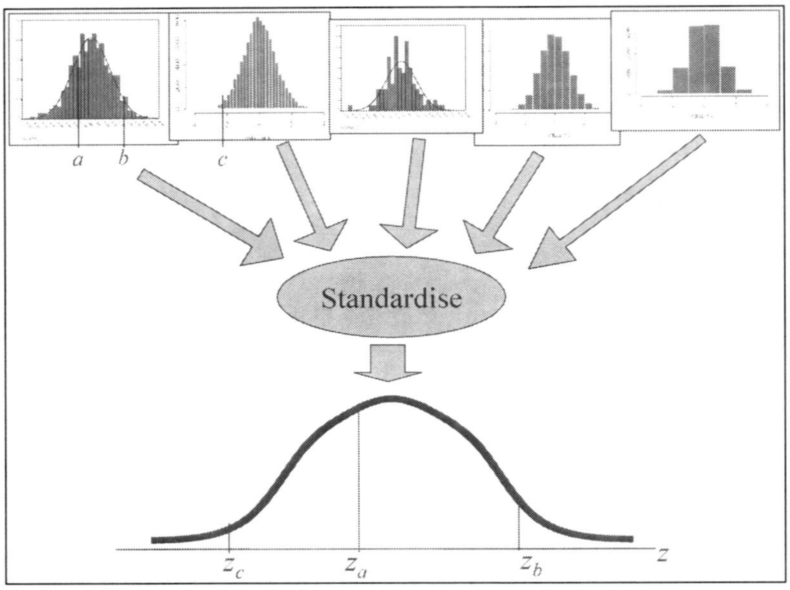

In the figure above, the five histograms are of completely unrelated variables that happen to be normally distributed. Values of each of these variables can be compared, however, by showing where they lie on the standard normal curve. The same proportion of observations will lie *to the right* of each of these values on the standard normal curve as they do on the original histogram. Similarly, the same proportion of observations will lie *to the left* each of these values on the standard normal curve as they do on the original histogram.

For example, point a lies just to the left of the mean in the first histogram. When we translate it onto the standard normal curve, it will have precisely the same relative position. Most importantly, the probability that z will lie to the left of z_a, the normalised value of a, is the same as the probability that the original values lie to the left of a. If we look now at point b from the same histogram, we can see that its relative position remains the same when we standardise it: it is a large value to the right of the mean in the histogram and it is a large value to the right of the mean in the standard normal curve when standardised.

Next consider point c which is from a completely different histogram. This is an extreme value at the lower end of the range of values for the second histogram. Note that the relative position of c is maintained when it is standardised. By standardising c we can also see whether it is a more or less extreme value compared to b and a which are from distributions of different variables by noting their relative positions on the standard normal curve.

So, to reiterate, we can standardise any observation from a normal distribution, that is, show where it fits on the standard normal distribution, by subtracting the mean from each value and dividing the result by the standard deviation. This is called the z-score = standardised value of any normally distributed observation. If we have information on the population of normally distributed variable x, we use the population mean and population standard deviation to calculate each value of the variable:

$$z_i = \frac{x_i - \mu}{\sigma}$$

where μ = population mean and σ = population standard deviation. Areas under the standard normal curve between different z-scores are equal to areas between corresponding values on any normal distribution. Because of this, tables of areas have been calculated for each z-score, so if you standardise your observation, you can find out the area to the right or left of it.

And because areas under density functions correspond to probabilities, if you standardise your observation these areas represent the probabilities of other observations lying to the right or left of it. This is such an important facility of the z-distribution that we shall devote the whole of the next chapter to computing z-scores and deriving associated probabilities.

2.6 The Central Limit Theorem

The reason that the normal distribution – and its standardised manifestation, the *z*-distribution – is so important is not because most social science variables are normally distributed (they are not), but because under certain conditions, the means of repeated samples from those variables will always have an approximately normal distribution, even if the individual values of the variable itself do not have a bell-shaped histogram. This is a law of nature. It is called the *Central Limit Theorem* (CLT).

More formal introductions to statistics provide mathematical proofs of the CLT. Even if you have the algebraic literacy necessary to follow the logic of this kind of proof, it is unlikely that it will improve your intuitive grasp of how the CLT works. Hence, such a proof is omitted here. We shall instead consider a numerical example that will hopefully help you grasp why the sampling distributions of the mean (the histogram of means from repeated samples) is always normal, providing the size of the samples we use is reasonably large, even if the underlying variable is not.

2.6.1 Distribution of Means from Repeated Samples

You have learned how to calculate the sample mean. But ask yourself this question: how would the mean of the variable you are interested in change if you were to collect another sample? Perhaps the mean of the new sample would be slightly higher or slightly less than that calculated from the first sample, but providing your sample is reasonably large, you would expect the averages of the two samples to be pretty similar. There is a small chance, however, that in collecting your second sample, you have selected a random sample that happens by chance to have a mean that is quite different from the mean of your first sample. If you collect another sample, and another, and another, you have hundreds of separate samples, each selected randomly, and each with different means. The random variation from sample to sample of the mean of a variable is called *sampling variation.* And if you plot a histogram of all the means you have calculated you have what is called the *sampling distribution of the mean.*

Example 2.6(a) Sampling Distribution of Means

To illustrate, let's suppose we have access to the selling prices of all properties on the south side of Glasgow area sold in the second half of 2004. Unusually, in this instance, we have information on the *population*, a total of 3,731 sales. Suppose further that we want to take a random sample of 100 prices from this population. A *random sample* is one where each observation in the population has an equal chance of entering our sample. How good an approximation of the population average house price will the mean of our random sample of 100 properties provide? And how would the sample mean vary if we were to take another random sample from the population of all house prices? To investigate we shall take repeated random samples of 100 properties, calculate the mean selling price of each sample, and plot a histogram of all the sample means we have calculated.

1. Open the **houseprices_pop_2004q3q4.sav** (the dataset is available from www.geebeejey.co.uk -- download it into the **C:\STATISTICS** folder on your hard drive; if this folder does not already exist, you will need to create it using My Computer). The 3,731 observations represent prices from the population of sales on the South Side of Glasgow in the second half of 2004.

2. Run descriptives on the **sellingprice** variable to calculate μ, the population mean, and run a histogram to verify that house prices do indeed have a *non*-normal distribution (remember that you can edit the chart by double clicking on it in the Output window – see Chapter 1 for more details):

```
GET FILE='C:\STATISTICS\Glasgow_houseprices_pop_2004q3q4.sav'.

DESCRIPTIVES VARIABLES=sellingprice .

GRAPH /HISTOGRAM=sellingprice /TITLE= 'Histogram of the Population of House Prices'.
```

Descriptive Statistics

	N	Minimum	Maximum	Mean	Std. Deviation
sellingprice	3731	13000.00	497250.0	109229.5	63557.35
Valid N (listwise)	3731				

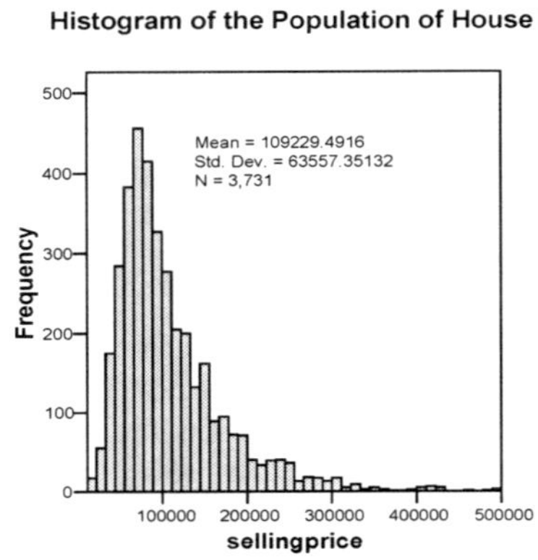

It is clear from the histogram that house prices are positively skewed. That is, the mean is pulled up by extreme values of selling price in the right tail of the distribution. Since properties cannot sell for negative values, there is a lower bound to the possible range of values and a short left tail to the distribution. The distribution is definitely not normal.

3. The **CLT** macro allows you to draw multiple random samples, and plots a histogram of the means of those samples. The macro works by taking a random sample from the file in memory, computing the mean and saving the mean of that sample as a separate single-cell data file in your current folder. It repeats this until the desired number of samples have been extracted and then combines all the single-cell data files into a single column called X_BAR and saves it as a new dataset. It then runs a histogram on the column of sample means contained in the X_BAR variable, and finally computes a table of descriptives.

4. To run the macro you need to enter the following syntax:

CLT variable=(sellingprice) nsample=(100) Npop=(3731) reps=(120).

where the items in parenthesis can be changed according to the desired specification. In this case, the variable we are interested in is **sellingprice**. So this is the name of the variable we have entered in the first set of brackets. We want to extract samples of size 100, so we enter '100' in the second set of brackets. We need to tell SPSS how large our population is. In this case it is 3,731, which we enter in the third set of brackets. Finally, we enter the number of repetitions – the number of samples we want to draw – in the fourth set of brackets. Let's go for 120.

If you select and run the above syntax you will be telling SPSS to extract 120 random samples on the **sellingprice** variable (each sample having 100 observations), and to compute the mean selling price in each sample; and finally to construct a histogram and table of descriptives of those means. Each time you run this routine you will get slightly different answers, but you should end up with a histogram of means that looks something like the following graph. (**Note that if you *do* decide to run the macro more than once, you will need to re-open the original house price data file each time prior to running the CLT macro**).

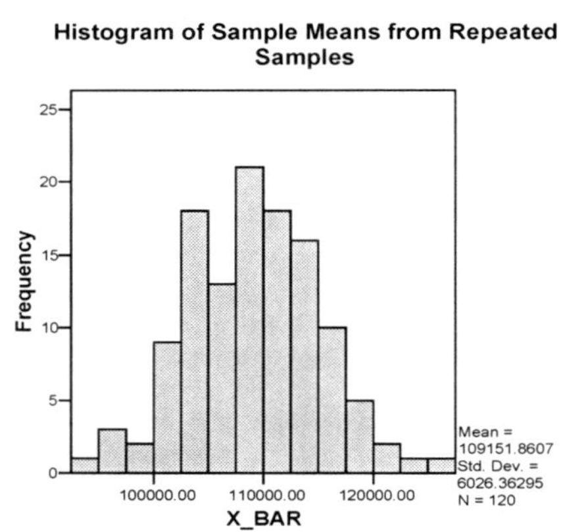

Descriptive Statistics

	N	Minimum	Maximum	Mean	Std. Deviation
X_BAR	120	94191.71	125245.5	109151.9	6026.363
Valid N (listwise)	120				

There are a number of important things to note from these results:

- First, the *distribution of sample means is approximately normal* even though the original variable is not normal (compare the histogram in step 2 of this exercise with the histogram obtained in step 5).

This result is universally true and is called the *Central Limit Theorem.* The theorem holds true providing the sample size is large. It is a fabulous discovery because it allows us to make probability statements about how close our sample results are to those we would obtain if we computed them for the population.

- Second, *the average of sample means* – the mean of means – equals £109,152, which is *almost exactly equal to the population mean* of £109,230 (a difference in fact of just £78!). This is not a coincidence – the laws of mathematics dictate that if we take an infinite number of random samples, the mean-of-sample-means will exactly equal the population mean. This is a very important finding because it implies that the sample mean offers us an *unbiased estimate* of the population mean. In other words, if we take enough samples, the mean of means will converge to the population mean. Any variation from sample to sample evens itself out in the long run.

- Third, as well as calculating the mean of means, we can also compute *the standard deviation of the mean* = £6,026. This standard deviation has a special name: *the standard error of the mean.* It is given this unique name to distinguish it from the standard deviation of the original variable (usually calculated using a single sample, or occasionally – as in the second step of this example – on the whole population). The standard error of the mean is very important because it tells us how much the sample mean varies from sample to sample. If the standard error is large, it suggests that sample means jump around a lot from sample to sample, and this makes it less likely that any single sample will give us a precise estimate of the population mean. If, on the other hand, the standard error is very small, it suggests that the mean computed from a single sample is likely to give a good estimate of the population mean.

- Unfortunately, we rarely know the true standard error of the mean. Even in our experiment of 120 random samples, the standard error we have calculated is only an estimate of the true standard error. We would need to take an infinite number of samples to deduce the exact value. In reality, we almost always have just one sample which, on the face of it, means we have no idea at all how the mean varies between samples. Thankfully, however, statisticians have found a clever way of approximating what the standard error is likely to be. Their solution rests on the fact that the standard deviation of a single sample is not unrelated to the standard error of the mean. Other things being equal, if the standard deviation of the original variable (as computed from a single sample) is large, then the standard error is also likely to be large. We will return to this below.

2.6.2 The Importance and Limitations of the CLT

To reiterate: even if a variable is not normally distributed, the distribution of means from random samples drawn from the population will be, provided n is large. While a few samples will have a mean that is way out of line with the population mean, most will be reasonably close. This is called the *Central Limit Theorem.*

The CLT is central to statistical inference because it enables us to take advantage of the very special properties of the normal distribution even when the variable we are concerned with is not normal. Suppose we don't know the shape of the population distribution of income, for example, but we want to estimate the population mean. We can usually only afford to take one sample (e.g. interview 100 people). How does the CLT help us?

The answer is that, because the sample mean is normally distributed, we can make use of the known values and probabilities associated with the z-distribution. In later sessions we shall look at how we can apply the properties of the z score to derive confidence intervals for the population mean from a single sample mean and conduct hypothesis tests. For now, it is sufficient to be convinced of the veracity of the CLT and to know that it will be crucial to solving the problem of inference. Before we can proceed any further we need to understand two key limitations of the CLT.

2.6.3 The First Limitation of the CLT: the Problem of Sample Size

The caveat we have continued to repeat every time we mention the Central Limit Theorem is *sample size.* We need to have plenty of observations in our sample for the theorem to work. The smaller the sample size, the less well the Central Limit Theorem tends to work. As far as the CLT is concerned, size does indeed matter. But how large is large? As the following example demonstrates, there is no simple answer, but a threshold of 30 observations is often used as a crude rule of thumb.

Exercise 2.6(b) The Impact on the CLT of Reducing the Sample Size

1. Open up the Glasgow_houseprices_pop_2004q3q4.sav file and re-run the CLT command with 60 observations. Copy and paste the histogram of means into a word processor, then re-run the CLT command again with 30 observations. Repeat for 20 observations, 10 and 5. Your syntax should look like this:

```
GET FILE='C:\STATISTICS\Glasgow_houseprices_pop_2004q3q4.sav'.
CLT variable=(sellingprice) nsample=(60) Npop=(3731) reps=(120).
GET FILE='C:\STATISTICS\Glasgow_houseprices_pop_2004q3q4.sav'.
CLT variable=(sellingprice) nsample=(30) Npop=(3731) reps=(120).
GET FILE='C:\STATISTICS\Glasgow_houseprices_pop_2004q3q4.sav'.
CLT variable=(sellingprice) nsample=(20) Npop=(3731) reps=(120).
GET FILE='C:\STATISTICS\Glasgow_houseprices_pop_2004q3q4.sav'.
CLT variable=(sellingprice) nsample=(10) Npop=(3731) reps=(120).
GET FILE='C:\STATISTICS\Glasgow_houseprices_pop_2004q3q4.sav'.
CLT variable=(sellingprice) nsample=(5) Npop=(3731) reps=(120).
```

and your histograms should look something like the following:

Sample size = 60

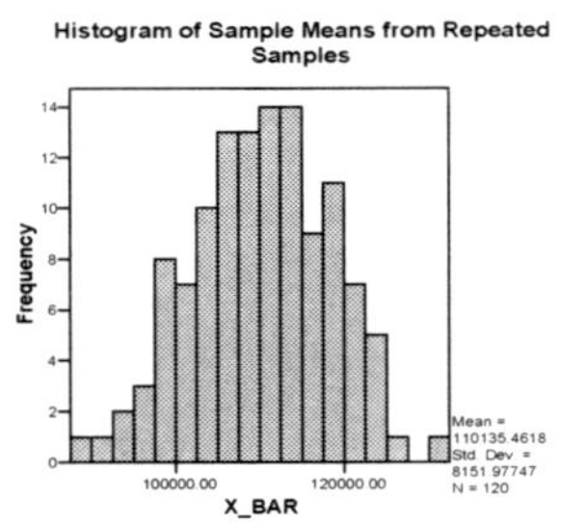

Sample size = 30

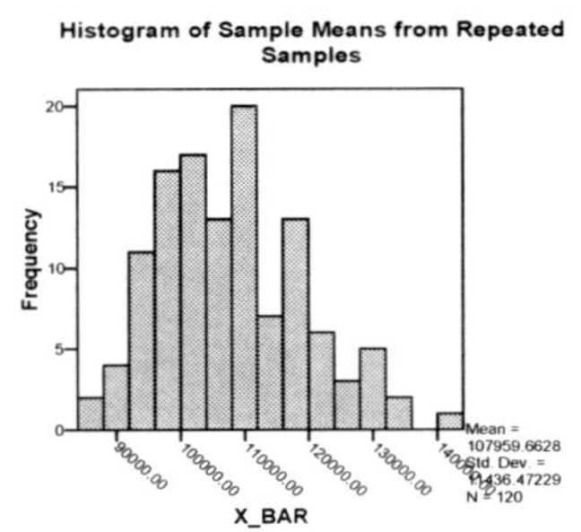

Sample size = 20

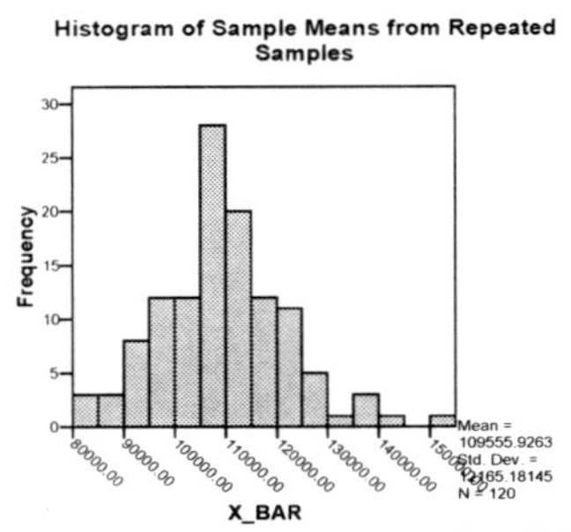

Sample size = 10

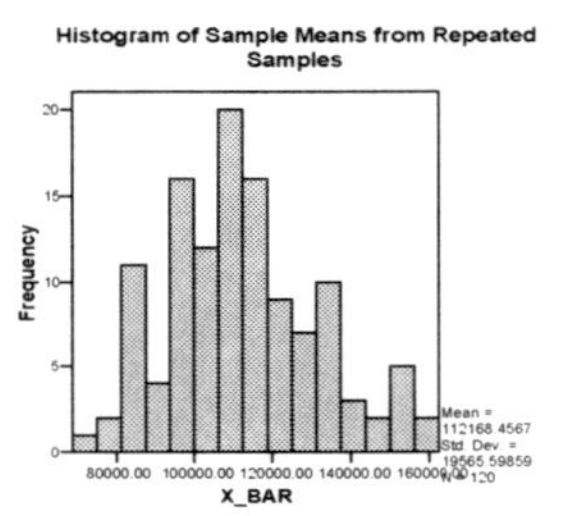

Sample size = 10

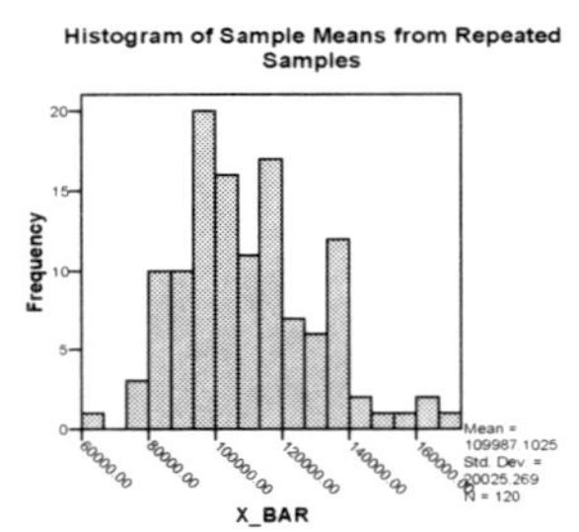

Sample size = 5

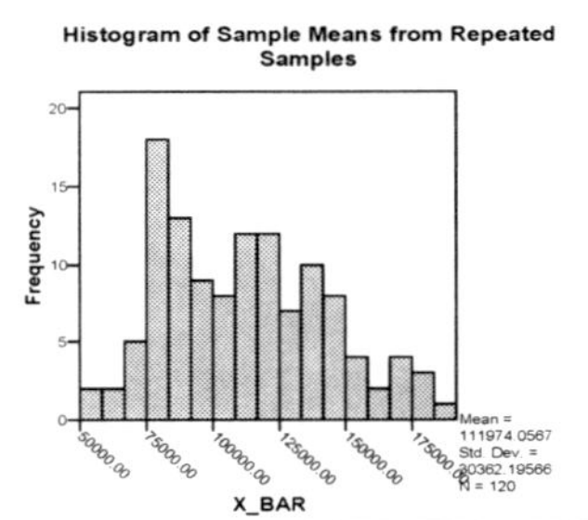

Note that two histograms have been presented for sample size = 10. This is not a mistake but included to demonstrate that if you run the CLT command twice with exactly the same sample sizes etc., you will obtain different results each time. This is because the selection of samples is random and the actual observations in each sample will vary each time.

Although the results vary from experiment to experiment, generally you will find that the histogram of means will become less normal in shape the smaller the sample size, particularly if the underlying variable is non-normal. In fact, the smaller the sample size, the more the distribution of means will resemble the histogram of the original variable. So you will notice that the histogram of means for sample size = 5 has a similarly skewed distribution to the house price histogram, whereas the sample size of 60 or 100 histograms are fairly symmetrical.

The increasing skew as sample size is reduced is worrying because it suggests that our estimate of the population mean will *no longer be unbiased.* Remember that the population mean equals £109,230. As the sample size gets smaller, the mean-of-means tends to systematically overestimate the population mean. If the skew of the original variable were the other way – a negative skew – we would find that the mean-of-sample-means would tend to underestimate the population mean. We then have to ask ourselves whether a biased estimator is of any use to us at all...

You will also find that the *standard error* rises significantly the smaller the sample size you use. In the last histogram (sample size = 5), the standard error of the mean equals £30,362, whereas it was just £6,026 in our first experiment (sample size = 100). This is a very important finding because it implies that the smaller the sample size, the greater the variation from sample to sample in the sample mean. So if our sample is small, we can be far less certain that the sample mean will be close to the population mean.

2.6.4 The Second Limitation of the CLT: the Problem of Unknown Standard Error

Usually when we take a sample and calculate the sample mean of a variable we do so as an estimate of the population mean. The question that we are continually trying to answer is, given the size of the sample, how close is it likely to be to the population mean? The CLT tells us that our sample mean is one of many potential sample means which make up a distribution of sample means, and that this distribution is normal. Consequently, we can take our observed sample mean and look at its relative position on the standard normal curve. But to do this, we need to know the standard error of the mean – the standard deviation of sample means – and the population mean:

$$z_i = \frac{\bar{x}_i - \mu}{\sigma_{\bar{x}}}$$

where:

μ = population mean

$\bar{x}_i$ = sample mean

$\sigma_{\bar{x}}$ = standard deviation of all the sample means, called the standard error of the mean

z_i = z score

But usually we don't know either the population mean or the standard error of the mean since we don't have access to data on the full population. Our experiments above have relied on us having access to data on the population, but this is rare in reality, and so we cannot take repeated samples to compute the standard error. And anyway, if we did have data on the population, why would we be interested in the standard error? Why would we bother taking a sample at all?!

Not knowing the population mean is the problem we started out with when we introduced the problem of inference and so is nothing new. We can simply rearrange our formula to give us the population mean (what we really would like to estimate) in terms of our sample mean (which we know) less (or plus) the product of z and the standard error of the mean:

$$\mu = \bar{x}_i - z_i \sigma_{\bar{x}}$$

This product of z and $\sigma_{\bar{x}}$ acts as an estimate of the random error surrounding our sample mean and is the basis for *confidence interval* estimation. To derive a confidence interval we choose a value of z reflecting an area on the standard normal curve that represents the confidence – such as 95% – we want to have that the population mean lies within our error term.

We will look in-depth at confidence intervals in subsequent chapters. The reason we are considering this formula now is to highlight the fact that we still need to know something about the population to calculate it: namely $\sigma_{\bar{x}}$ the standard error of the mean. As we have noted, this parameter is rarely known, so how can we approximate it?

Statisticians began to unravel this Gordian Knot by exploring whether the standard deviation within the sample you have selected will tell you something about the standard error of the mean. They reasoned that the spread of any one sample and the spread of all sample means would be related because the sample is drawn, after all, from the same population. We would expect the variability of the possible sample means to be related to the variability of the population, which in turn is estimated by our sample standard deviation. The mean and standard deviation will be closer to mean and standard deviation of the population the larger is n. So the variability of the sample mean decreases as the sample size increases. More specifically,

$$\sigma_{\bar{x}} = \frac{\sigma}{\sqrt{n}} \rightarrow \frac{s}{\sqrt{n}} \text{ as } n \rightarrow \infty$$

That is, provided n is large, we can use s, the sample standard deviation, as an approximation for σ, the population standard deviation. So, for large samples, we can create confidence intervals for the population mean from the sample mean and standard deviation using the following formula:

$$\mu = \bar{x}_i \pm z^* \frac{s}{\sqrt{n}}$$

where z^* is the value of z associated with the level of confidence we are seeking. For example, if we say that we want to be 95% sure that the population mean lies between a and b, the z^* corresponds to the values of z that correspond to the central 95% of the standard normal curve. We shall learn in the next chapter how to compute z^*. With this information, we have all we need to derive the desired bounds for the population mean.

2.7 Student's t-Distribution

We have established that we can approximate the standard error of the mean using $s/\sqrt{n}$ rather than $\sigma/\sqrt{n}$. However, when we substitute for the standard error of the mean in this way, the statistic does *not* have a true normal distribution: its distribution is slightly different from the normal distribution and is called the *t-distribution.* It is sometimes called "Student's t-distribution" because its inventor William Gosset published under the pseudonym, "Student". The t-distribution varies according to sample size so there is actually a different density curve for each sample size.

For small sample sizes, you will find that the spread is slightly larger than the normal distribution due to the substitution of s for σ, but because s tends towards σ as the sample size rises, the t-distribution tends towards the normal curve the larger the sample size. In fact, for samples over say 100, the t-distribution is virtually indistinguishable from the normal distribution.

2.7.1 *Assumption and Implication:*

A key assumption we have to make however when using t-distribution, is that the variable in question is normally distributed. In reality, few variables are normal, but the effect of non-normality in the original variable lessens as the sample size increases (because the Central Limit Theorem starts to kick in). There following strategy summarises when we should and shouldn't use the t-distribution:

i) If the sample size is *small*, and the variable is *normal*, we can use the t-distribution.

ii) If the sample size is *large*, and the variable is *non*-normal, we can still use the t-distribution.

iii) But if the sample size is *small*, and the variable is *non*-normal, we can't use the t-distribution (or we do so with caution!).

2.8 What about Proportions?

So far our examples of sampling distributions have all been with regard to continuous (or 'scale') variables. In other words, we have been concerned with comparing the mean of our sample observations on a continuous variable with the mean of the population of observations on that variable. But what if our variable is categorical? Suppose we want to know the proportion of post graduate students from working class backgrounds or the proportion of attacks that are racially motivated. Once we have taken our respective samples, we don't calculate a mean for such variables but a proportion (or if you prefer, a percent). So our sample of post graduate students would yield an estimate of the proportion from working class backgrounds and our sample of people who have been attacked would yield an estimate of the number that were racially motivated. Now, suppose we were to take repeated samples. What would the histogram of sample proportions look like? In both cases the distribution of proportions would be normal.

To illustrate this further, consider the following experiment: with his back to the audience, a lecturer randomly throws 30 sweets into the audience and records the proportion of the 30 catchers that were male. He repeats the experiment several times, recording the proportion of male catchers each time. If the class is split equally between males and females, what would the proportion of male catchers be on average (assuming they are all equally good catchers)? You would of course expect the long run proportion of male catchers to be 50%. You would also find that the proportion of male catchers from repeated samples would have an approximately normal distribution. In other words, the Central Limit Theorem does indeed apply to categorical variables: the sampling distribution of the proportion will be approximately normal provided the sample size is large.

Exercise 2.8: Proportions and the Central Limit Theorem

Open the Glasgow_houseprices_pop_2004q3q4.sav and create a new variable called 'over100k' which equals zero if the house price is less than or equal to £100,000, and equals one if the house price is greater than £100,000. If you calculate the average of this variable it will give you the proportion of properties over £100K, so you can treat it as a proportion.

Run a histogram on **over100k**. Does it look as you expected? Now obtain the sampling distribution of the **over100k** variable using the CLT syntax (let the sample size = 100, and use two hundred repetitions).

The full set of syntax needed to complete this exercise is as follows:

```
GET FILE='C:\STATISTICS\Glasgow_houseprices_pop_2004q3q4.sav'.
COMPUTE over100k = 0.
IF(sellingprice > 100000) over100k = 1.
EXECUTE.
DESCRIPTIVES  VARIABLES=over100k  .
GRAPH /HISTOGRAM=over100k /TITLE= 'Histogram: Proportion of House Prices > £100k'.
CLT  variable=(over100k)  nsample=(100)  Npop=(3731)  reps=(200).
```

Answer:

The histogram of **over100k** should look like the graph below on the left, where as the sampling distribution of the proportion should look like the histogram on the right:

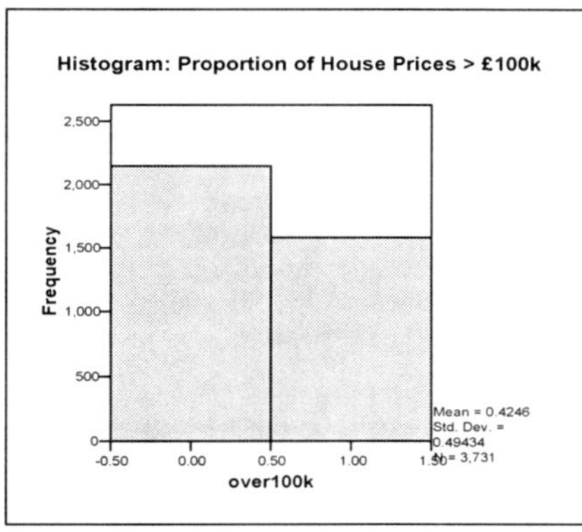

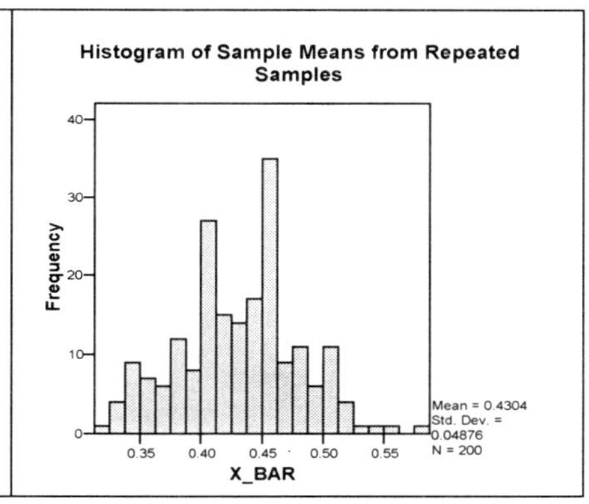

2.9 Conclusion

This chapter has been rather different from the first, and indeed from the remaining chapters of this book, in that it has been largely theoretical. We have run through a plethora of new concepts, and you may feel somewhat haggard at this point, if not a little bewildered. Worry not! We shall reiterate the key finds as we need them. Nevertheless I would recommend re-reading this chapter until the concepts become reasonably clear. This will give you greater confidence as you proceed.

The key ideas you need to grasp at this stage are as follows:

- The meaning of the terms *random* and *probability*.
- The basic laws of probability and how the difference between the law for independent events and contingent events leads us to a method for testing the existence of a relationship between two categorical variables.
- The meaning of *random sample* and *sampling distribution*.
- The Central Limit Theorem, the intuition behind it and its limitations.
- The purpose and limitations of the t-distribution.

2.10 Further Study

1) Use SPSS help system to find out all you can about P-P plots and Q-Q plots. Click on Graph, P-P plot, then click on the Help button in the P-P window. For information on Normal Probability plots you can click on the little graph in the Help window. This is copied below (note that P-P plots can be made for all sorts of weird and wonderful distributions – but we are only interested in P-P plots for the normal distribution):

   P-P Plots: SPSS Definition:
   Plots a variable's cumulative proportions against the cumulative proportions of any of a number of test distributions. Probability plots are generally used to determine whether the distribution of a variable matches a given distribution. If the selected variable matches the test distribution, the points cluster around a straight line. (Click the icon at right to see an example.) Available test distributions include beta, chi-square, exponential, gamma, half-normal, Laplace, Logistic, Lognormal, normal, pareto, Student's t, Weibull, and uniform. Depending on the distribution selected, you can specify degrees of freedom and other parameters. You obtain probability plots for transformed values. Transformation options include natural log, standardize values, difference, and seasonally difference. You can specify the method for calculating expected distributions, and for resolving "ties," or multiple observations with the same value.

   Normal P-P chart:
   The cumulative proportion for a single numeric variable is plotted against the cumulative proportion expected if the sample were from a normal distribution. If the sample is from a normal distribution, points will cluster around a straight line. Minimum specification: one or more numeric variables. A separate plot will be produced for each variable.

2) Open the **Glasgow_houseprices_pop_2004q3q4.sav data.** Run a normal probability plot (called a P-P plot in SPSS) on the **sellingprice** variable and comment on the meaning of the charts you produce. How does your conclusion compare with the judgement you would have reached from looking at the histograms of **sellingprice**?

---

3 Calculating *z*-Scores

Aim:
This chapter considers the practicalities of translating values to and from the standard normal curve.

Objectives:
By the end of this chapter, you should be able to understand how to calculate the probabilities associated with *z*-scores using a variety of methods. You should also be able to calculate the *z* for any value of a normally distributed variable *x*. Combining these two skills will allow you to calculate the probabilities associated with any value of a normally distributed variable. For example, if height is normally distributed, you will be able to compute the probability that height is less than 6', or the probability that height lies between 5'2" and 5'10". You should also be able to understand how the *z*-distribution is relevant even to variables that are not normally distributed. This is because the sample means from repeated samples are normally distributed even if the variable in question is not normally distributed, a principle known as the Central Limit Theorem (a key assumption behind this theorem, however, is that the sample size is large).

Further Reading:
D. S. Moore and G. P. McCabe, *Introduction to the Practice of Statistics,* 4th Ed., Freeman, New York, Chapter 5 and section 1.3.
Gonick, L. and Smith, W. (1993) *Cartoon Guide to Statistics*, Harper Collins, New York, Chapters 3 to 6.

Plan:

3.1 Introduction

In the previous chapter we saw how the sampling distribution of the mean was always normal for large samples. In other words, if we take repeated samples from the population, and calculate the mean value in each sample, we will find that the histogram of the sample means will have a bell-shaped distribution. And if we take enough samples, we will find that the mean of all the sample means will equal the population mean.

These are useful discoveries. For although typically we only have one sample in real-life research situations, these theorems allow us to make inferences about the population mean from the information in our sample, and to conduct hypothesis tests. For example, if the assumption in government documentation is that average income among single parent families is £20,000 per year, but the mean income from our sample of 200 randomly selected single parent households is only £15,000, knowing that sample means follow a normal distribution will allow us to work out the probability that our observations are drawn from a freak sample. We can, in other words, calculate the probability of selecting a sample with a mean of £15,000 when the true population mean (as assumed by government) is £20,000. This probability has an alternative interpretation, however. Suppose we think that the assumption made by government about mean income is in fact rather suspect. The probability we have computed can be interpreted as telling us *how likely we are to be wrong* if we *reject* the hypothesis that the government assumption is correct. That is, it tells us the *probability of false rejection* (also called the *significance level*).

Knowing that the sampling distribution of the mean is normal and that the mean of sample means equals the population mean, also allows us to compute *confidence intervals*. For any given sample mean, and predetermined level of confidence, we can work out the upper and lower limits of a likely range of values of the population mean. For example, if we want to compute a and b so that we are 95% confident that the population mean lies between a and b, the normality of the sampling distribution allows us to compute these bounds. Our calculation would run as follows: first we would take advantage of the fact that all normal distributions are related and that all points on a particular sampling distribution can be converted into equivalent points on the standard normal curve – the z-distribution. The flip-side of this fact is that any point on the z-distribution can be translated onto any sampling distribution. This means that once we have computed z_a and z_b, the lower and upper bounds of the central 95% of the standard normal curve, we can translate these values onto particular sampling distribution, such as that associated with the income of single parent households. In other words we can find the values of income, a and b, that correspond to z_a and z_b, and hence identify where the central 95% of all sample mean incomes lie. Given that the central point of our sampling distribution is always the mean-of-means – which we know equals the population mean – we can be 95% sure that the population mean income lies between income a and income b.

We have some way to go before we can actually calculate confidence intervals and hypothesis tests so these terms will no doubt seem rather vague at this stage. What is already apparent, however, is that the standard normal curve is central to the calculation of both hypothesis tests and confidence intervals. In hypothesis tests, we want to compute the probability that our sample is atypical, and to do this we translate the mean of our data onto the z-distribution to work out the probability that we could observe a sample with an average as far away from the true population mean as ours is from our *assumed* population mean. In confidence interval estimation our calculations run the opposite way. We first calculate the bounds of the central 95% of the z-distribution and then translate these bounds onto our particular sampling distribution.

We are, therefore, unable to proceed any further without fully understanding how to calculate probabilities associated with particular z values, and how to compute z values from particular probabilities. We also need to know how to translate values from the z-distribution onto our sampling distribution and visa versa. So our goals in this chapter are less theoretical than in the previous chapter – we are simply learning how to do particular calculations – but no less important.

3.2 Calculating the Probabilities Associated with z-Scores

We shall, in this section, learn three methods of how to compute the area (probability) of particular sections under the standard normal curve. First, we shall learn how to make the calculation using tables of values (published in the back-pages of almost all traditional textbooks on introductory statistics). Second, we shall learn how to make the calculation using standard SPSS commands. We shall discover that this is rather long-winded so our third approach is to make use of the macro commands written to accompany this book.

3.2.1 Calculating Probabilities Associated with z-Scores Using Tables

The traditional way of computing the probability associated with a particular z-score is to make use of published tables. Because the standard normal curve is fully described by a unique mathematical formula, it is possible to compute the area of *any* vertical segment under the z-curve. However, this formula is rather complicated, despite the fact that it only actually has two things in it that can vary – the mean and the standard deviation. (To derive the standard normal curve, as opposed to any other normal distribution, the mean is set at zero and the standard deviation is set at one.) So statisticians have made a living from computing the probabilities associated with particular z-scores and publishing them as tables.

Of course, we would need a table with an infinite number of rows and columns to make the calculation for every value of z. So such tables only offer probabilities for a selection of values. Whilst the calculated values are carefully selected to maximise their usefulness, the tables inevitably only provide an approximation for most of the calculations we want to make. This is not necessarily a bad thing since students of statistics – and not a few professionals – have a tendency to present confidence intervals and hypothesis tests with a spurious degree of accuracy. That is, they compute the appropriate statistics using a computer package to seven decimal places, even though the sample they are using was not a true random sample and even though there are huge errors in the measurement of the variable they are considering. Nevertheless, it is hard to justify adding further imprecision into our calculations when –

with the aid of modern technology – we can calculate areas under the z-curve with near-perfect precision. Still, it is worth learning how to use these tables since they provide good practice in manipulating areas under the z-distribution, which is no bad thing.

At the back of this text you will find a set of tables. The first of these, Table A, presents the area under the standard normal curve to the left of z. The first column lists the values of z. The figures in the subsequent column headings represent the second decimal place of the z value. So if you want to find the area to the left of -3.14, you run your finger down the z column until you get to 3.10, then you go along that row until you get to the column headed .04. The value in that unique cell should be .0008, which means that the area to the left of $-3.14 = 0.0008$.

Since areas under density curves can be interpreted as probabilities, we can say that this table records $\Pr(z < z_i)$ which is the probability under the standard normal curve that z will be less than z_i, where z_i is the specific z value you choose. Note that probabilities are only presented for negative values of z. This is in fact all we need. Because the normal distribution is symmetrical, if we know the area of the left tail, we can work out the area of the equivalent right tail, and from this we can work out the area in-between because we know that the total area under the curve equals one. Notice also that the z values don't get any more negative than –3.49. This is because the probability of z being less than –3.49 (or z being greater than +3.49) is so infinitesimally small that it's not worth knowing.

Example 3.2.1(a) Calculate the probability that z is less than –3.4

Run your finger down the column of figures under z in Table A. You won't have to go very far since –3.4 is the very first row. The second decimal place of –3.4 is 0, so we need the probability listed in the column headed ".00", which is **0.0003**. So we can say $\Pr(z < -3.4) = 0.0003$, which is a very small probability indeed (there is less than a tenth of 1 percent chance that z will be less than –3.4).

Example 3.2.1(b) Calculate the probability that z is less than –1.23

We want the value identified by the row of –1.2 and the column .03 which is **.1093**. That is, there is a 11% chance that z is less than –1.23.

Example 3.2.1(c) Calculate the probability that z is greater than 2.34

Table A only lists the probabilities associated with negative values of z. However, because the distribution is symmetrical around $z = 0$, the probability that z is less than a negative value is equal to the probability that z is greater than the equivalent positive value. So, $\Pr(z > 2.34) = \Pr(z < -2.34)$, which is identified by running your finger down the column of z values until you get to –2.3, then moving along that row until you get to the column headed .04. The value you should arrive at is .0096. In other words, $\Pr(z > 2.34) = \Pr(z < -2.34) =$ .96%, which is a hair's-breadth short of one percent.

Example 3.2.1(d) Calculate the probability that z lies between –1.96 and 1.96

We know that the area between $z = -1.96$ and $z = 1.96$ is equal to 1 minus the sum of two probabilities: the probability that z is less than –1.96 and the probability that z is greater than 1.96. The probability that z is less than –1.96 can be found from Table A by going along the $z = -1.90$ row until you get to the column headed ".06". The figure you arrive at is .0250. Because the distribution is symmetrical, this means that the probability that z is greater than the positive value of 1.96 is also equal to .0250. So the sum of the probabilities in the two tails associated with ±1.96 is .0250 + .0250 = .05. So to compute $\Pr(-1.96 < z < 1.96)$ we must simply calculate 1 – 0.05 = 0.95. So, $\Pr(-1.96 < z < 1.96) = 0.95$, which is the same as saying that 95% of z-values lie between ±1.96.

3.2.2 *Calculating Probabilities Associated with z-Scores using SPSS Commands*

It is not a problem for SPSS to calculate the probability that z is less than a particular value. There is a slight inconvenience, however, in that the command to compute the probabilities associated with z values only works if you already have a data file open, and rather irritatingly it will compute the probability for each row in your data file. So, suppose you have a blank data sheet and you want to calculate the probability that z is less than –3.14. To compute this in SPSS you have to create a variable using the following syntax (we have called the new variable **Pr_z_lt_zi** but you can call it what you like):

```
COMPUTE Pr_z_lt_zi = CDFNORM(–3.14).
EXECUTE.
```

Now, if you run this syntax when your data file is blank, you will get an error message, so first open a data file or place an arbitrary value in the first cell of your empty data file, and *then* run the syntax. Unfortunately, depending on how your version of SPSS has been installed, you may find that only two decimal places are displayed in the data window for your new variable. You can correct this by using the FORMATS command which sets the overall width of a variable as it appears in the data sheet window, and also the number of decimal places. The format is determined by the code entered in brackets, such as F5.4. More generally, *Fw.d* is used if you want to specify the variable is numeric. *F* denotes the format type (numeric), *w* represents the variable width, and *d* represents the number of decimal places. For example, if we want our variable *X* to have width = 6, and 2 decimal places, we enter FORMATS *X* (F6.2). In this case, we want **Pr_z_lt_zi** to have width 5, and 4 decimal places, hence F5.4 is entered in the brackets. Assuming you have at least one cell of data in your Data View window, the following syntax should achieve the desired result:

```
COMPUTE Pr_z_lt_zi = CDFNORM(–3.14).
FORMATS Pr_z_lt_zi (F5.4).
EXECUTE.
```

If you return to your Data View window after running this syntax you should find that you have a variable called Pr_z_lt_zi with the same value for all rows of your data, each value equal to **.0008**. An alternative to using the FORMATS command is to go to **Edit**, **Options**, **Data**, and increase the number of decimal places to the desired level. Any new variables you create will have the stipulated number of decimal places. Note that the value you enter in brackets in the CDFNORM function does not have to be a negative value. For example, if you enter 3.14 in the brackets you would be telling SPSS to calculate the area under the *z*-distribution to the left of 3.14. Since this area is most of that under the entire distribution, you would expect $\Pr(z < 3.14)$ to be close to 1, and indeed you would be right. Try it and see – the value of **Pr_z_lt_zi** in your Data View window should change to **.9992**. This is, of course, equivalent to $1 - \Pr(z < -3.14) = 1 - 0.0008$.

Example 3.2.2 Find Pr(z < –0.95) using the CDFNORM function in SPSS

Type the following syntax:

```
COMPUTE Pr_z_lt_zi = CDFNORM(–0.95).
FORMATS Pr_z_lt_zi (F5.4).
EXECUTE.
```

The values of your **Pr_z_lt_zi** variable should now all equal **0.1711**. In other words, the probability that *z* is less than –0.95 equals 0.1711, or 17.11%.

Now repeat the exercises set out in examples **3.2.1a** to **3.2.1d** above, using SPSS commands and compare your answers with those obtained using Table A.

3.2.3 Calculating Probabilities Associated with z-Scores using the SPSS Macros

The macros (and installation instructions) referred to below and in the remainder of the book can be obtained from www.geebeejey.co.uk. Once you have installed the macros and run the "macro call" (see installation instructions) you should be able to run the macros as explained below.

We use four macros in this section, **pz_lt_zi** (calculates the probability that z is less than z_i), **pz_gt_zi** (calculates the probability that z is greater than z_i), **pz_lg_zi** (calculates the probability that z is less than z_{iL} or greater than z_{iU}), **pz_gl_zi** (calculates the probability that z is greater than z_{iL} AND less than z_{iU}).

pz_lt_zi

pz_lt_zi (?) calculates the probability that z is less than z_i. For example, typing and running the following,

```
pz_lt_zi (–3.4).
```

would result in the output presented below (notice the full stop at the end of the command – without it the command won't run). Note that the results verify the figure we obtained in Example 3.2.1a above using Table A.

```
Run MATRIX procedure:

 Prob(z < zi) for a given zi
        zi        Prob
   -3.40000     .00034
```

The figure you enter in brackets does not have to be negative. For example, suppose you want to know Pr(z < 1.36). The probability you are after is equal to the shaded area in the diagram below. To calculate this area, you would enter,

pz_lt_zi (1.36) .

which would result in the output presented in the right-hand pane below:

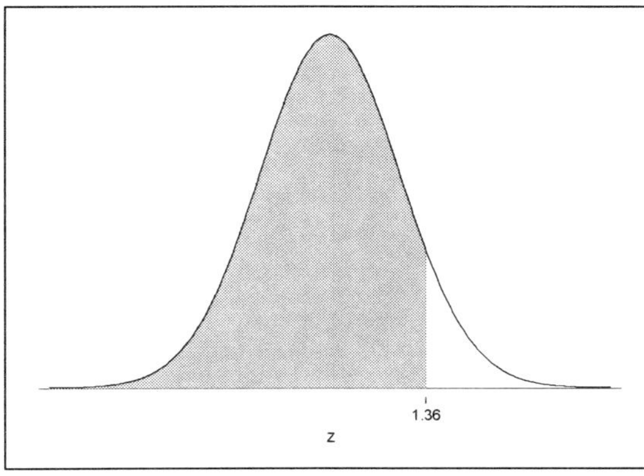


```
Prob(z < zi) for a given zi
        ZI        PROB
   1.36000      .91309
```

That is, there is a 91.31% chance that z is less than 1.36, which is equivalent to saying that 91.31% of z lie below 1.36.

pz_gt_zi

pz_gt_zi (?) calculates the probability that z is greater than z_i. For example, suppose you want to calculate Pr(z > –2.897), equal to the shaded area in the diagram below.

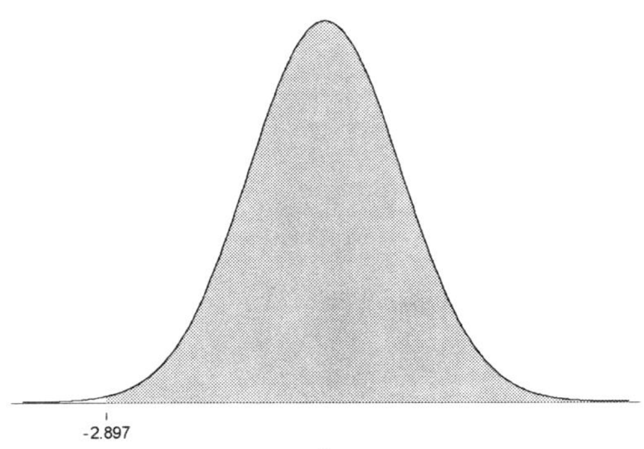

To compute this probability you would enter **pz_gt_zi (–2.897).** resulting in the following output:

```
Prob(z > zi) for a given
zi
        ZI        PROB
   -2.89700     .99812
```

which says that 99.812% of z lie above –2.897.

pz_lg_zi

pz_lg_zi zil=(?) ziu=(?). calculates the probability that z is less than ziL or greater than ziU. For example, suppose you want to compute the probability that z lie in the two tails bounded by ±2. This equals $\Pr((z < z_{iL})$ OR $(z > z_{iU}))$, as illustrated by the sum of the shaded areas in the diagram below:

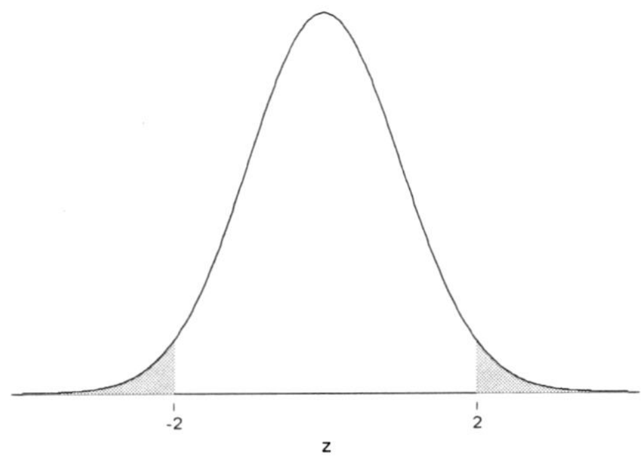

To compute it you would enter, **pz_lg_zi zil=(−2) ziu=(2).** resulting in the following output:

```
Prob((z < ziL) OR (z > ziU)) for a given
zi
        ZIL            ZIU           PROB
   -2.00000       2.00000        .04550
```

which can be interpreted as telling us that just 4.5% of z lie outside of the range −2 to 2.

pz_gl_zi

pz_gl_zi zil=(?) ziu=(?). calculates the probability that z is greater than ziL AND less than ziU. For example, suppose you want to compute the probability that z lies in the range bounded by ±2. This equals $\Pr(z_{iL} < z < z_{iU})$, as illustrated by the shaded area in the diagram below:

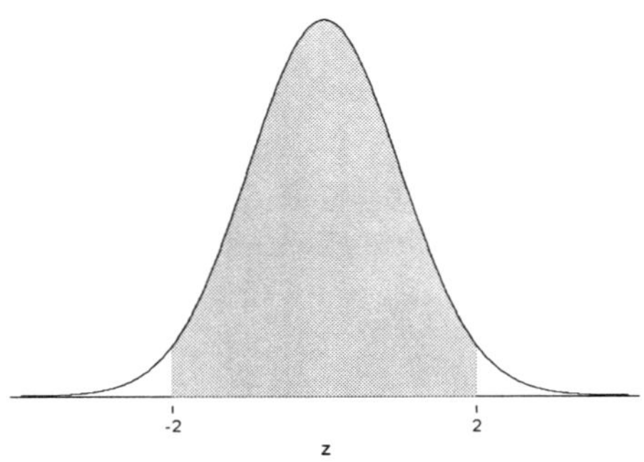

To compute the size of this area you would enter, **pz_gl_zi zil=(−2) ziu=(2).** resulting in the following output:

```
Prob(ziL < z < ziU)) for a given zi
        ZIL            ZIU           PROB
   -2.00000       2.00000        .95450
```

which tells us that 95.45% of z lie in the range −2 to 2.

Exercise 3.2 Calculating the Probabilities Associated with z-scores

For each of the following exercises, draw an appropriate diagram of the z-distribution to help you understand the problem, then compute the probabilities using both Table A and the relevant macro command.

1. Find the proportion of z-scores that are less than 1.8.
2. Find the proportion of z-scores that are less than 3.
3. Find the probability that z is less than 2.
4. Find the following probabilities using the standard normal table:

a. Prob(0 < z < 1.87) i.e. the probability that *z* lies between 0 and 1.87
b. Prob(–1.11 < z < 0) i.e. the probability that *z* lies between –1.11 and 0.
c. Prob(–1.18 < z < 0)
d. Prob(–1.26 ≤ z < 2.11)
e. Prob(–2.06 < z ≤ 0.63)
f. Prob(z ≥ 1.47)
g. Prob(z < 2.05)
h. Prob(z < –0.99)
i. Prob(z > –1.05)
j. Prob(0.86 ≤ z ≤ 1.72)
k. Prob(z < 1.58)
l. Prob(–1.96 < z < –1.28)
m. Prob(0 < z < 1.83)
n. Prob(–2.08 < z < 0.63)

Answers to Exercise 3.2

Only look at these answers once you have had a go yourself.

1. Find the proportion of *z*-scores that are less than 1.8.

   First sketch your density curve (see figure below where the shaded area represents the probability that *z* is less than 1.8). Then, from Table A, look up 1.80 and you will find that Prob(z < 1.8) = 0.9641. In SPSS, type **pz_lt_zi (1.8).** which should give you the following text (presented to the right of the diagram below) in the Output window:

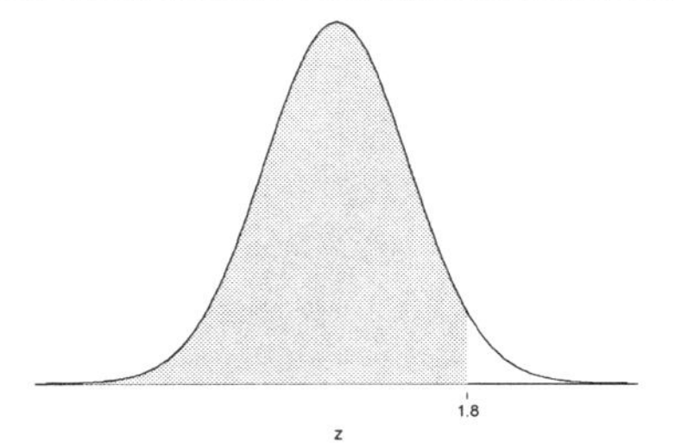


```
Prob(z < zi) for a given zi
      ZI          PROB
   1.80000      .96407
```

2. Find the proportion of *z*-scores that are less than 3.

   First sketch your curve (see below where again the shaded area represents the probability we are trying to estimate). Then, in the tables look up 3.0, which will give the following: Prob(*z* < 3) = **.9987** .In SPSS: type **pz_lt_zi (3.0).** which should result in the following text appearing in the output window:

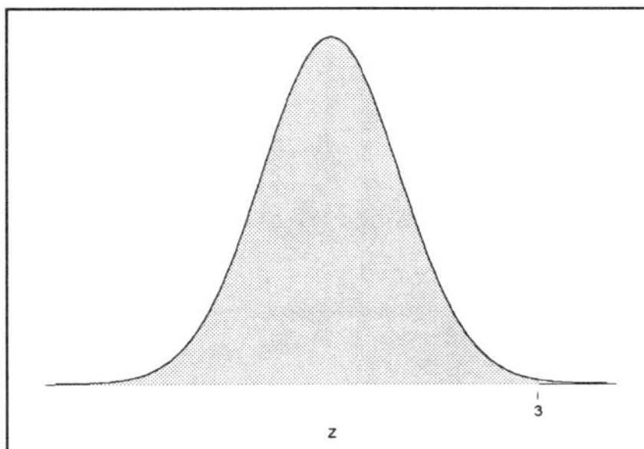


```
Prob(z < zi) for a given zi
      ZI          PROB
   3.00000      .99865
```

3. Find the probability that *z* is less than 2.

   First sketch your graph (see below – again the shaded area represents the probability we are trying to estimate). Then from the tables look up 2.0, Prob(z < 2) = .9772. In SPSS type **pz_lt_zi (2.0).** which will result in the following output:

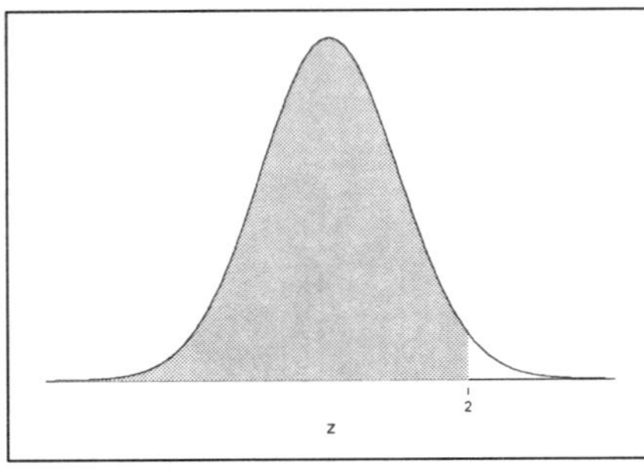


```
Prob(z < zi) for a given zi
        ZI          PROB
   2.00000        .97725
```

4. Find the following probabilities using the standard normal table:

   a. Prob(0< z < 1.87)   i.e. the probability that z lies between 0 and 1.87

First sketch your curve (see diagram below – the shaded area represents the probability we are trying to estimate). Then from Table A look up the probability associated with z < –1.87, from which you should be able to work out that Prob(z < 1.87) = 0.9693. Then take away 0.5 since 50% of z values are less than 0:

Prob(0< z < 1.87) = Prob(z < 1.8) – 0.5 = 0.9693 – 0.5 = 0.4693

In SPSS, type **pz_gl_zi zil=(0) ziu=(1.87).** which tells you that 46.9% of z lies between zero and 1.87.

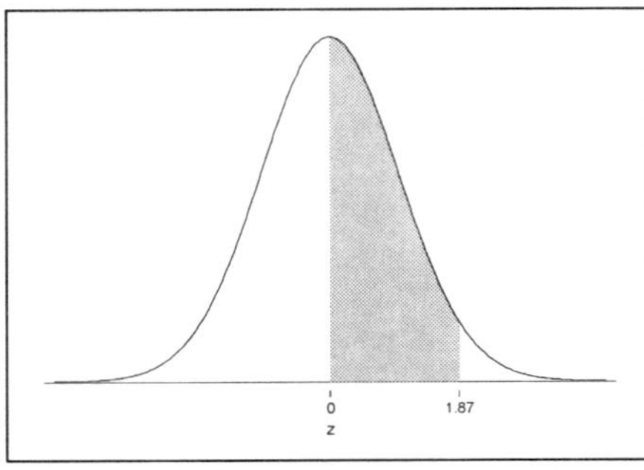


```
Prob(ziL < z < ziU) for a given zi
       ZIL         ZIU         PROB
    .00000     1.87000       .46926
```

b. Prob(–1.11 < z < 0)   i.e. the probability that z lies between –1.11 and 0.

First sketch your density curve (see diagram below – the shaded area represents the probability we are trying to estimate). If you are using Table A you can make use of the fact that the z-distribution is symmetric, which implies that the probability we are trying to compute is the same as the probability that z lies between 0 and 1.11. So, in Table A look up the probability that z < 1.11. Then take away 0.5 from the probability you have located (0.5 is the area to the left of zero under the curve):

Prob(–1.11 < z < 0)   = Prob(0 < z < 1.11)
                          = Prob(z < 1.11) – 0.5
                          = .8665 – 0.5
                          = .3665

If you are using SPSS to make the calculation, type **pz_gl_zi zil=(–1.11) ziu=(0).** which tells you that 36.7% of z lies between –1.11 and 0.

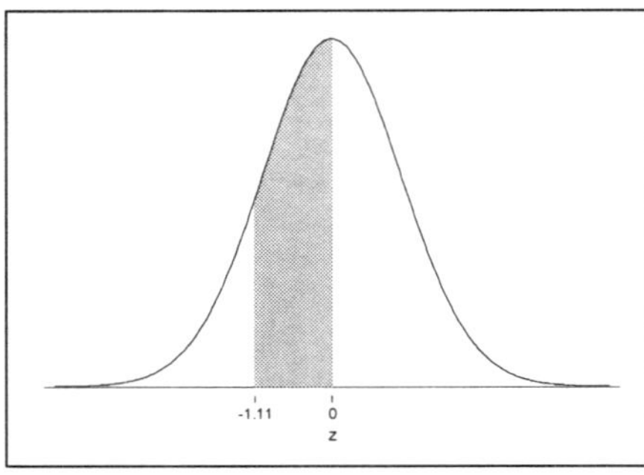


```
Prob(ziL < z < ziU) for a given zi
       ZIL         ZIU         PROB
  -1.11000      .00000       .36650
```

c. Prob(–1.18 < z < 0)

First sketch your curve (see diagram below – the shaded area represents the probability we are trying to estimate). Using Table A: because the z-distribution is symmetrical, this is the same as the probability that *z* lies between 0 and 1.18. So, in the tables look up the probability that $z < 1.18$ and take away 0.5 from it:

$$\begin{aligned} \text{Prob}(-1.18 < z < 0) &= \text{Prob}(0 < z < 1.18) \\ &= \text{Prob}(z < 1.18) - 0.5 \\ &= .3810 - 0.5 \end{aligned}$$

Using SPSS: Type **pz_gl_zi zil=(–1.18) ziu=(0).** which tells you that 38.1% of *z* lie between –1.18 and 0.

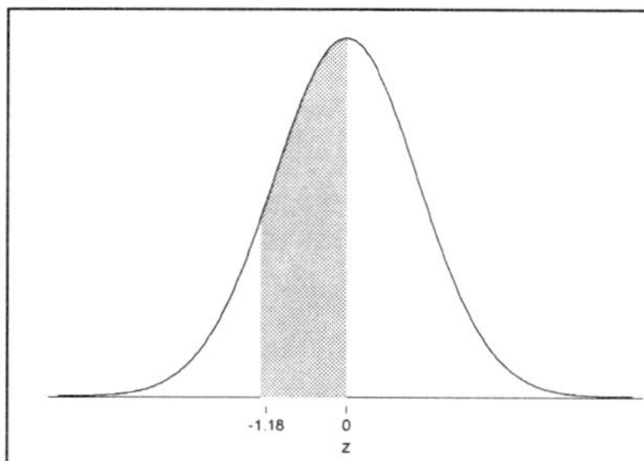


```
Prob(ziL < z < ziU) for a given zi
     ZIL          ZIU          PROB
  -1.18000       .00000       .38100
```

d. Prob(–1.26 ≤ *z* < 2.11)

First sketch the standard normal curve (see diagram below – the shaded area represents the probability we are trying to estimate). Because the *z* variable is continuous, probabilities associated with weak inequalities, ≥ and ≤, are the same as those associated with strong inequalities, > and <. So, $\Pr(z \leq z_i) = \Pr(z < z_i)$. With this in mind, sketch the probability we want to compute as a shaded area under the standard normal curve. If you were using the tables you would then make use of the fact that:

$$\begin{aligned} \text{Prob}(-1.26 \leq z < 2.11) &= \text{Prob}(z < 2.11) - \text{Prob}(z \leq -1.26) \\ &= .982571 - .103835 \\ &= .878736 \end{aligned}$$

In SPSS type, **pz_lt_zi (–.2).** which should give the following output:

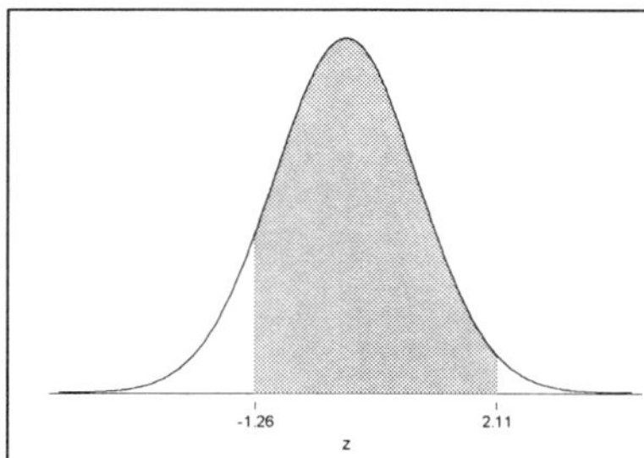


```
Prob(ziL < z < ziU) for a given zi
     ZIL          ZIU          PROB
  -1.26000      2.11000       .87874
```

In the remaining answers, only the SPSS method will be presented, and less detail given.

e. Prob(–2.06 < *z* ≤ 0.63)

This is similar to the previous question, since:

Prob(–2.06 < *z* ≤ 0.63) = Prob(z ≤ 0.63) – Prob(z ≤ –2.06)

```
Prob(ziL < z < ziU) for a given zi
   ZIL          ZIU          PROB
 -2.06000      .63000       .71595
```

f. Prob(z ≥ 1.47)

First sketch your z-distribution (see diagram below – the shaded area represents the probability we are trying to estimate). We can do this two ways: either we can make use of the fact that Prob(z ≥ 1.47) = Prob(z < –1.47) which SPSS can calculate directly, or we can make use of the fact that Prob(z ≥ 1.47) = 1 – Prob(z < 1.47) which would be the way we would have to calculate it if we were using Table A. In SPSS you would type, **pz_gt_zi (1.47).** and obtain the output in the right-hand box below.

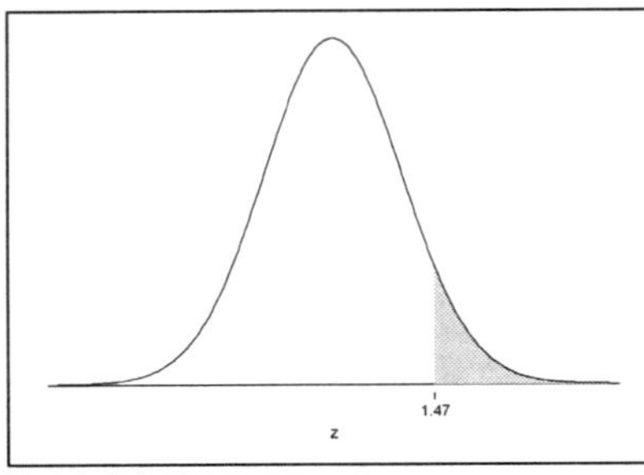


```
Prob(z > zi) for a given zi
            ZI          PROB
       1.47000        .07078
```

Because z is a continuous variable, the probability of z being greater than or equal to 1.47 is the same as the probability that z will be greater than 1.47 (the probability that z exactly equals 1.47 is infinitesimally small) which equals 0.071.

g. Prob(z < 2.05)

First sketch your z-distribution (see diagram below – the shaded area represents the probability we are trying to estimate). In SPSS type: **pz_lt_zi (2.05).** which will give you the output presented in the right-hand box below.

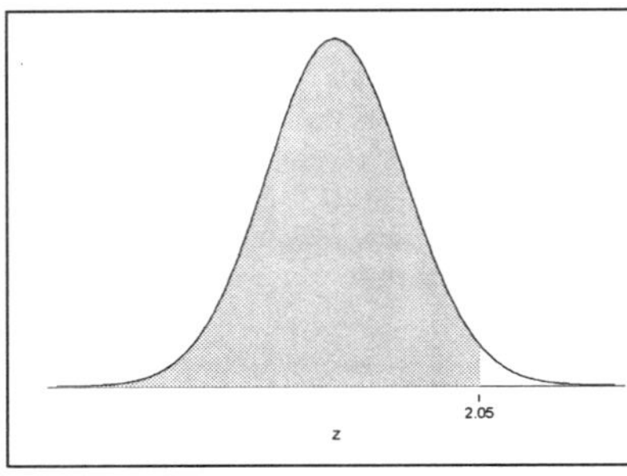


```
Prob(z < zi) for a given zi
            ZI          PROB
       2.05000        .97982
```

So Prob(z < 2.05) = **.97982**

h. Prob(z < –0.99)

First sketch your z-distribution (see diagram below – the shaded area represents the probability we are trying to estimate). In SPSS type: **pz_lt_zi (–0.99).** which should give you the following output:

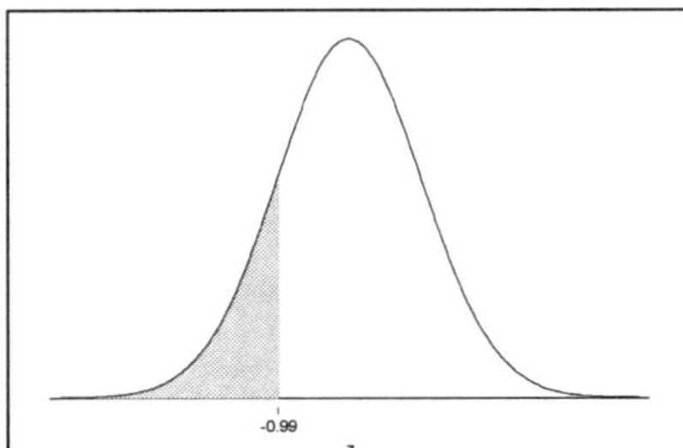


```
Prob(z < zi) for a given zi
            ZI          PROB
       -.99000        .16109
```

which says that Prob(z < –.99) = **.16109**

i. Prob(z > –1.05)

Because the z-distribution is symmetrical, this is equivalent to the probability that z will be less than 1.05 (draw a z-score distribution diagram to confirm this): Prob(z > –1.05) = Prob(z < 1.05). Macro syntax and output are presented below:

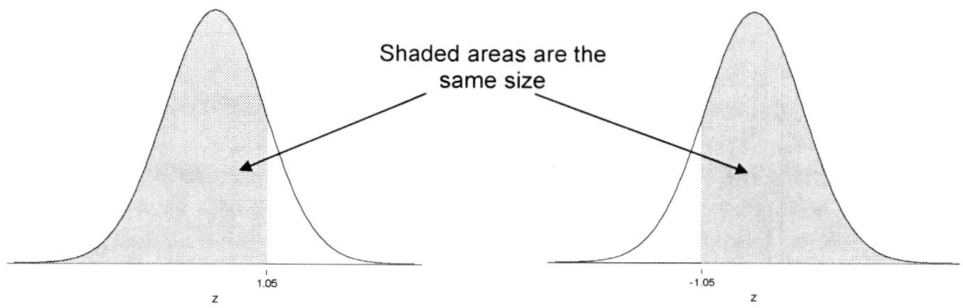

pz_lt_zi (1.05).

Prob(z < zi) for a given zi	
ZI	PROB
1.05000	.85314

pz_gt_zi(–1.05).

Prob(z > zi) for a given zi	
ZI	PROB
-1.05000	.85314

j. Prob(0.86 ≤ *z* ≤ 1.72)

First sketch your *z*–distribution (see diagram below – the shaded area represents the probability we are trying to estimate). The tables will give us the probability that *z* is less than 1.72 (i.e. the area under the curve to the left of 1.72). If we take away from this area the region to the left of 0.86 (i.e. probability that *z* < 0.86) then we have the desired area. In SPSS, type: **pz_gl_zi zil=(0.86) ziu=(1.72).**

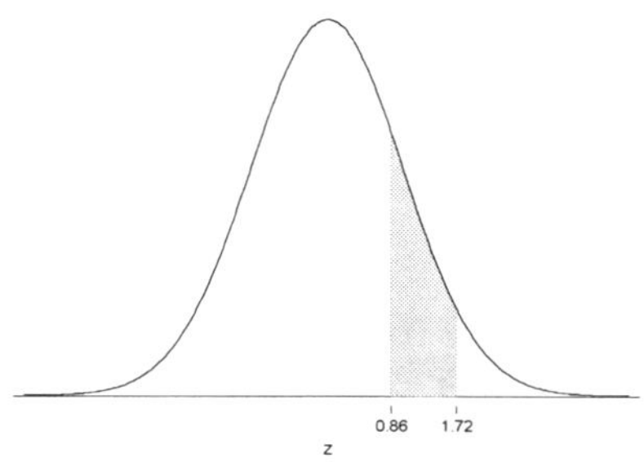

Prob(ziL < z < ziU) for a given zi		
ZIL	ZIU	PROB
.86000	1.72000	.15218

k. Prob(z < 1.58)

pz_lt_zi(1.58).

Prob(z < zi) for a given zi	
ZI	PROB
1.58000	.94295

l. Prob(0 < *z* < 1.83)

pz_gl_zi zil=(0) ziu=(1.83).

Prob(ziL < z < ziU) for a given zi		
ZIL	ZIU	PROB
.00000	1.83000	.46638

m. Prob(–2.08 < *z* < 0.63)

pz_gl_zi zil=(–2.08) ziu=(0.63).

Prob(ziL < z < ziU) for a given zi		
ZIL	ZIU	PROB
-2.08000	.63000	.71689

From the tables,

Prob(–2.08 < z < 0.63) = Prob(z < 0.63) – Prob(z < –2.08)
= .735653 – .018763
= 0.71689

3.2.4 *Z-score Problems: Finding a Probability from a Given z*

So far we have been looking at how to calculate the probabilities associated with particular values of z. But suppose that you are given a probability and you need to find the values of z associated with it.

Knowing the probability alone will not give you sufficient information to work out the corresponding z values. You will also need to be given some clue as to which segment under the z-distribution the probability refers. For example, if you are asked to find the z values associated with a probability of 0.95, then you would have to reply that there are in fact an infinite number of possible z values that could be used (any two that bound an interval which makes up 95% of the z-distribution).

However, if you were told to find the z values associated with the central 95% of a normal distribution, then you would be able to give a more precise answer, since all normal distributions are symmetrical, and so the central 95% equals 2 × 47.5% – two areas either side of the line of symmetry. In terms of the z-distribution, the line of symmetry runs through zero, and so we would be looking for the value of z associated with 47.5% to the left of zero. Since the whole area to the left of zero equals 50%, you know that the left tail associated with the value of z you are looking for has an area of 0.5 – 0.475 = 0.025.

In other words, you are looking for z_i such that $\Pr(z < z_i) = 0.025$. How would you find this value of z_i? Recall that the figures in the body of Table A are probabilities associated with the left tail of the z-distribution. So, what you need to do is look for 0.025 in the body of the table and then look at the row and column headings to locate the value of z it is associated with.

Finding the probability 0.025 in the body of the table shouldn't be too difficult since you will notice that the probabilities increase in value as you move left and down through the cells of the table. You should find that the unique value of z associated with the left tail area of 0.025 is in fact **–1.96**. In other words, $\Pr(z < -1.96) = 0.025$.

So, by manipulating the areas under the z curve, you can use Table A to find the z-values associated with any given central probability (such as the central 95%, or central 99%, or central 30%). Even though the process is rather cumbersome, it is a method worth practicing since it will reinforce your understanding of the standard normal curve.

An alternative way of finding the z-values associated with given probabilities is to use the set of macro commands included in the suite of macros downloadable from www.geebeejey.co.uk . These macros and how to use them are summarised below:

zi_lt_zp

zi_lt_zp p = (?). calculates the value of z_i such that $\text{Prob}(z < z_i) = \text{PROB}$ for a given PROB. For example, suppose you wanted to find the value of z_i such that $\text{Prob}(z < z_i) = 0.06$. From your knowledge of the standard normal curve you know that this relates to a small area in the left tail (as in the graph below).

To obtain a precise value for z_i you would type,

zi_lt_zp p = (0.06).

and as a result you would obtain the output presented in the right box below.

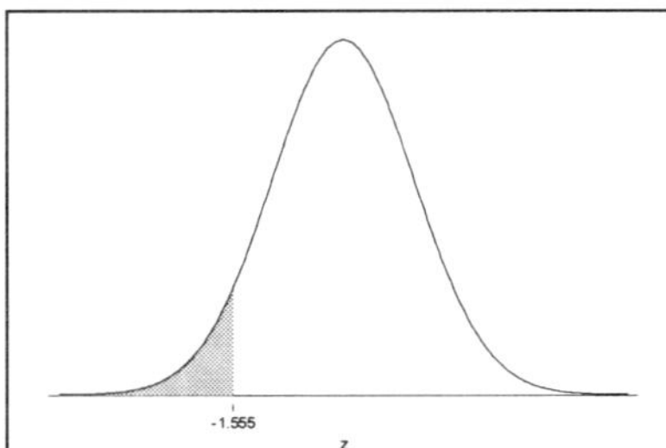


```
Value of zi such that Prob(z < zi) = PROB when
PROB is given
         ZI           PROB
    -1.55477        .06000
```

zi_gt_zp

zi_gt_zp p = (?). calculates the value of z_i such that Prob(z > zi) = PROB for a given PROB. (This is somewhat redundant, of course, since you can make use of the symmetry of the normal distribution and enter 1-PROB into the previous syntax). Suppose you want to find the value of z_i such that Prob($z > z_i$) = 0.06. That is, find the value of z_i above which there is only 6% of z_i. You would guess that the graph would look something like the diagram below. To obtain a precise value for z_i you would type:

zi_gt_zp p = (0.06).

and as a result you would obtain:

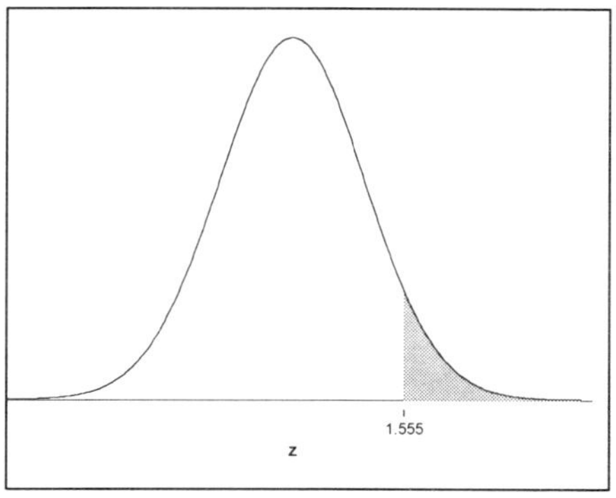


```
Value of zi such that Prob(z > zi) = PROB
when PROB is given
          ZI          PROB
     1.55477        .06000
```

3.2.5 *Z-scores that Bound Central Probabilities*

Very often you are given a probability, such as the central probability (for example, the middle 99% of the normal distribution) and your task is to calculate the z_i scores that bound it. This can be done using the following syntax:

zi_gl_zp

zi_gl_zp p=(?). calculates the value of z_i such that Prob($-z_i < z < z_i$) $= p$, when p is given. In other words, it calculates the z_i for a given central probability. For example, suppose you want the values of z_i that bound the central 99% of z, then you would type,

zi_gl_zp p=(0.99) .

which tells you that the central 99% of values are bounded by + and – 2.576:

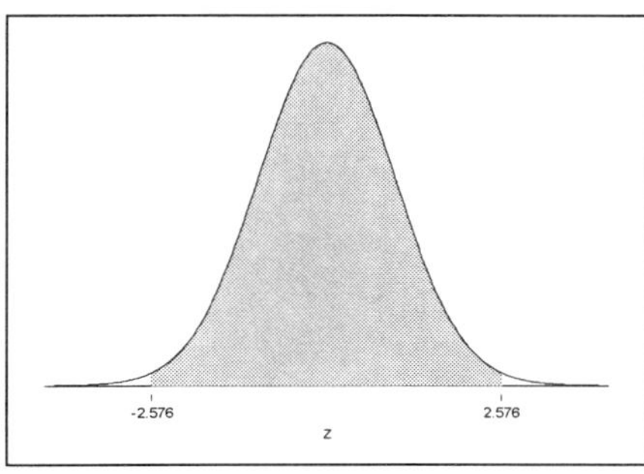


```
Value of zi such that Prob(-zi < z < zi)  =
PROB, when PROB is given
     ZIL        ZIU         PROB
  -2.57583   2.57583      .99000
```

Suppose again that you want the values of z_i that bound the central 95% of z, then you would type,

zi_gl_zp p=(0.95) .

which yields the following output for the middle 95% of the normal distribution:

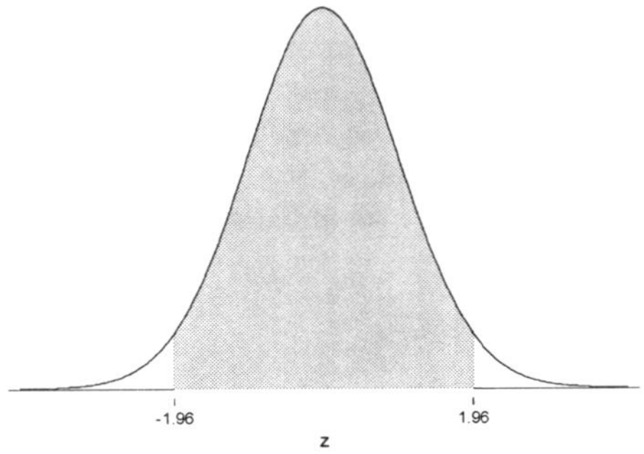


```
value of zi such that Prob(-zi < z
< zi)  = PROB, when PROB is given
   ZIL           ZIU           PROB
-1.95996      1.95996        .95000
```

Exercise 3.2.5 Find the values of z associated with given probabilities

1. Find a value z_i such that:

   a. Prob($z \geq z_i$) = 0.06   i.e. the probability that z is greater than z_i is 0.06.
   b. Prob($z > z_i$) = 0.95
   c. Prob($z < z_i$) = 0.80

2. Find z_i such that 95% of z-scores are above z_i. That is, Prob($z > z_i$) = 95%.

3. Find z_i such that Prob($-z_i < z < z_i$) = 95%.

Answers:

Attempt to answer the questions yourself before looking at the answers.

1. Find a value z_i such that:

   a. Prob($z \geq z_i$) = 0.06   i.e. the probability that z is greater than z_i is 0.06.

   Here we are given the probability and need to find the value of z_i associated with it.

   The tables we have been using only list the probabilities for z *less than* a particular value. We can still work out z_i because we know that Prob($z > z_i$) = 1 – Prob($z < z_i$) = 0.06. In other words,

   Prob($z < z_i$)   = 1 – 0.06
                      = 0.94.

   If we now look up 0.94 in the body of the table we find that the nearest z-score is 1.56. That is: **z_i = 1.56.**

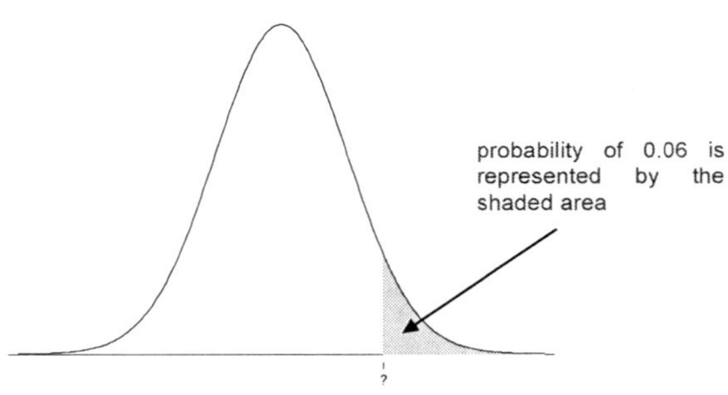

To do this in SPSS we would type, **zi_gt_zp p = (0.06).** resulting in the following output:

```
Value of zi such that Prob(z > zi) = PROB when PROB is given
         ZI          PROB
    1.55477        .06000
```

That is, Prob($z \geq$ **1.55477**) = 0.06

b. Prob($z > z_i$) = 0.95

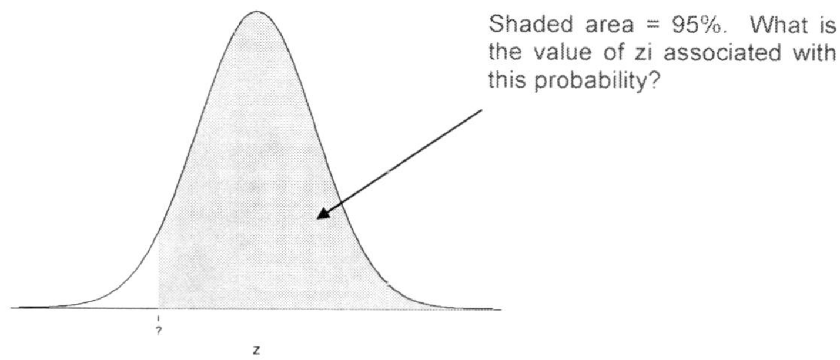

Prob($z > z_i$) = 1 – Prob($z < z_i$) = 0.95, therefore, Prob($z < z_i$) = 1 – 0.95 = 0.05. If we now try to look up 0.05 in the body of the table we find that we cannot find it because in the table we have been using, the lowest probability is 0.5 because only values of z_i that are greater than zero are considered. So this method won't work here. For 95% of *z*-scores to be greater than z_i, we know that z_i must be negative, so we can re-write the question as: find z_i such that Prob($z > -z_i$) = 0.95. Because the distribution is symmetrical, we know that:

Prob($z > -z_i$) = Prob($z < z_i$) = .95.

If we look up 0.95 in our table it gives us a *z-score* of 1.65. So,

Prob($z > -1.65$) = Prob($z < 1.65$) = .95.

That is: $\mathbf{z_i = -1.65}$

To do this in SPSS we would simply type **zi_gt_zp p = (0.95).**

```
Value of zi such that Prob(z > zi) = PROB when PROB is given
          ZI          PROB
    -1.64485      .95000
```

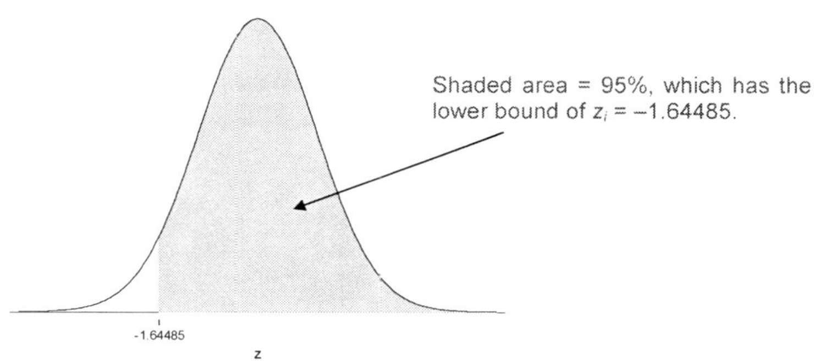

c. Prob($z < z_i$) = 0.8

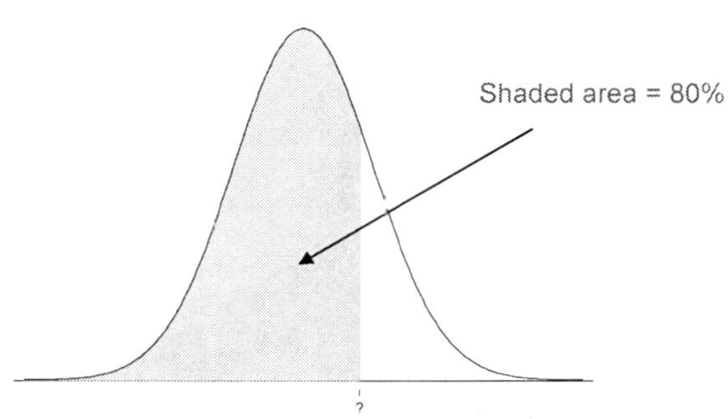

To compute this using macro syntax we would type: **zi_lt_zp p = (0.8).**

```
Value of zi such that Prob(z < zi) = PROB when PROB is given
          ZI          PROB
      .84162      .80000
```

Again, this is relatively straightforward in the tables. We just look up 0.8 in the body of the table and find the nearest *z* value to be 0.84, Prob($z < 0.84$) = 0.8, so $\mathbf{z_i = 0.84}$

2. Find z_i such that 95% of *z*-scores are above z_i. That is, Prob($z > z_i$) = 95%.

   See 1.2 question 5(b): $\mathbf{z_i = -1.65}$

3. Find z_i such that Prob($-z_i < z < z_i$) = 95%.

   Here we have to find the values of z_i which bound the middle 95% of the distribution. If you draw the *z*-curve diagram for this area, you will see that it is equal to the probability that *z* is less than z_{iU} (the whole area to the left of z_{iU}) minus the probability that *z* is less than z_{iL} (the lower-tail area), where $z_{iL} = -z_{iU}$:

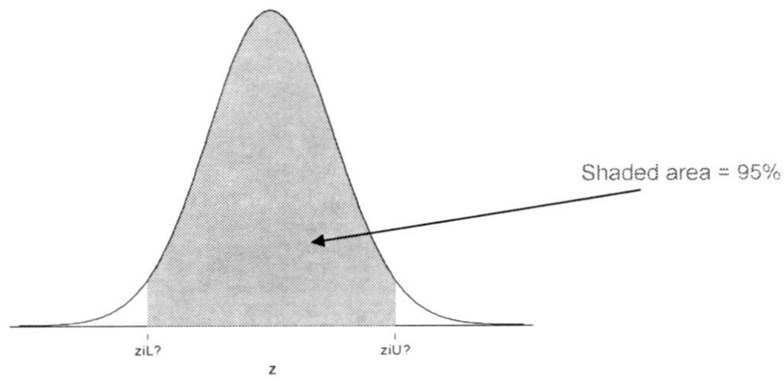

   We know the value of the tail areas since they are symmetrical:

   Area of lower-tail = area of upper-tail = $\frac{1-0.95}{2} = \frac{0.05}{2} = 0.025$

   So we know that Prob($z < -z_i$) = Prob($z > z_i$) = 0.025. The table only lists probabilities for $z < z_i$, so we must take 0.025 away from 1 to give the entire area to the left of z_i that we need to look up, i.e. Prob($z < z_i$) = 1 – 0.025 = 0.975. If we look up 0.975 in the body of the table, we find that z_i = **1.96**. In other words, Prob(–1.96 < *z* < 1.96) = 95%. The following matrix syntax allows you to simply enter the central probability in order to calculate values for z_i:

   zi_gl_zp p = (0.95).

```
Value of zi such that Prob(-zi < z < zi)  = PROB, when PROB is given
        ZIL           ZIU          PROB
   -1.95996       1.95996        .95000
```

3.3 Calculating z for a Normally Distributed Variable, x

For a particular value x_i of a normally distributed variable x, we can calculate the associated standardised normal value, z_i, by subtracting the population mean, and dividing by the population standard deviation,

$$z_i = \frac{x_i - \mu}{\sigma}$$

So, we can standardise any value of x provided we know the population mean and population standard error of the mean. And once you have standardised a value (i.e. converted it to a z-score), then you can use it to calculate probabilities under the standard normal curve knowing that these probabilities correspond to probabilities under the original distribution of x.

Exercise 3.3 Calculating z for a normally distributed variable, x, where population mean and population standard deviation are known

1. If x = 12, the population mean = 9 and the SE of the mean is 3, what is the *z-score*? Once you have calculated the *z-score*, calculate the probability that x > 12. (N B. this will equal the probability that $z > z_i$ where z_i is the standardised value for x = 12. I.e. Prob(x > 12) = Prob($z > z_i$)).

2. If x = 3.9, the population mean = 5.4, and the population standard deviation is 2, what is the z–score for 3.9? What is the probability that x < 3.9?

3. You know that the height of all 18 year old males is normally distributed with a mean of 1.8m and a standard deviation of 1.2m. What proportion of 18year olds are < 2m tall?

4. The weight of all newly born babies is normally distributed with a mean of 3kg and a standard deviation of 4kg.

   (a) What proportion of newly born babies weigh less than the average?
   (b) What proportion of newly born babies weigh less than 2kg?
   (c) What proportion of babies weigh between 2kg and 4kg?
   (d) How do your answers to (a), (b) and (c) change if the standard deviation were only 2kg?

5. You know that the mean height of all 20yr old females is normally distributed with mean = 1.5m and s.d. = 1.4m. (a) what is the height below which 50% of all 20yr old females lie? (b) what is the height below which 40% of all 20yr old females lie? How do the answers change if the mean is 1.7m and the standard deviation is 1.2m?

Answers

Attempt to answer the questions yourself before looking at the answers.

1. If x = 12, the population mean = 9 and the population standard deviation is 3, what is the *z-score*? Once you have calculated the *z-score*, calculate the probability that x > 12. (N.B. this will equal the probability that $z > z_i$ where z_i is the standardised value for X = 12. I.e. Prob(x > 12) = Prob($z > z_i$)).

   Assuming that X is normally distributed: first calculate the z-score for x_i which is calculated using the following formula:

$$z_i = \frac{x_i - \mu}{\sigma}$$

   where,

x_i	=	a particular value of a normally distributed variable x
z	=	standardised value for x
μ	=	population mean value of x
σ	=	population standard deviation of x.

   We are given the the values of x_i, σ, and μ in the question:

x_i	=	12
μ	=	9
σ	=	3

$$z_i = \frac{x_i - \mu}{\sigma} = \frac{12 - 9}{3} = \mathbf{1}$$

The crucial thing to understand here is that the probability that $x_i > 12$ is exactly equal to the probability that z > 1 (assuming that x is normally distributed).

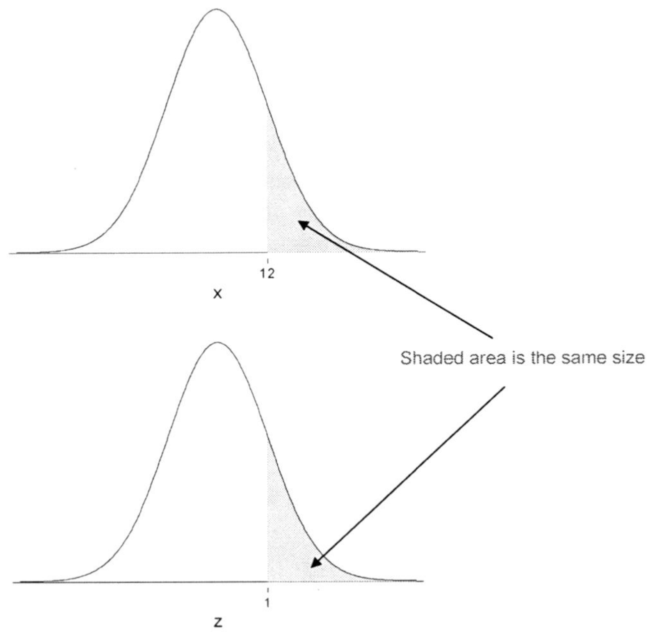

So to find Prob(x > 12) we just need to find Prob($z > z_i$) and we can use the **pz_gt_zi** syntax to do this:

pz_gt_zi(1).

```
Prob(z > zi) for a given zi
        ZI          PROB
   1.00000        .15866
```

So we now know that 15.87% of *z* lie above 1. Which means that we now also know that 15.87% of x lie above 12. We can confirm this by doing the calculation by hand. If we look up a value for *z* in the table (or use SPSS), it will give us the probability that *z* is less than that value. But we want the probability that *z* is *greater than* a particular value. We know that we can get round this problem by taking advantage of the fact that 1 minus the probability of $z < z_i$ is equal to the probability that *z* is greater than z_i:

Prob(*x* > 12)	=	Prob(*z* > 1)
	=	1 – .841345
	=	**0.1587**

That is, 15.87% of x are greater than 12. It is not surprising that the probability is relatively small if you take into account the fact that the mean of *x* is 9 and that the standard deviation is fairly small (= 3). So most of *x* are grouped around the mean value of 9, with only 15.87% greater than 12.

2. If *x* = 3.9, the population mean = 5.4, and the population standard deviation is 2, what is the *z*-score for 3.9? What is the probability that *x* < 3.9?

Assuming that x is normally distributed:

x_i	=	a particular value of a normally distributed variable x	=	3.9
μ	=	population mean value of x	=	5.4
σ	=	population standard deviation of x.	=	2

$$z_i = \frac{x_i - \mu}{\sigma} = \frac{3.9 - 5.4}{2} = -1.5 / 2 = \mathbf{-0.75}$$

If *x* is normally distributed, we know that Prob(*x* < 3.9) = Prob(*z* < –.75)

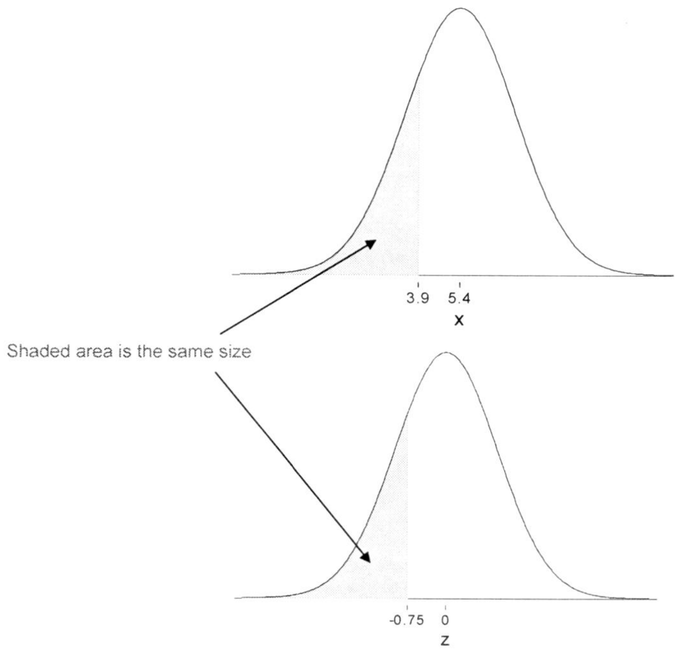

So we simply need to calculate the proportion of *z-scores* that lie below –0.75, and we can do this by entering the following SPSS macro command **pz_lt_zi (–0.75).** which results in the following output:

```
Prob(z < zi) for a given zi
        ZI         PROB
   -.75000       .22663
```

These results tell us that 22.66% of *z* lie below –0.75, the corollary of which is that 22.66% of *x* fall below 3.9:

Prob($x < 3.9$) = Prob($z < -.75$) = **0.2266**

That is, 22.66% of *x* are less than 3.9.

3. You know that the height of all 18 year old males is normally distributed with a mean of 1.8m and a standard deviation of 1.2m. What proportion of 18year olds are < 2m tall?

x_i	=	height of 18 year olds	=	2
μ	=	population mean of x = mean height of all 18yr olds	=	1.8
σ	=	population standard deviation of x.	=	1.2

Because height is normally distributed, we know that, Prob(height < 2m) = Prob($z < z_i$), where z_i is the standardised value for $x = 2$. First we need to calculate z_i:

$$z_i = \frac{x_i - \mu}{\sigma} = \frac{2 - 1.8}{1.2} = \frac{0.2}{1.2} = 0.1667$$

Now that we have calculated $z_i = 0.1667$, we can calculate Prob(height < 2m) = Prob($z < 0.1667$), which we can compute using the following macro syntax, **pz_lt_zi (0.1667).**

```
Prob(z < zi) for a given zi
        ZI         PROB
    .16670       .56620
```

Therefore, Prob(height < 2m) = **.56620.** That is, 56.62% of 18year old males are less than 2m tall.

4. The weight of all newly born babies is normally distributed with a mean of 3kg and a standard deviation of 4kg.

   (a) What proportion of newly born babies weigh less than the average?
   (b) What proportion of newly born babies weigh less than 2kg?
   (c) What proportion of babies weigh between 2kg and 4kg?
   (d) How do your answers to (a), (b) and (c) change if the standard deviation were only 2kg?

x	=	weight of newly born babies		
μ	=	population mean of x = mean weight of all babies	=	3kg
σ	=	population standard deviation of x	=	4kg

(a) Because weight is normally distributed, and this distribution is symmetrical, we know that 50% of values will be less than the mean. To show this is true, we can apply the *z-score* method: Prob(weight < 3kg) = Prob($z < z_i$), where z_i is the standardised value for x = 3. First we need to calculate z_i:

$$z_i = \frac{x_i - \mu}{\sigma} \quad = \quad \frac{3-3}{4} = \frac{0}{4} = 0$$

Now that we have calculated z_i = 0, we can calculate Prob(Weight < 3kg) = Prob(z < 0). That 50% of z lie below zero is confirmed below: **pz_lt_zi (0).**

```
Prob(z < zi) for a given zi
        ZI          PROB
     .00000       .50000
```

Therefore, Prob(Weight < 3kg) = **.5000.** That is, 50% of newly born babies weigh less than the mean, as expected.

(b) Prob(weight < 2kg) = Prob($z < z_i$) where z_i is the standardised value for x = 2. First we need to calculate z_i:

$$z_i = \frac{x_i - \mu}{\sigma} \quad = \quad \frac{2-3}{4} = \frac{-1}{4} = -0.25$$

Now that we have calculated zi = –0.25, we can calculate Prob(Weight < 2kg) = Prob(z < –0.25) using the following macro syntax, **pz_lt_zi (–0.25).** which results in the following output:

```
Prob(z < zi) for a given zi
        ZI          PROB
    -.25000       .40129
```

Thus, Prob(Weight < 2kg) = .40129. That is, 40.13% of newly born babies weigh less than 2kg. It is not surprising that this proportion is so large given the very large standard deviation which suggests a fairly flat normal distribution in the original variable.

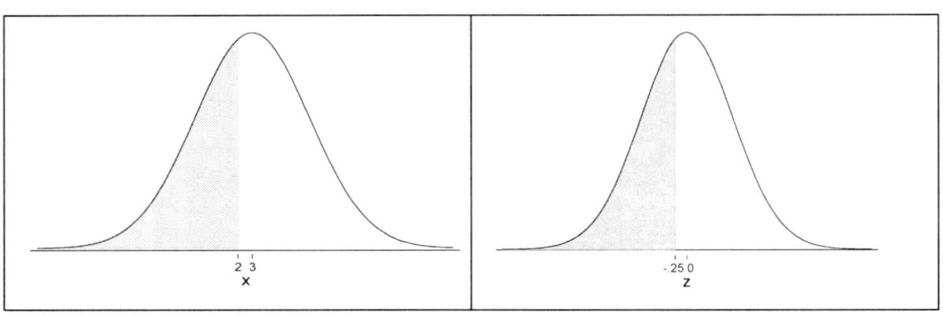

5. You know that the mean height of all 20yr old females is normally distributed with mean = 1.5m and standard deviation = 1.4m.

(a) Because height is normally distributed we know that 50% of all heights lie below the population mean which is 1.5m. This is confirmed if we apply the **zi_lt_zp** syntax which calculates the value of zi such that Prob(z < zi) = PROB for a given PROB. Here, PROB = 0.5 so we type in **zi_lt_zp p=(0.5).** which yields:

```
Value of zi such that Prob(z < zi) = PROB when PROB is given
       ZI         PROB
   .00000       .50000
```

(b) To answer this we need to find xi for which Prob(height < h*) = 40%. Because height is normally distributed we can take advantage of the fact that: Prob(height < xi) = Prob(z < –zi) = 40%. We knew that zi would be negative because only 40% is less than it, Prob(height < xi) = Prob(z < –zi) = 40%. If we look up 0.6 in the body of the tables, or use the following syntax: **zi_lt_zp p = (0.5).**

```
Value of zi such that Prob(z < zi) = PROB when PROB is given
       ZI         PROB
  -.25335       .40000
```

We find that the associated z-score is 0.25. That is Prob(height < xi) = Prob(z < –0.25) = 40%. We now need to rearrange the formula for z and write it in terms of x which is what we are trying to find:

$$z_i = \frac{x_i - \mu}{\sigma}$$

Multiply both by sigma,

$$z_i \sigma = x_i - \mu$$

and add the population mean to both sides to get:

$$z_i \sigma + \mu = x_i$$

$$x_i = z_i \sigma + \mu$$

So, x_i = –0.25 × 1.4 + 1.5 = 1.15m. That is, 40% of all 20yr old females are less than 1.15m tall.

How do the answers change if the mean is 1.7 and the standard deviation is 1.2?

(c) Because height is normally distributed we know that 50% of all heights lie below the population mean which is now 1.7m.

(d) We know that z = –0.25 and that $x = z\,\sigma + \mu$. Plug in the new values for the mean and standard deviation and you get

$$x_i = -0.25 \times 1.2 + 1.7$$
$$= \mathbf{1.4m}$$

That is, 40% of all 20yr old females are less than 1.4m tall.

3.4 Distribution of Sample Means

Because sample means are always normally distributed around the population mean (provided the sample sizes are > 30), we can calculate *z*-scores for a particular *sample mean* if we know the population mean and population standard error of the mean (i.e. the standard deviation of sample means):

$$z_i = \frac{\bar{x}_i - \mu}{\sigma_{\bar{x}}}$$

where :

μ = population mean

$\bar{x}_i$ = sample mean

$\sigma_{\bar{x}}$ = standard deviation of all the sample means, called the standard error of the mean

z_i = z - score

This formula tells us that, if we have taken a sample and calculated its mean, $\bar{x}$, and we happen to know both the population mean (very unlikely in reality, but often we have some assumption or hypothesis about it) and the standard error of the mean (even less likely in reality, though we are usually able to approximate it), then we can then calculate the *z-score* using the formula above. This is a crucial insight because it allows us to apply the skills we have developed in estimating areas under the *z*-distribution, not only to variables that are normally distributed (such as height), but also to variables that do not follow a bell-shaped distribution (such as income). The formula takes advantage of the Central Limit Theorem which says that the sampling distribution of the mean is always normal for large samples.

Exercises on Applying the Central Limit Theorem when the population mean and standard deviation are known

1. If the sample mean income is £25,000, population mean income is £20,000, and the population standard error of the mean is £2000, what is the z-score for the sample mean? What proportion of sample means (from all possible large samples) would be less than £25,000? What proportion would be greater than £25,000?

2. If the sample mean inside leg measurement of gerbils is 2.7cm, the population mean is 3cm and the standard error of the mean is 4, what is the z-score for the sample mean? What proportion of all possible large samples of gerbils have inside leg measurements of less than 2.7cm?

Answers

Attempt to answer the questions yourself before looking at the answers.

Because sample means are always normally distributed around the population mean (provided the sample sizes are > 30), we can calculate *z-scores* for a particular sample mean if we know the population mean and population standard error of the mean (i.e. the standard deviation of sample means):

$$z_i = \frac{\bar{x}_i - \mu}{\sigma_{\bar{x}}}$$

1. If the sample mean income is £25,000, population mean income is £20,000, and the population standard error of the mean is £2,000, what is the z-score for the sample mean? What proportion of sample means (from all possible large samples) would be less than £25,000? What proportion would be greater than £25,000?

   (a) Start off with the formula for *z*:

$$z_i = \frac{\bar{x}_i - \mu}{\sigma_{\bar{x}}} \qquad z_i = \frac{25000 - 20000}{2000} = 2.5$$

(b) We can then use this z-score to calculate the proportion of sample means that would be less than £25,000 because we know that, Prob(sample mean income < £25000) = Prob(z < 2.5). We can calculate this using the following macro syntax, zi_lt_zp p = (0.25).

```
Prob(z < zi) for a given zi
        ZI          PROB
   2.50000        .99379
```

Prob(sample mean income < £25000) = 0.99379. That is, 99.38% of sample mean incomes are less than £25,000. The proportion is so large because of the very small standard deviation which means that most sample mean incomes in this distribution are very close to the mean. (If the standard deviation was £20,000, for example, rather than £2,000, then the z-score would be 0.25, and the proportion of incomes less than £25K would be around sixty percent.).

(c) The proportion greater than £25,000 is simply 1–0.993790 = 0.00621. That is 0.62% of sample mean incomes are greater than £25K.

2. If the sample mean inside leg measurement of gerbils is 2.7cm, the population mean is 3cm and the standard error of the mean is 4, what is the z-score for the sample mean? What proportion of all possible large samples of gerbils have inside leg measurements of less than 2.7cm?

(a) Calculate the *z-score*:

$$z_i = \frac{\bar{x}_i - \mu}{\sigma_{\bar{x}}} = \frac{2.7 - 3}{4} = -0.075$$

(b) Now that we have computed the *z-score* we can calculate the proportion less than this score knowing that, Prob(sample mean < 2.7) = Prob(z < –0.075). We can calculate this using the following macro syntax, **zi_lt_zp p = (–0.075).** which results in the following output:

```
Prob(z < zi) for a given zi
        ZI          PROB
   -.07500        .47011
```

That is, 47.01% of all possible sample mean inside leg lengths are less than 2.7cm.

3.5 How to Create Your Own z-Table

Follow the steps below to create your own standard normal table! It's a useful exercise to work through since you'll learn some useful new SPSS commands along the way (such as NEW FILE, FLIP, and RENAME VARIABLES). NEW FILE simply creates a new blank data sheet. FLIP transposes the datasheet (i.e. converts columns to rows). We use RENAME VARIABLES to create more useful names than those automatically assigned by SPSS.

```
*STEP 1: create a new blank file.

NEW FILE.

*STEP 2: enter –3.4 in the first cell, and hit <Enter>.

*STEP 3: the variable you have created will have automatically been assigned a name (e.g. VAR0001)
* So rename it as v1.

RENAME VARIABLES (VAR00001 = v1).

*STEP 4: Calculate a second variable, v2, which equals the first + 0.1, then a third variable etc.

COMPUTE v2 = v1 + 0.1.
COMPUTE v3 = v2 + 0.1.
COMPUTE v4 = v3 + 0.1.
COMPUTE v5 = v4 + 0.1.
COMPUTE v6 = v5 + 0.1.
COMPUTE v7 = v6 + 0.1.
COMPUTE v8 = v7 + 0.1.
COMPUTE v9 = v8 + 0.1.
COMPUTE v10 = v9 + 0.1.
COMPUTE v11 = v10 + 0.1.
COMPUTE v12 = v11 + 0.1.
```

```
COMPUTE v13 = v12 + 0.1.
COMPUTE v14 = v13 + 0.1.
COMPUTE v15 = v14 + 0.1.
COMPUTE v16 = v15 + 0.1.
COMPUTE v17 = v16 + 0.1.
COMPUTE v18 = v17 + 0.1.
COMPUTE v19 = v18 + 0.1.
COMPUTE v20 = v19 + 0.1.
COMPUTE v21 = v20 + 0.1.
COMPUTE v22 = v21 + 0.1.
COMPUTE v23 = v22 + 0.1.
COMPUTE v24 = v23 + 0.1.
COMPUTE v25 = v24 + 0.1.
COMPUTE v26 = v25 + 0.1.
COMPUTE v27 = v26 + 0.1.
COMPUTE v28 = v27 + 0.1.
COMPUTE v29 = v28 + 0.1.
COMPUTE v30 = v29 + 0.1.
COMPUTE v31 = v30 + 0.1.
COMPUTE v32 = v31 + 0.1.
COMPUTE v33 = v32 + 0.1.
COMPUTE v34 = v33 + 0.1.
COMPUTE v35 = v34 + 0.1.
EXECUTE.

*STEP 5: Now transpose the whole data sheet using the FLIP command.

FLIP VARIABLES = ALL.

*STEP 6: rename var001 as z.

RENAME VARIABLES (var001 = z).

*STEP 7: Compute the probability using CDFNORM, then label the variable.
*and then format the variable as numeric of width = 5 and decimal places = 4.

COMPUTE DM2eq0 = CDFNORM(z).
VARIABLE LABELS  DM2eq0 'Value of second decimal place on z = 0'.
FORMATS DM2eq0 (F5.4) .

*STEP 8: Create DM2eq1 by taking away 0.01 from z and repeat for all 9 decimal places.

COMPUTE DM2eq1 = CDFNORM(z -.01).
VARIABLE LABELS  DM2eq0 'Value of second decimal place on z = 1'.
FORMATS DM2eq1 (F5.4) .
COMPUTE DM2eq2 = CDFNORM(z -.02).
VARIABLE LABELS  DM2eq0 'Value of second decimal place on z = 2'.
FORMATS DM2eq2 (F5.4) .
COMPUTE DM2eq3 = CDFNORM(z -.03).
VARIABLE LABELS  DM2eq0 'Value of second decimal place on z = 3'.
FORMATS DM2eq3 (F5.4) .
COMPUTE DM2eq4 = CDFNORM(z -.04).
VARIABLE LABELS  DM2eq0 'Value of second decimal place on z = 4'.
FORMATS DM2eq4 (F5.4) .
COMPUTE DM2eq5 = CDFNORM(z -.05).
VARIABLE LABELS  DM2eq0 'Value of second decimal place on z = 5'.
FORMATS DM2eq5 (F5.4) .
COMPUTE DM2eq6 = CDFNORM(z -.06).
VARIABLE LABELS  DM2eq0 'Value of second decimal place on z = 6'.
FORMATS DM2eq6 (F5.4) .
COMPUTE DM2eq7 = CDFNORM(z -.07).
VARIABLE LABELS  DM2eq0 'Value of second decimal place on z = 7'.
FORMATS DM2eq7 (F5.4) .
COMPUTE DM2eq8 = CDFNORM(z -.08).
VARIABLE LABELS  DM2eq0 'Value of second decimal place on z = 8'.
FORMATS DM2eq8 (F5.4) .
COMPUTE DM2eq9 = CDFNORM(z -.09).
VARIABLE LABELS  DM2eq0 'Value of second decimal place on z = 9'.
FORMATS DM2eq9 (F5.4) .
EXECUTE.

*STEP 9: Save your data file.

SAVE OUTFILE='C:\STATISTICS\TABLE A standard normal probabilities.sav'.
```

3.6 Copies of the Macro Commands Used in this Chapter

You should not have to type in these programs yourself as they are in the QUANTSCOMMANDS.SPS file which can be downloaded, along with installation instructions, from www.geebeejey.co.uk. The macro programs are presented below for those brave enough to browse through them and maybe even attempt to write some macros of their own. Note that each of the macros below start with the word **DEFINE**. This is the command used to tell SPSS that you are about to create a new macro command. After the word **DEFINE** comes the name of the macro. Note also that the second line of each macro tells SPSS to open the following file: **'C:\QUANTS\one.sav'**. This is one of the files you need to download from www.geebeejey.co.uk. If you don't have access to the internet, the file is easy to create: it is just a an SPSS data file with the number 1 in the first cell and nothing else (actually, you could put any number in there) and then saved the file as '**one.sav**' in the **C:\QUANTS** folder on your hard-drive (if this folder doesn't exist, you'll need to create it using My Computer).

Each macro-program needs to be "called" (i.e. highlighted and run) before the respective command will work. So, if you are not installing the full set of files from www.geebeejey.co.uk but you want to run the **pz_lt_zi** command, for example, first type in the program below into your syntax file, then run it, then use the **pz_lt_zi** command as explained earlier in this chapter.

```
DEFINE pz_lt_zi (!POSITIONAL !ENCLOSE('(',')')).
GET FILE='C:\QUANTS\one.sav'.
compute Zi_Var = !1 .
COMPUTE PROB = CDFNORM(Zi_Var).
EXECUTE.
MATRIX.
GET PROB_VAR /VARIABLES = PROB.
GET Zi_Var /VARIABLES = Zi_Var.
COMPUTE Prob = PROB_VAR(1).
COMPUTE zi = Zi_Var(1).
COMPUTE ANSWER = {zi, PROB}.
PRINT ANSWER / FORMAT "F10.5" /Title = " Prob(z < zi) for a given zi " / CLABELS = zi, Prob.
END MATRIX.
!ENDDEFINE.
```

If all you want to do is use the macros as required in the exercises of this book, then you don't need to do all this. You just need to install the macros as explained under the Downloads section of www.geebeejey.co.uk . However, if you want to learn how to write your own macros for SPSS, then browsing through these and other macros will be useful. An excellent source for SPSS macros covering a massive range of empirical tasks is as www.spsstools.net offer new routines, automated tasks, and thousands of extra facilities that greatly expand the versatility of the standard SPSS package. Also, the **spssbase.pdf** file that comes with your version of SPSS will also prove a useful resource. You should be able to access it by opening SPSS, clicking on **Help** and selecting **Command Syntax Reference**, which should open up a pdf file of around 1,800 pages. Towards the end of that document you'll find an appendix called *Using the Macro Facility* (or similar) which will take you through the various macro facilities available in SPSS and the steps you need to follow to learn how to use them. If you cannot find this pdf document, it is likely that you inadvertently chose not to include it when you first installed SPSS on your computer, so you'll need to go back to the original installation CD.

3.6.1 Macros used in this chapter

(See above for the program for **pz_lt_zi**, and see Appendices at the back of the book for details of other macro commands).

```
DEFINE pz_gt_zi (!POSITIONAL !ENCLOSE('(',')')).
GET FILE='C:\QUANTS\one.sav'.
compute Zi_Var = !1 .
COMPUTE PROB = 1 - CDFNORM(Zi_Var).
EXECUTE.
MATRIX.
GET PROB_VAR /VARIABLES = PROB.
GET Zi_Var /VARIABLES = Zi_Var.
COMPUTE Prob = PROB_VAR(1).
COMPUTE zi = Zi_Var(1).
COMPUTE ANSWER = {zi, PROB}.
PRINT ANSWER / FORMAT "F10.5" /Title = " Prob(z > zi) for a given zi " / CLABELS = zi, Prob.
```

```
END MATRIX.
!ENDDEFINE.

DEFINE pz_lg_zi (zil = !ENCLOSE('(',')')  / ziu =  !ENCLOSE('(',')')).
GET FILE='C:\QUANTS\one.sav'.
compute ZiL_Var = !zil .
compute ZiU_Var = !ziu .
EXECUTE.
COMPUTE PROBL = CDFNORM(ZiL_Var).
COMPUTE PROBU = 1 - CDFNORM(ZiU_Var).
COMPUTE PROBLG = PROBL + PROBU.
EXECUTE.
MATRIX.
GET PROB_VAR /VARIABLES = PROBLG.
GET ZiL_Var /VARIABLES = ZiL_Var.
GET ZiU_Var /VARIABLES = ZiU_Var.
COMPUTE Prob = PROB_VAR(1).
COMPUTE ziL = ZiL_Var(1).
COMPUTE ziU = ZiU_Var(1).
COMPUTE ANSWER = {ziL, ziU, PROB}.
PRINT ANSWER / FORMAT "F10.5" /Title = " Prob((z < ziL) OR (z > ziU)) for a given zi " / CLABELS = ziL, ziU, Prob.
END MATRIX.
!ENDDEFINE.

DEFINE pz_gl_zi (zil = !ENCLOSE ('(',')')  / ziu = !ENCLOSE('(',')')).
GET FILE='C:\QUANTS\one.sav'.
compute ZiL_Var = !zil .
compute ZiU_Var = !ziu .
EXECUTE.
COMPUTE PROBL = CDFNORM(ZiL_Var).
COMPUTE PROBU = 1 - CDFNORM(ZiU_Var).
COMPUTE PROBLG = 1 - (PROBL + PROBU).
EXECUTE.
MATRIX.
GET PROB_VAR /VARIABLES = PROBLG.
GET ZiL_Var /VARIABLES = ZiL_Var.
GET ZiU_Var /VARIABLES = ZiU_Var.
COMPUTE Prob = PROB_VAR(1).
COMPUTE ziL = ZiL_Var(1).
COMPUTE ziU = ZiU_Var(1).
COMPUTE ANSWER = {ziL, ziU, PROB}.
PRINT ANSWER / FORMAT "F10.5" /Title = " Prob(ziL < z < ziU) for a given zi " / CLABELS = ziL, ziU, Prob.
END MATRIX.
!ENDDEFINE.

DEFINE zi_lt_zp (p = !ENCLOSE('(',')')).
GET FILE='C:\QUANTS\one.sav'.
COMPUTE Zi = PROBIT(!p).
EXECUTE.
MATRIX.
GET Zi_VAR /VARIABLES = Zi.
COMPUTE Zi = Zi_VAR(1).
COMPUTE PROB= {!p}.    /*Enter the given probability into the curly brackets*/
COMPUTE ANSWER = {Zi, PROB}.
PRINT ANSWER / FORMAT "F10.5" /Title = " Value of zi such that Prob(z < zi) = PROB when PROB is given" /
CLABELS = zi, PROB.
END MATRIX.
!ENDDEFINE.

DEFINE zi_gt_zp (p = !ENCLOSE('(',')')).
GET FILE='C:\QUANTS\one.sav'.
COMPUTE Zi = PROBIT(1-!p).
EXECUTE.
MATRIX.
GET Zi_VAR /VARIABLES = Zi.
COMPUTE Zi = Zi_VAR(1).
COMPUTE PROB= {!p}.    /*Enter the given probability into the curly brackets*/
COMPUTE ANSWER = {Zi, PROB}.
PRINT ANSWER / FORMAT "F10.5" /Title = " Value of zi such that Prob(z > zi) = PROB when PROB is given" /
CLABELS = zi, PROB.
END MATRIX.
!ENDDEFINE.
DEFINE zi_gl_zp (p = !ENCLOSE('(',')')).
GET FILE='C:\QUANTS\one.sav'.
COMPUTE PROB = !p.
COMPUTE PROBLG = 1 - !p.
COMPUTE PROBL = PROBLG / 2.
```

```
COMPUTE ZiL_Var = PROBIT(PROBL).
COMPUTE ZiU_Var = -1 * ZiL_Var .
EXECUTE.
MATRIX.
GET PROB_VAR /VARIABLES = PROB.
GET ZiL_Var /VARIABLES = ZiL_Var.
GET ZiU_Var /VARIABLES = ZiU_Var.
COMPUTE Prob = PROB_VAR(1).
COMPUTE ziL = ZiL_Var(1).
COMPUTE ziU = ZiU_Var(1).
COMPUTE ANSWER = {ziL, ziU, PROB}.
PRINT ANSWER / FORMAT "F10.5" /Title = " Value of zi such that Prob(-zi < z < zi)  = PROB, when PROB is given  " /
CLABELS = ziL, ziU, Prob.
END MATRIX.
!ENDDEFINE.
```

4 Confidence Intervals

Aim:
To introduce confidence interval estimation.

Objectives:
By the end of this chapter, you should be able to calculate large and small sample confidence intervals for one mean; confidence intervals for means and proportions from two populations and be able to compute the sample size needed to arrive at a given margin of error for an estimate of the mean or proportion.

Further Reading:
D. S. Moore and G. P. McCabe, *Introduction to the Practice of Statistics,* 4th Ed., Freeman, New York, sections 6.1 (p. 415-429) and 7.1 (p.491-494). See also p.501-503; p.532; p.538; p.572; p.578-581; p.589.

Plan:

4.1 Introduction

A core theme of this book is *inference*. You will have gathered by now that statistical inference is concerned with how we derive conclusions about the population from our sample. The rationale for inference comes from the laws of probability: if our sample is a random selection of observations drawn from the population (*random* simply means that each individual in the population has an equal chance of entering our sample), then we can estimate the probability of observing our sample given the assumed value of the population mean. If the probability is estimated to be small, this might lead us to question our assumed hypothesis about the population mean. Alternatively, we can estimate intervals within which the population mean is likely to lie; likely enough to satisfy a prior level of confidence. It is this latter approach, known as *confidence interval* estimation, with which we shall concern ourselves in this chapter. The former method is known as *hypothesis testing* and is the subject of later chapters.

Confidence intervals are a very useful way of incorporating *sampling variation* into our estimate of the population mean. Sampling variation is the random variation in results from sample to sample. It is not caused by measurement error, or human error, or mistakes by computers. We assume, for now, that all these sources of error do not exist. Sampling variation refers only to the differences one naturally observes in the make up of individual samples drawn randomly from the same population. It would be worth reviewing the sampling distribution sections of Chapter 2 at this stage since they demonstrate how the mean of samples vary. The variation is not without order, however. You will recall that the *Central Limit Theorem* stipulates that the mean from repeated random samples of the same size will be normally distributed. Since all normal distributions are related to the *standard normal curve* we can translate our desired level of confidence from the central section of the z-distribution onto the sampling distribution associated with our current sample. Because we can easily calculate the values of z that bound any central area of the standard normal curve, and because we can convert any value of z into the equivalent value on our sampling distribution, we can estimate where the population mean will lie.

Practical application of confidence interval estimation will be aided by the use of the following macro commands:

Confidence Intervals (CI)	
Macro command	Definition
CI_L1M	Large sample CI for one mean
CI_S1M	Small sample CI for one mean
CI_S2MP	Small independent samples CI for difference between 2 means (pooled variance)
CI_S2MD	Small independent samples CI for difference between 2 means (different variances)
CI_L1P	Large sample CI for one proportion (presents output for both Traditional and Wilson methods of calculation)
CI_L2P	Large sample CI for comparing two proportions (presents output for both Traditional and Wilson methods of calculation)
N_L1M	Sample size for desired margin or error for the mean

These commands estimate confidence for different types of variable and for different data scenarios. The final command is rather different. It allows us to estimate the size of sample we need to obtain the desired degree of accuracy in estimating a particular variable – very useful in the sample design stage of a research project.

4.2 Large Sample Confidence Interval for the Mean

Usually we do not know either the population mean or population standard error of the mean. You will recall from Chapter 2 that the standard error of the mean is the standard deviation of sample means from sample to sample. Although the true value of the standard error of the mean is rarely known, a simple approximation is obtained by dividing the sample standard deviation by the square root of the sample size:

$$\frac{s}{\sqrt{n}} \approx \sigma_{\bar{x}}$$

where s is the sample standard deviation, n is the sample size, and $\sigma_{\bar{x}}$ is the standard error of the mean. We can then calculate the z-score for any sample mean, provided we know the population mean by using the following formula:

$$z_i = \frac{\bar{x}_i - \mu}{s/\sqrt{n}}$$

This formula is not usually much use as it stands, however, because we rarely know the population mean either. However, we can use it to test hypotheses we may have about the population mean (the procedure for hypothesis testing is introduced in Chapter 5). For now, though, we will concern ourselves with the other useful application of the formula which arises when we rearrange it in a way that allows us to calculate a likely range of values for the population mean:

$$\mu = \bar{x}_i \pm z^* \frac{s}{\sqrt{n}}$$

That is, we can think of the sample mean $\bar{x}$ as an estimate of the population mean μ with a margin of error equal to $z^*(s/\sqrt{n})$, where z^* is the value of z associated with the level of confidence we want our estimate to achieve. For example, we might want to say that that we are 95% confident that the population mean income of single parent households lies between a and b. Because we know that the sampling distribution of mean incomes is normal, and that the mean of all sample means – the central line of symmetry of our sampling distribution – equals population mean income, we can use the standard normal curve to estimate the values of a and b. We learned in the previous chapter how to calculate the z

values associated with any central area of the z curve, so we know already how to calculate z_a and z_b, the z values associated with the central 95% of the z-distribution.

Exercise 4.2(a) Large Sample Confidence Interval for One Mean

Find z_i such that Prob($-z_i < z < z_i$) = 95%.

Here we have to find the values of z_i which bound the middle 95% of the distribution. If you draw the z-curve diagram for this area, you will see that it is equal to the probability that z is less than z_i minus the probability that z is less than $-z_i$ (the lower-tail area):

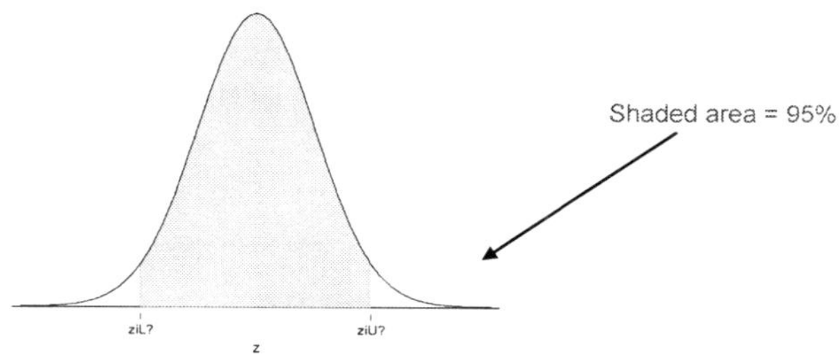

We know the value of the tail areas since they are symmetrical:

Area of lower-tail = area of upper-tail = $\frac{1-0.95}{2} = \frac{0.05}{2} = 0.025$

So we know that Prob($z < -z_i$) = Prob($z > z_i$) = 0.025. The table only lists probabilities for $z < z_i$. So we must take 0.025 away from 1 to give the entire area to the left of z_i that we need to look up, i.e. Prob($z < z_i$) = 1 – 0.025 = 0.975. If we look up 0.975 in the body of the table, we find that z_i = **1.96**. In other words, Prob($-1.96 < z < 1.96$) = 95%. The following matrix syntax allows you to simply enter the central probability in order to calculate values for z_i:

zi_gl_zp p = (0.95).

```
Value of zi such that Prob(-zi < z < zi)  = PROB, when PROB is given
         ZIL          ZIU         PROB
    -1.95996     1.95996       .95000
```

So in this case, $z_a = -1.96$ and $z_b = 1.96$, and we know that 95% of z-values lie between these two values. All we need to do to estimate a and b is convert these z-scores into their equivalent values on our sampling distribution of mean incomes. To do this we apply the above formula:

$$\mu = \bar{x}_i \pm z^* \frac{s}{\sqrt{n}}$$

$$= \bar{x}_i \pm 1.96 \frac{s}{\sqrt{n}}$$

Since we know the sample standard deviation s, the sample mean x-bar, and the sample size n, we have allow we need to compute the intervals for the population mean, μ.

4.2.1 Three Steps of Confidence Interval Estimation for Large Samples

Calculating confidence intervals is less confusing if you follow the following three steps:

Step 1: **Choose the appropriate formula and decide on the level of confidence.**

Where you want to estimate the interval for a *population* and where you have a *large sample*, the formula is as described above:

$$\mu = \bar{x}_i \pm z^* \frac{s}{\sqrt{n}}$$

But if you are calculating the confidence interval for a *proportion*, or you are using a *small sample*, then a different formula is needed, as we shall discover. Therefore, the first step of confidence interval estimation is to identify the correct formula to use. You also need to choose the desired level of confidence. In textbook exercises this is usually specified for you, but in your own research you will have to decide for yourself. A confidence level of 95% is traditional in social science.

Step 2: **Find the value for z^* such that: Prob($-z^* < z < z^*$) = Confidence Level**

Step 3: **Calculate the confidence interval by substituting your values for the sample mean, z^* and your approximation for the standard error of the mean ($s/\sqrt{n}$).**

Exercise 4.2(b) The Three Steps of Confidence Intervals

Suppose you are interested in the disappearance of thousands of civil servants and other workers during Joseph Stalin's *Great Purge* in Soviet Russia 1936-38. One of the questions you are interested in is the average age of the workers when they disappeared. Your thesis is that Stalin felt most threatened by older, more established 'enemies', and so you anticipate their average age to be over 50. Unfortunately, you only have access to 506 records on the age of individuals when they disappeared.

You have calculated the average age in this sample to be 56.2 years, which would appear to confirm your thesis. The standard deviation of your sample was found to be 14.7 years. Assuming that your 506 records constitute a random sample from the population of those who disappeared (a questionable assumption?), calculate the 95% confidence interval for the population mean age. Does your expected value for the population average age fall below the interval? Compute also the 99% confidence interval and reconsider whether your theorised average age still falls below the range of possible values for the population mean.

Answer:

Attempt the question yourself before referring to the answer below.

Before progressing with any calculations, it is usually worth summarising the information you have and the specific problems you are faced with in a way that relates it to the formula you are going to use. So, for the example in question, we can say that:

n = 506
$\overline{x}$ = 56.2
s = 14.7

We need to find: (i) 95% confidence interval; (ii) 99% confidence interval and comment. We can now run through the 3 steps of calculating the confidence interval:

(i) 95% confidence interval:

Step 1: **Choose the appropriate formula and decide on the level of confidence.**

We want to estimate the interval for a *population mean* given that we have a *large sample*, so the formula is:

$$\mu = \overline{x}_i \pm z^* \frac{s}{\sqrt{n}}$$

Confidence level has been specified as 95%.

Step 2: **Find the value for z^* such that Prob($-z^* < z < z^*$) = 95%.**

We find this by first identifying the middle 95% of the z-distribution:

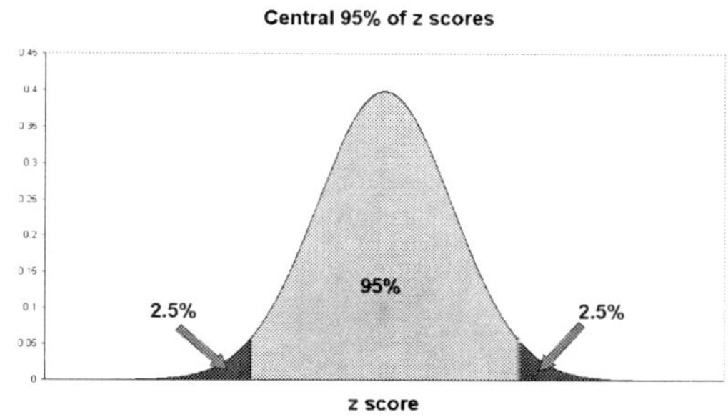

We can see that this leaves two tails of 2.5%. We can find $-z^*$ by finding the value of z_i below which the lowest 2.5% of z values lie. This can be found by looking up 0.025 in the body of the z table (Table A) which tells us that the value for $-z^*$ is 1.96, which is plotted below:

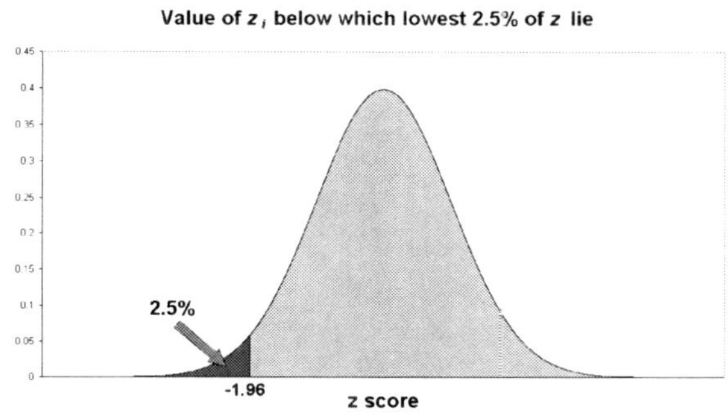

To find the value of $+z^*$ we simply take advantage of the fact that the normal distribution is symmetrical. If 2.5% of z lies below –1.96, then we know that 2.5% lies above 1.96 as illustrated in the following diagram.

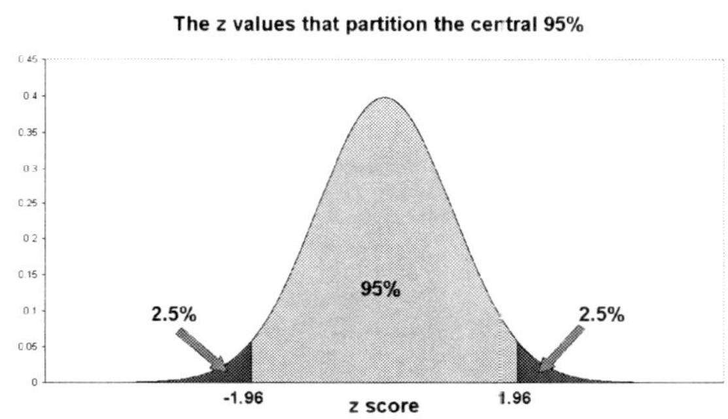

So, Prob($-z^* < z < z^*$) = Prob($-1.96 < z < 1.96$) = 95%. Alternatively we could use the following SPSS macro syntax introduced in the previous chapter for finding the central 95%: **zi_gl_zp p = (0.95).**

```
Value of zi such that Prob(-zi < z < zi)  = PROB, when PROB is given
       ZIL         ZIU        PROB
  -1.95996     1.95996      .95000
```

Step 3: **Calculate the confidence interval.**

By substituting the known values for the sample mean, z^* and our approximation for the standard error of the mean ($s/\sqrt{n}$) into the formula for the population mean we can obtain the desired confidence interval:

$$\mu = \bar{x}_i \pm z^* \frac{s}{\sqrt{n}}$$
$$= 56.2 \pm 1.96 \times \frac{14.7}{\sqrt{506}}$$
$$= 56.2 \pm 1.281$$

The error associated with using the sample mean as an estimate of the population mean is therefore 1.281 years. Put another way, we are 95% certain that the population age of missing workers was between 54.92 years and 57.481 years. Note that this range of likely values of the population mean age is clearly above our guesstimate of the population mean of 50 years, so our theory appears to be verified by the data.

SPPS Macros: An alternative method is to use the following syntax which will do steps 2 and 3 for you. It is strongly recommended that you learn to do the 3 steps yourself and use the macro only as a way of checking your results:

CI_L1M **CI_L1M** calculates the large–sample CI for one mean. After typing this command you need to specify the sample size, n, the sample mean, x_bar, the sample standard deviation, s, and the desired confidence level, c:

CI_L1M n = (?) x_bar = (?) s = (?) c = (?).

Exercise 4.2.1: Continued...

So, for the problem at hand we would type: **CI_L1M n = (506) x_bar = (56.2) s = (14.7) c = (0.95).** which would result in the following output:

```
Large sample confidence interval for the population mean
         N      X_BAR        ZIL          SE         ERR      LOWER       UPPER
 506.00000   56.20000   -1.95996      .65349     1.28083   54.91917    57.48083
```

The figures under the LOWER and UPPER column headings are the results we are most interested in since they define the confidence interval for the population mean and verify our earlier calculation.

(ii) 99% confidence interval

If we re-run the syntax, changing only the confidence level:

CI_L1M n = (506) x_bar = (56.2) s = (14.7) c = (0.99).

we can see from the output below that the confidence interval has widened slightly. We can be 99% certain that the population age of missing workers was between 54.517 years and 57.883 years. Note that this interval for the population mean is clearly above our guesstimate of the population mean of 50 years.

```
Large sample confidence interval for the population mean
         N      X_BAR        ZIL          SE         ERR      LOWER       UPPER
 506.00000   56.20000   -2.57583      .65349     1.68329   54.51671    57.88329
```

The interval would also widen if we had a larger standard deviation in our sample and/or if the sample size was smaller. For example, if we had only a sample of 50 records with a standard deviation of 25, we would get a confidence interval for the population mean for which the lower bound would be below that of our guesstimate of the population mean age of 50 years: **CI_L1M n = (50) x_bar = (56.2) s = (25) c = (0.99).**

```
Large sample confidence interval for the population mean
         N      X_BAR        ZIL          SE         ERR      LOWER       UPPER
  50.00000   56.20000   -2.57583     3.53553     9.10693   47.09307    65.30693
```

Exercise 4.2.(c) Calculating the Confidence Interval for the mean when you have a large sample:

In the following questions, work out the solution by hand and then run the syntax to check your results:

1. As an economic historian, you are interested in the average age of the heads of household who had their homes repossessed in Scotland during the Great Depression. Records are kept at local sheriff court archives, and from an examination of a sample of 200 records from across Scotland, you find that the average age of head of household was 34.5 years with standard deviation of 20 years. What is the 90% confidence interval for the mean age?

n	=	200
$\overline{x}$	=	34.5
s	=	20
Confidence level	=	90%

Step 1: Formula is:

$$\mu = \bar{x}_i \pm z^* \frac{s}{\sqrt{n}}$$

with confidence level of 90%.

Step 2: Find the value for z^* such that Prob($-z^* < z < z^*$) = 90%

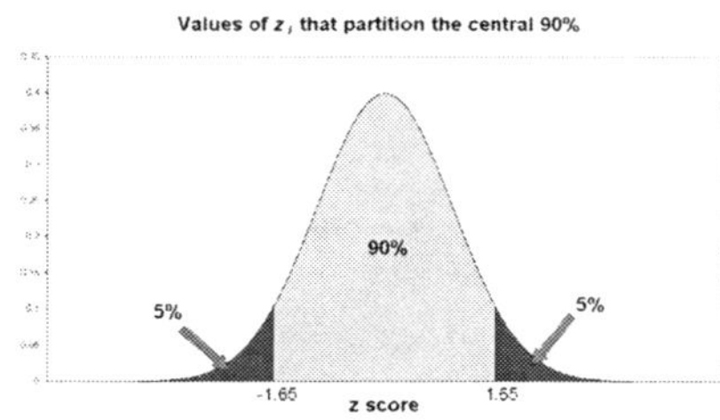

Step 3: substitute the known values for s, n and x-bar into the formula:

$$\begin{aligned}\mu &= \bar{x}_i \pm z^* \frac{s}{\sqrt{n}} \\ &= 56.2 \pm 1.65 \times \frac{20}{\sqrt{200}} \\ &= 34.5 \pm 2.33\end{aligned}$$

We can therefore say that we are 90% confident that the average age of repossessed heads-of-household was no less than 32.2 years and no greater than 36.8 years. The information presented in the question can be entered into the syntax as follows:

CI_L1M n = (200) x_bar = (34.5) s = (20) c = (0.90).

which verifies our manual calculation:

Large sample confidence interval for the population mean

N	X_BAR	ZIL	SE	ERR	LOWER	UPPER
200.00000	34.50000	-1.64485	1.41421	2.32617	32.17383	36.82617

2. For your dissertation, you interview 78 nurses and ask them their weight. The average weight within your sample turns out to be 70kg with a standard deviation of 20kg. What is the 95% confidence interval for the mean weight of all nurses?

n	=	78
$\bar{x}$	=	70
s	=	20
Confidence level	=	95%

Step 1: Formula is:

$$\mu = \bar{x}_i \pm z^* \frac{s}{\sqrt{n}}$$

with confidence level of 95%.

Step 2: Find the value for z^* such that Prob($-z^* < z < z^*$) = 95%

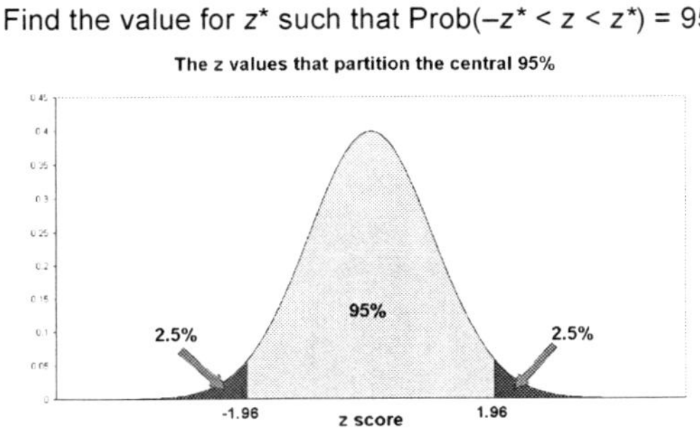

So, Prob($-z^* < z < z^*$) = Prob($-1.96 < z < 1.96$) = 95%.

Step 3: Calculate the confidence interval by substituting your values for the sample mean, z* and your approximation for the standard error of the mean (s/√n).

$$\mu = \bar{x}_i \pm z^* \frac{s}{\sqrt{n}}$$
$$= 70 \pm 1.96 \times \frac{20}{\sqrt{78}}$$
$$= 70 \pm 4.44$$

So we are 95% certain that the population mean weight for nurses lies between 65.56kg and 74.44kg. We can verify our results using the following syntax command in SPSS:

CI_L1M n = (78) x_bar = (70) s = (20) c = (0.95).

which results in the following output:

```
Large sample confidence interval for the population mean
         N       X_BAR        ZIL          SE         ERR       LOWER       UPPER
  78.00000    70.00000   -1.95996     2.26455     4.43844    65.56156    74.43844
```

3. For your dissertation, you interview 90 teenage girls, randomly selected from across Glasgow about how they would rate the Government's sexual health advice service. You find that, on an ascending scale of zero to 100, the average rating given is 45.3 with a standard deviation of 35.2. What is the 99% confidence interval for the mean rating of official sexual health advice by all Glaswegian teenage girls?

n	=	90
$\bar{x}$	=	45.3
s	=	35.2
Confidence level	=	99%

Step 1: Formula is:

$$\mu = \bar{x}_i \pm z^* \frac{s}{\sqrt{n}}$$

with confidence level of 99%.

Step 2: Find the value for z* such that Prob(–z* < z < z*) = 99%

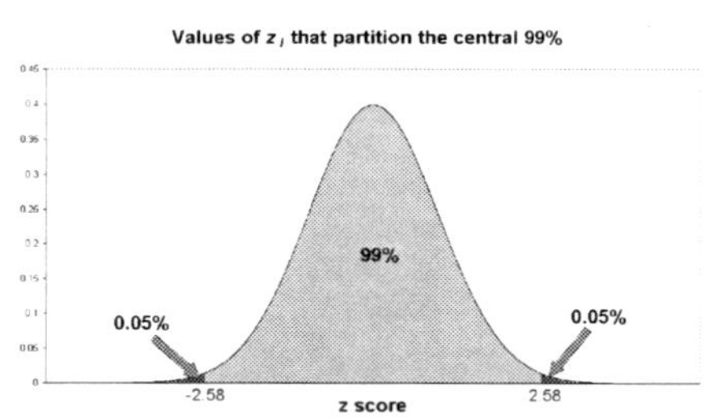

So, Prob(–z* < z < z*) = Prob(–2.58 < z < 2.58) = 99%.

Step 3: Calculate the confidence interval by substituting your values for the sample mean, z* and your approximation for the standard error of the mean (*s*/√*n*).

$$\mu = \bar{x}_i \pm z^* \frac{s}{\sqrt{n}}$$
$$= 45.3 \pm 2.58 \times \frac{35.2}{\sqrt{90}}$$
$$= 45.3 \pm 9.57$$

So we are 99% certain that the population mean rating of official sexual health advise for teenage girls in Glasgow lies between 35.7 and 54.9. We can confirm our results using the following SPSS macro command:

CI_L1M n = (90) x_bar = (45.3) s = (35.2) c = (0.99).

which results in the following output:

```
Large sample confidence interval for the population mean
        N       X_BAR        ZIL         SE         ERR      LOWER      UPPER
  90.00000   45.30000   -2.57583    3.71041    9.55737   35.74263   54.85737
```

4. As an Occupational Therapist, you are interested in how long it takes amputees to recover from their operation and reach a reasonable level of proficiency with their prosthetic replacement. You decide to take a sample of 150 amputees and find an average recovery time of 97.5 days, with a standard deviation of 60. What is the 90% confidence interval for the population mean recovery time?

n	=	150
$\bar{x}$	=	97.5
s	=	*60*
Confidence level	=	*90%*

<u>*Step 1:*</u> Formula is:

$$\mu = \bar{x}_i \pm z^* \frac{s}{\sqrt{n}}$$

with confidence level of 90%.

<u>*Step 2:*</u> Find the value for z* such that Prob(–z* < z < z*) = 90%

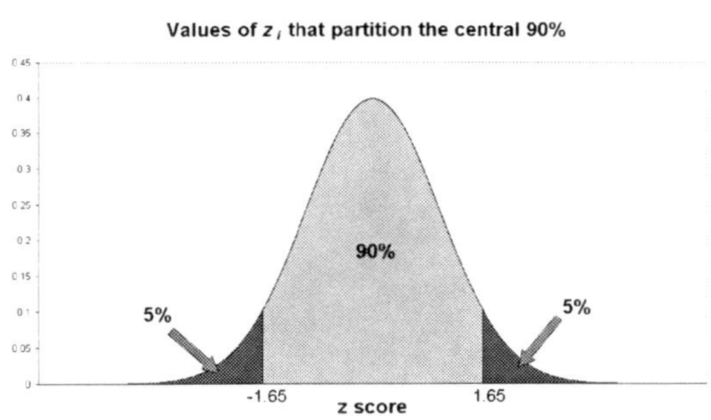

<u>*Step 3:*</u> Compute interval:

$$\mu = \bar{x}_i \pm z^* \frac{s}{\sqrt{n}}$$
$$= 97.5 \pm 1.65 \times \frac{60}{\sqrt{150}}$$
$$= 97.5 \pm 8.08$$

Thus, we are 90% certain that the population mean recovery time lies between 89.4 days and 105.6 days. We can verify our results by using the following macro command:

CI_L1M n = (150) x_bar = (97.5) s = (60) c = (0.90).

which results in the following output. The macro results are very slightly different due to their greater accuracy.

```
Large sample confidence interval for the population mean
        N       X_BAR         ZIL          SE         ERR       LOWER       UPPER
150.00000    97.50000    -1.64485     4.89898     8.05810    89.44190   105.55810
```

5. For your dissertation you attempt to estimate the exposure to toxic substances of workers in the chemical industry in the post war period. You have examined a random sample of 354 records from the archives of random medical tests from a range of firms from that period. This sample has been provided by the industry with a press release stating that the average exposure score is 194.35. The government had previously stated that retrospective collective compensation claims from workers could only proceed if there was evidence that the average exposure of all workers in the industry exceeded the threshold of 200 set down in European health and safety legislation. You examine the dataset and calculate the standard deviation of the sample scores to be 142.98. Do you think the compensation claim has grounds to proceed?

n	=	354
$\overline{x}$	=	194.35
s	=	142.98
Confidence level	=	?

<u>*Step 1:*</u> Formula is:

$$\mu = \overline{x}_i \pm z^* \frac{s}{\sqrt{n}}$$

We shall initially select a confidence level of 99%.

<u>*Step 2:*</u> Find the value for z* such that Prob(–z* < z < z*) = 99%

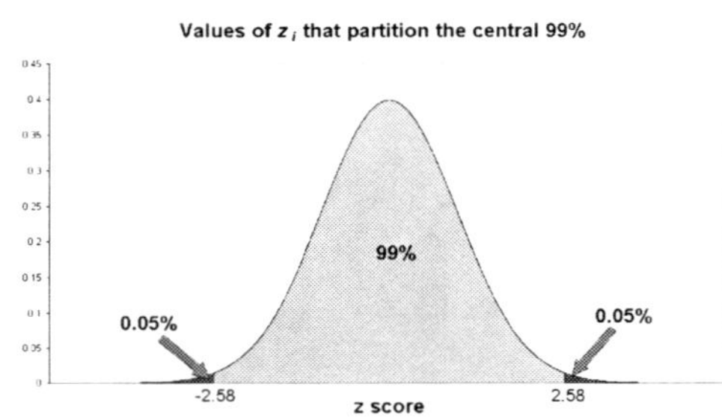

So, Prob(–z* < z < z*) = Prob(–2.58 < z < 2.58) = 99%.

<u>*Step 4:*</u> Calculate the confidence interval by substituting your values for the sample mean, z*, and your approximation for the standard error of the mean ($s/\sqrt{n}$).

$$\begin{aligned}\mu &= \overline{x}_i \pm z^* \frac{s}{\sqrt{n}} \\ &= 194.35 \pm 2.58 \times \frac{142.98}{\sqrt{354}} \\ &= 194.35 \pm 19.61\end{aligned}$$

So we are 99% certain that the population mean toxic exposure score of workers in the post war chemical industry lies between 175.25 and 213.45. Thus, the population mean could well lie above the European threshold of 200 and so the workers have an argument for proceeding with the compensation claim. We can verify our results using the following macro syntax:

CI_L1M n = (354) x_bar = (194.35) s = (142.98) c = (0.99).

which results in the following output. The intervals are slightly different due to the greater precision of the macro method.

```
Large sample confidence interval for the population mean
        N       X_BAR         ZIL          SE         ERR       LOWER       UPPER
354.00000   194.35000    -2.57583     7.59930    19.57450   174.77550   213.92450
```

You might want to consider how much you would have to reduce your confidence level for the health and safety threshold to lie above the interval for the population mean. Try reducing the confidence level in the syntax until this happens. You will notice from the following output for a confidence level of just 55%, that it is still possible for the population mean to lie within the interval:

CI_L1M n = (354) x_bar = (194.35) s = (142.98) c = (0.55).

```
Large sample confidence interval for the population mean
       N       X_BAR        ZIL          SE          ERR       LOWER        UPPER
 354.00000  194.35000    -.75542     7.59930     5.74063   188.60937   200.09063
```

You will notice, however, that a 54% confidence interval will lie just below the 200 threshold. In other words, we can only be 54% certain that the population mean toxic exposure score lies outside the 188.737 to 199.962 range:

CI_L1M n = (354) x_bar = (194.35) s = (142.98) c = (0.54).

```
Large sample confidence interval for the population mean
       N       X_BAR        ZIL          SE          ERR       LOWER        UPPER
 354.00000  194.35000    -.73885     7.59930     5.61472   188.73528   199.96472
```

4.3 Small Sample Confidence Intervals for the Population Mean

The z-score method of calculating confidence intervals can only be applied if your sample size is greater than 30. What do you do if it is smaller than this? As discussed in Chapter 2, Student found a way of adjusting the normal distribution so that confidence intervals could be calculated for small samples. His adjusted distribution is called the t-distribution. Note that his method only works if *the variable in question is normally distributed,* though the greater the sample size, the less of problem it is if the original variable is non-normal. This is because the t-distribution tends towards the normal distribution anyway as the sample size increases. Note also that, as the sample size increases, the Central Limit Theorem will start to apply. In short, the larger the sample, the smaller the distortionary effect on t-test results of non-normality in the original variable. The fact that the t-distribution becomes virtually identical to the standard normal curve as the sample size increases, leads many statisticians to make little use of the z-distribution in practice, applying the t distribution whether the sample size is small or large, knowing that in large samples it will give the same results.

To find the confidence interval estimate of the population mean using the t-distribution, first find a value t_i such that $\text{Prob}(-t_i < t < t_i) = K$, where K is the desired confidence interval. Degrees of freedom (needed to compute the t-value) are calculated as $n - 1$. Then calculate the confidence interval using the following formula:

$$\mu = \bar{x} \pm t_i \frac{s}{\sqrt{n}}$$

where

$\bar{x}$ = the sample mean
s = the sample standard deviation
n = the sample size.

As with z-values, you can calculate t-statistics using SPSS syntax. Simply use the **IDF.T(prob,df)** function in the Transform, Compute, Functions menu (but note that you have to have at least one cell of data in your data editor for this to work). This function computes the value of t associated with a given area of the left tail. For example, suppose you want to find the value of t associated with a 95% confidence interval for a sample of 80 observations. You have enough information to work out that the size of the left tail is 0.025 and the degrees of freedom are 79, so you would enter the following syntax:

```
COMPUTE tval = IDF.T(0.025,79) .
EXECUTE .
```

Note that the degrees of freedom for this syntax is calculated as n–1. If you go to the Data View window you will see that SPSS has returned the figure **–1.99** for the variable **tval**, which is the appropriate t value from the Student's t-distribution, with **df** degrees of freedom, for which the cumulative probability (i.e. the area to the left of the t-value) is **prob** (in this case prob was set at 2.5%).

You can alternatively use the following syntax :

CI_S1M CI_S1M calculates the small-sample CI for one mean. Applying this syntax to Stalin's *Great Purge* example above, we would first summarise the information we have been given:

n = 506
$\overline{x}$ = 56.2
s = 14.7
Confidence level = .95

We would then enter these details into the macro syntax as follows,

CI_S1M n = (506) x_bar = (56.2) s = (14.7) c = (0.95).

which would result in the following output:

```
Small sample confidence interval for the population mean
        N      X_BAR         TIL          SE        ERR      LOWER      UPPER
506.00000   56.20000    -1.96467      .65349    1.28390   54.91610   57.48390
```

If we compare this with the 95% confidence interval run using the z-score we find that they are almost identical (see below). This is because, as we noted earlier, the t-distribution tends towards the normal distribution as the sample size increases, and in this example, the sample was relatively large (506).

```
Large sample confidence interval for the population mean
        N      X_BAR         ZIL          SE        ERR      LOWER      UPPER
506.00000   56.20000    -1.95996      .65349    1.28083   54.91917   57.48083
```

The implication of this is that you can use the t-distribution to do all your confidence interval calculations, whether small or large samples.

Exercise 4.3 Computing small sample confidence intervals

1. As a war historian, you are interested in the average survival time of soldiers on the front line in the First World War. There are over 1,000 records available for examination at the Ministry of Defence, but because of the considerable time and cost of accessing these records, you decide to examine a random sample of just 16 records. Your sample reveals an average of 18.7 weeks, with a standard deviation of 2.8 weeks. Find the 90% confidence interval estimate of the mean survival time of all soldiers on the front line.

Answer:

You should answer the question in full using the formula as demonstrated above and using the macro syntax (presented below) to check your answer.

n = 16
$\overline{x}$ = 18.7
s = 2.8
Confidence level = 90%

CI_S1M n = (16) x_bar = (18.7) s = (2.8) c = (0.90).

```
Small sample confidence interval for the population mean
       N      X_BAR         TIL          SE        ERR      LOWER      UPPER
16.00000   18.70000    -1.75305      .70000    1.22714   17.47286   19.92714
```

We are therefore 90% confident that the average survival time of all soldiers on the front line in the First World War lay between 17.5 weeks and 19.9 weeks.

2. For your PhD, you want to estimate the number of times an American phrase or pronunciation occurs in a typical 5 minute conversation between teenage youths in Liverpool. Because of the time taken to build up sufficient rapport with such youths for them to speak in a relaxed and typical way, you only manage to observe 23 such conversations. The average number of Americanisms in 5 minute conversations amongst your small sample is 137.71, with a standard deviation of 69.56. What is the 95% confidence interval of the average incidence of Americanisms for all youths in Liverpool?

Answer:

You should answer the question in full using the formula as demonstrated above and using the macro syntax (presented below) to check your answer.

n = 23
$\bar{x}$ = 137.71
s = 69.56
Confidence level = 95%

CI_S1M n = (23) x_bar = (137.71) s = (69.56) c = (0.95).

```
Small sample confidence interval for the population mean
          N      X_BAR      TSTAR         SE        ERR      LOWER      UPPER
   23.00000  137.71000   -2.07387   14.50426   30.08000  107.63000  167.79000
```

We can be 95% confident that an American phrase or pronunciation enters a typical 5 minute conversation among youths in Liverpool between 108 and 168 times on average.

3. As a political scientist you have been researching the political perspectives of students from working class backgrounds. You have surveyed 36 students, asking them to rate on an ascending scale of 0 to 100 their preference for the public ownership of the means of production. The average rating in your sample is 59.75 with a standard deviation of 42.93. What can you say from your small sample about the political perspectives of working class students as whole?

Answer:

You should answer the question in full using the formula as demonstrated above and using the macro syntax (presented below) to check your answer.

n = 36
$\bar{x}$ = 59.75
s = 42.93
Confidence level = 95% (assumed)

CI_S1M n = (36) x_bar = (59.75) s = (42.93) c = (0.95).

```
Small sample confidence interval for the population mean
          N      X_BAR        TIL         SE        ERR      LOWER      UPPER
   36.00000   59.75000   -2.03011    7.15500   14.52542   45.22458   74.27542
```

We are therefore 95% certain that the preference for public ownership score among students from working class backgrounds lies between 45.2 and 74.3. Because of the small sample size and relatively large standard deviation, this is a very wide confidence interval for the population mean score.

Note though that the standard deviation given in the exercise is implausible since it suggests that some scores were more than a hundred (e.g. just one standard deviation more than the mean gives you a score of over a hundred). Either the data was wrongly coded or the standard deviation incorrectly calculated. You should always think about the plausibility of your results before basing any further analysis on them!

There is a further problem with this type of data: the public ownership preference score is bounded at zero and 100. However, the formula we have used to calculate the confidence interval does not know that the range of feasible values has these bounds. It is quite plausible, then, for either the lower or the upper bound of the confidence interval to lie outside of the range of feasible values for the variable itself.

4.4 Small Independent Samples CI for the Difference Between 2 Means

Sometimes we want to compare the means of two independent populations. For example, suppose we have a sample mean height from a population of girls of a particular age, $\bar{x}_1$, and a sample mean height from a population of boys, $\bar{x}_2$. It just so happens that $\bar{x}_1$ is greater than $\bar{x}_2$, but is this difference a freak result arising from sampling variation, or does it reflect true differences in height between the population of boys and the population of girls? One way of tackling this sort of problem is to estimate the confidence interval for the difference in the two means. This will tell us the range of likely values for that difference the in the whole population. If the confidence intervals overlap then there is no real evidence that the two populations have different means. However, if the confidence intervals do *not* overlap, then it is likely that the population means are indeed different.

The following calculations assume that the two populations (and hence the two samples) are independent (i.e. someone in the first population can occur in the second). This is distinct from situations where the researcher observes the same person before and after a treatment (for such experiments we use the *Paired Samples Confidence Interval* described briefly below).

There are two formulae for calculating the confidence interval for comparing two population means: one assumes equal (or *homogeneous*) variances across the two populations, and the other assumes unequal (or *heterogeneous*) variances across the two populations. We shall consider each in turn:

4.4.1 Pooled variance

When the two populations we are considering have similar variance, σ^2, we derive $\sigma^2_{\bar{x}_1-\bar{x}_2}$, the *variance of the difference in sample means*, as follows:

$$\sigma^2_{\bar{x}_1-\bar{x}_2} = \text{variance of}(\bar{x}_1 - \bar{x}_2) = \sigma^2\left(\frac{1}{n_1}+\frac{1}{n_2}\right),$$

We can now calculate the confidence interval for the difference in population means as follows:

$$\mu_1 - \mu_2 = (\bar{x}_1 - \bar{x}_2) \pm z^* S.E.$$

where S.E. is the standard error of the difference in means we are looking at in repeated samples from the two populations (standard error = standard deviation of a sampling distribution). If we know the common variance of the two populations, σ^2 (unlikely given that we usually only have information on samples), then we can write the confidence interval formula for the difference in population means as follows:

$$\mu_1 - \mu_2 = (\bar{x}_1 - \bar{x}_2) \pm z^* \sigma\sqrt{\left(\frac{1}{n_1}+\frac{1}{n_2}\right)}.$$

If we only have sample information (nearly always the case), we can estimate the value of common standard deviation σ using the pooled estimator s_p:

$$s_p = \sqrt{\frac{(n_1-1)s_1^2 + (n_2-1)s_2^2}{n_1+n_2-2}}$$

However, if we replace σ with s_p we should really use the t distribution (though in large samples the difference between z and t based calculations will be negligible), giving us the following formula for computing the confidence interval for differences in population means:

$$\mu_1 - \mu_2 = (\bar{x}_1 - \bar{x}_2) \pm t^* s_p \sqrt{\left(\frac{1}{n_1} + \frac{1}{n_2}\right)}$$

where the degrees of freedom are given by,

$df = n_1 + n_2 - 2$

and the t value, t^*, is calculated for the required level of confidence.

Example 4.4.1 Pooled Variance confidence interval for the difference between two means.

For example, suppose the mean height of girls, in our sample of ten, equals 100 cm (s.d. = 30cm), and the mean height of 12 boys is 94cm (sd = 31cm), then the 95% confidence interval for the difference in population means would be computed as follows:

First, choose the appropriate formula:

$$\mu_1 - \mu_2 = (\bar{x}_1 - \bar{x}_2) \pm t^* s_p \sqrt{\left(\frac{1}{n_1} + \frac{1}{n_2}\right)}$$

Second, compute t^*, which the is value of t associated with the central 95% of the t-distribution when $df = n_1 + n_2 - 2$:

$df = 10 + 12 - 2 \quad = \quad 20$

We can see from the tables that the t value associated with an upper-tail of 0.025 with 20 degrees of freedom is 2.086.

Third, compute s_p:

$$s_p = \sqrt{\frac{(n_1 - 1)s_1^2 + (n_2 - 1)s_2^2}{n_1 + n_2 - 2}}$$

$$s_p = \sqrt{\frac{(10 - 1)900 + (12 - 1)961}{10 + 12 - 2}} = \sqrt{18671 / 20} = 30.55$$

and substitute this along with t^* into the CI formula:

$$\mu_1 - \mu_2 = (100 - 94) \pm 2.086 \times 30.55\sqrt{\left(\frac{1}{10} + \frac{1}{12}\right)}$$

$= 6 \pm 63.73(.428)$

$= 6 \pm 27.27$

The confidence interval is so wide because the sample sizes are so small.

You can check this result using the following macro command for SPSS:

CI_S2Mp **CI_S2Mp** calculates the small Independent Samples CI for differences between 2 means (pooled variance). The arguments for this command are entered as follows:

CI_S2Mp n1=(10) n2=(12) x_bar1=(100) x_bar2=(94) s1=(30) s2=(31) c=(.95).

which results in the following output:

```
CI for the difference between 2 population means
   SAMPDIFF          SP         TIL          SE         ERR        LOWER        UPPER
    6.00000    30.55405    -2.08596    13.08246    27.28954    -21.28954    33.28954
```

4.4.2 Different Variance

When the variances of our two populations are likely to be different, we use the following formula to compute the confidence interval for the difference between two means:

$$\mu_1 - \mu_2 = (\bar{x}_1 - \bar{x}_2) \pm t^* \sqrt{\left(\frac{s_1^2}{n_1} + \frac{s_2^2}{n_2}\right)}$$

where the degrees of freedom needed to calculate t* are given by the smaller of n_1-1 and n_2-1:

$df = \min[n_1-1, n_2-1]$

CI_S2Md — **CI_S2Md** calculates small Independent Samples CI for differences between 2 means (different variances), where the arguments are entered in the same way as CI_S2Mp.

Example 4.4.2 Heterogeneous Variance confidence interval for the difference between two means.

If we run this method on the child height example above, we find that the interval widens slightly for the same level of confidence:

CI_S2Md n1=(10) n2=(12) x_bar1=(100) x_bar2=(94) s1=(30) s2=(31) c=(.95).

```
CI for the difference between 2 population means (different variance)
   SAMPDIFF         TIL          SE         ERR       LOWER        UPPER
    6.00000    -2.26216    13.04160    29.50215   -23.50215     35.50215
```

4.4.3 The Test for Equality of Variances

How do you decide whether variances are equal or not? Sometimes the answer is obvious, but other times we would like to know whether the apparent different in variances in our samples are not entirely due to sampling variation. Appropriate tests for the equality of variance are considered in Chapter 6 under the discussion of small independent samples significance test for equality of two means.

4.4.4 Small Sample Matched Pairs

When our two samples are paired, that is, we have two sets of observations on the same subjects as in a "before and after" trial, we can compute the mean difference between the two sets of results and then apply the one sample confidence interval procedure.

4.5 Large Sample Confidence Intervals for Proportions

The following syntax calculates the confidence interval for a large sample proportion using both the traditional method and the Wilson method, the latter being the most reliable. For example, if 8,527 of your sample of 11,096 Scottish households regularly drink Iron Bru, the following syntax will provide the confidence interval for the population proportion of Iron Bru drinkers:

CI_L1P Traditional & Wilson Large sample CI for a Single Proportion where the arguments are entered as follows: CI_L1P n=(?) x=(?) c=(?). Entering the details of our Iron Bru problem into the syntax,

CI_L1P n=(11096) x=(8527) c=(.95).

would result in the following output:

```
Traditional Large sample CI for one proportion
      ptrad       zstar    se_trad       etrad    low_trad      up_trad
    .768475   -1.959964    .004004     .007848     .760627      .776323

Wilson Large sample CI for one proportion
      pwlsn       zstar    se_wlsn       ewlsn    low_wlsn      up_wlsn
    .768378   -1.959964    .004004     .007848     .760530      .776226
```

As it happens, there is very little difference between the Traditional and Wilson methods in this particular example. It is always best to use the latter method which corrects for estimation problems when the proportion we are dealing with is close to zero or one. In this case, we use the Wilson method to estimate with 95% confidence that between 76.1% and 77.6% of households are frequent Iron Bru drinkers. If, however, we had only a sample of 100, and 98 them said they regularly drank the famous Scottish beverage, then we would find much greater differences between the Wilson and Traditional estimates. Verify this by re-running the syntax with n=100 and x=98 (notice how the upper bound on the Traditional estimate of the confidence interval lies outside of the feasible range of the proportion).

4.5.1 Using the Syntax When You Only Have p *and* n*:*

Sometimes you only have p, the sample proportion, and you don't have x. You can of course calculate x by multiplying n by p. So in the above example, if you were told only that $p = 0.055$ and that $n = 400$, you would calculate $x = 0.055 \times 400 = 22$, and enter the arguments accordingly into the **CI_L1P** command.

Exercises 4.6 Calculating Confidence Intervals for Proportions:

1. Consider the following email from a Consultant Paediatrician and the associated Powerpoint slide (based on a real-life statistical problem). The data refer to the number deaths of children with Leukaemia (numerator) over the total number in the sample (denominator). There are four samples: two in the "early" period (samples taken of children with Leukaemia in 1995-98) and two in the "late" period (samples taken of children with Leukaemia in 1998-2002). The first sample in each period is of children given 5 courses of chemotherapy. The second sample in each period is of children given 4 courses of chemotherapy.

   You would think that 5 courses of chemotherapy would result in fewer deaths than 4 courses, but the picture seems less straightforward and so rather puzzling. To solve Dr X's problem, answer the following questions:

   (i) Derive a confidence interval for the proportion of deaths of children who underwent **5** courses in the **Early** period.
   (ii) Derive a confidence interval for the proportion of deaths of children who underwent **4** courses in the **Early** period and compare with (i).
   (iii) Derive a confidence interval for the proportion of deaths of children who underwent **5** courses in the **Late** period.
   (iv) Derive a confidence interval for the proportion of deaths of children who underwent **4** courses in the **Late** period and compare with (iii).
   (v) Derive a confidence interval for the proportion of deaths of children who underwent **5** courses in the combined periods.
   (vi) Derive a confidence interval for the proportion of deaths of children who underwent **4** courses in the combined periods and compare with (v).

From: DrX@nhs.uk>
To: "'G.Pryce@socsci.gla.ac.uk'"
Subject: Data on Leukemia
Date: Tue, 26 Nov 2004 15:04:32 -0000
X-Mailer: Internet Mail Service (5.5.2653.19)

Hi Gwilym,
I trust you are having a good day. Sorry to bother you but I have a Statistical problem and was wondering if you could help. This slide shows the results of a clinical trial where the survival rate following four and five courses of chemotherapy was compared. The deaths mentioned refer to deaths in remission (i.e. toxic deaths). The interesting point of the slide is that in the first half of the trial 5 courses did better but in the second half 4 did better. To my non-statistical mind there are an awful lot of numbers on the slide -if one was to show it to people like myself, which things could be left out without compromising any accuracy? Maybe telling me what it all meant might help. Our statisticians are in Oxford and not available to help. Can you help?
Dr X

	Deaths/Patients	
Period of Study	**5 courses**	**4 courses**
Early	41/240	66/240
Late	153/375	106/379
Subtotal:	194/615	172/619

Answer:

(i) To derive a confidence interval for the proportion of deaths of children who underwent **5** courses in the **Early** period we would enter the following syntax, **CI_L1P n=(240) x=(41) c=(.95).** which would result in the following output:

```
Traditional Large sample CI for one proportion
      PTRAD       ZSTAR     SE_TRAD       ETRAD    LOW_TRAD     UP_TRAD
    .170833   -1.959964     .024294     .047616     .123218     .218449

Wilson Large sample CI for one proportion
      PWLSN       ZSTAR     SE_WLSN       EWLSN    LOW_WLSN     UP_WLSN
    .176230   -1.959964     .024392     .047807     .128422     .224037
```

(ii) To derive a confidence interval for the proportion of deaths of children who underwent **4** courses in the **Early** period and compare with (i) we would enter the following syntax, **CI_L1P n=(240) x=(66) c=(.95).** which would yield the following output,

```
Traditional Large sample CI for one proportion
      PTRAD       ZSTAR     SE_TRAD       ETRAD    LOW_TRAD     UP_TRAD
    .275000   -1.959964     .028822     .056491     .218509     .331491

Wilson Large sample CI for one proportion
      PWLSN       ZSTAR     SE_WLSN       EWLSN    LOW_WLSN     UP_WLSN
    .278689   -1.959964     .028703     .056257     .222432     .334945
```

Note that the 95% confidence intervals for the two sets of courses in the early period overlap (see graph below, constructed in Excel using the Stock High-Low chart option):

Five courses in the early period (sample proportion = 17.08%) 95% CI = (12.8%, 22.4%)
Four courses in the early period (sample proportion = 27.50%) 95% CI = (22.2%, 33.5%)

So, the difference between the two sample proportions may simply be due to sampling variability.

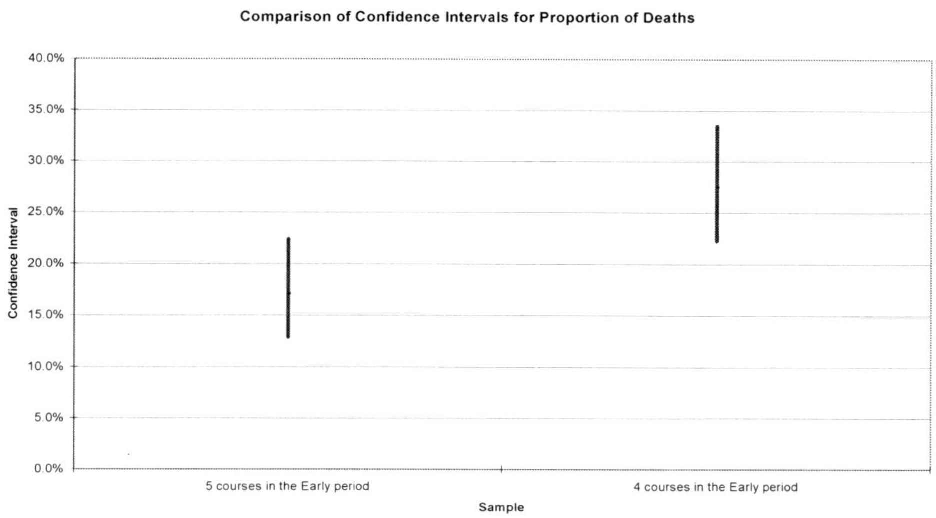

(iii) To derive a confidence interval for the proportion of deaths of children who underwent **5** courses in the **Late** period we would enter the following syntax: **CI_L1P n=(375) x=(153) c=(.95).** which would result in the following output:

Traditional Large sample CI for one proportion

PTRAD	ZSTAR	SE_TRAD	ETRAD	LOW_TRAD	UP_TRAD
.408000	-1.959964	.025379	.049742	.358258	.457742

Wilson Large sample CI for one proportion

PWLSN	ZSTAR	SE_WLSN	EWLSN	LOW_WLSN	UP_WLSN
.408971	-1.959964	.025254	.049497	.359474	.458468

(iv) To derive a confidence interval for the proportion of deaths of children who underwent 4 courses in the Late period and compare with (iii) we would enter the following syntax: **CI_L1P n=(379) x=(106) c=(.95).** resulting in the following output:

Traditional Large sample CI for one proportion

PTRAD	ZSTAR	SE_TRAD	ETRAD	LOW_TRAD	UP_TRAD
.279683	-1.959964	.023056	.045188	.234495	.324871

Wilson Large sample CI for one proportion

PWLSN	ZSTAR	SE_WLSN	EWLSN	LOW_WLSN	UP_WLSN
.281984	-1.959964	.022992	.045064	.236920	.327048

The 95% confidence intervals for the two sets of courses in the **late** period do not overlap which means that the difference cannot be ascribed to sampling variation alone:

Five courses in the late period (sample proportion = 40.80%) 95% CI = (35.9%, 45.9%)
Four courses in the late period (sample proportion = 27.97%) 95% CI = (23.7%, 32.7%)

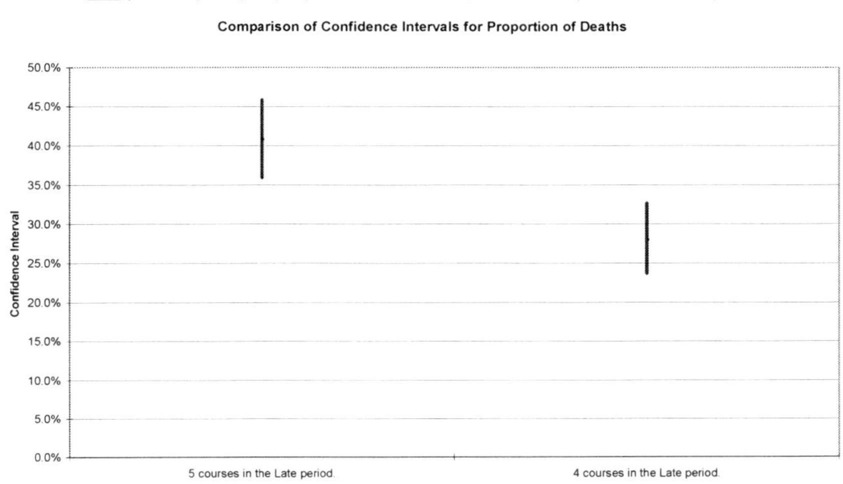

(v) To derive a confidence interval for the proportion of deaths of children who underwent 5 courses in the combined periods we would enter the following syntax: **CI_L1P n=(615) x=(194) c=(.95).** which would result in the following output:

```
Traditional Large sample CI for one proportion
      PTRAD       ZSTAR    SE_TRAD       ETRAD    LOW_TRAD     UP_TRAD
    .315447   -1.959964    .018738     .036726     .278721     .352173

Wilson Large sample CI for one proportion
      PWLSN       ZSTAR    SE_WLSN       EWLSN    LOW_WLSN     UP_WLSN
    .316640   -1.959964    .018697     .036645     .279995     .353284
```

(vi) To derive a confidence interval for the proportion of deaths of children who underwent 4 courses in the combined periods we would enter the following syntax, **CI_L1P n=(619) x=(172) c=(.95).** which would result in the following output:

```
Traditional Large sample CI for one proportion
      PTRAD       ZSTAR    SE_TRAD       ETRAD    LOW_TRAD     UP_TRAD
    .277868   -1.959964    .018005     .035288     .242579     .313156

Wilson Large sample CI for one proportion
      PWLSN       ZSTAR    SE_WLSN       EWLSN    LOW_WLSN     UP_WLSN
    .279294   -1.959964    .017975     .035230     .244064     .314524
```

Again, note that the 95% confidence intervals for the two sets of courses in the **combined** periods also overlap:

Five courses in the *combined* periods (sample proportion = 31.55%) 95% CI = (35.9%, 45.9%)
Four courses in the *combined* periods (sample proportion = 27.79%) 95% CI = (23.7%, 32.7%)

Dr X would need much larger samples to derive the narrower confidence intervals needed to identify the true differences in the proportions between different treatments.

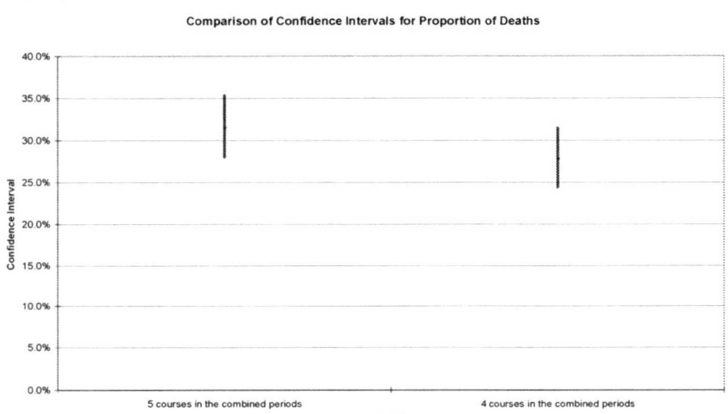

<u>Summary:</u>

The six confidence intervals we have estimated can be summarised as follows:

		Lower	Upper	Sample p
(i)	5 courses in the Early period	12.8%	22.4%	17.1%
(ii)	4 courses in the Early period	22.2%	33.5%	27.5%
(iii)	5 courses in the Late period	35.9%	45.8%	40.8%
(iv)	4 courses in the Late period	23.7%	32.7%	28.0%
(v)	5 courses in the combined periods	28.0%	35.3%	31.5%
(vi)	4 courses in the combined periods	24.4%	31.5%	27.8%

Dr X could present this information without recourse to numbers by using a high-low graph to compare all six confidence intervals. Where two intervals overlap, there is no significant difference between the proportions (that is, we cannot say with any degree of confidence that the difference isn't simply due to random sampling variability). What is odd, is that there appears to be a significant difference between the early and late 5 course proportions: the confidence intervals are far apart and so it is highly unlikely that the difference between the death rates is due to sampling variability only.

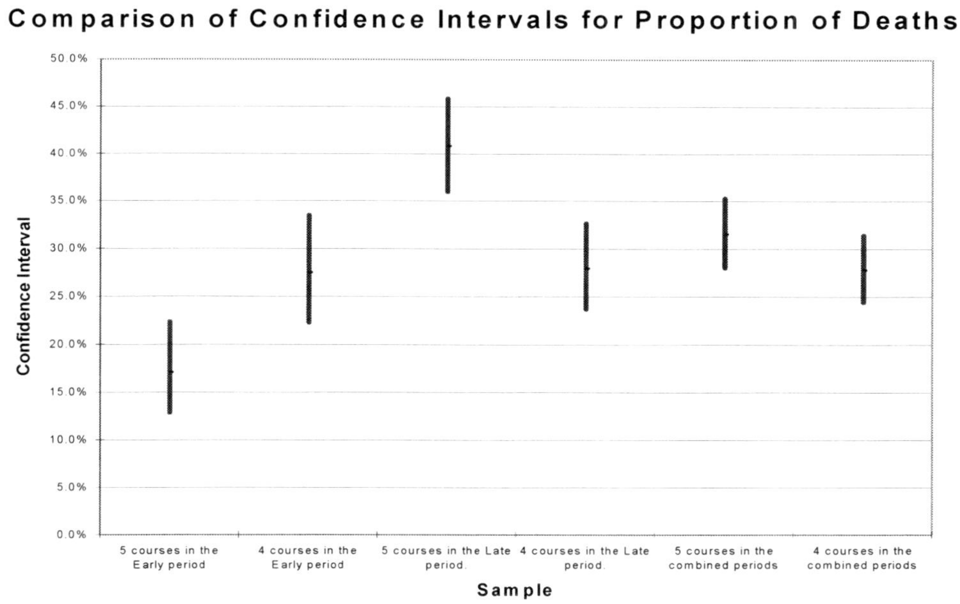

4.6 Calculating Confidence Intervals for Original Data

Whilst SPSS does not have set routines for calculating confidence intervals from summary information (i.e. when you are only given information on the mean, standard deviation and sample size, as in the above exercises), it does have facilities for calculating confidence intervals when you have the full data on a sample. We shall now consider how you would compute confidence intervals when you have access to the full data set. Note, however, that even when you have access to the original sample data, you can still use the macro commands you have been learning. Simply calculate the mean, standard deviation and sample using the Descriptives function we introduced in Chapter 1. For example, if you have data on a variable called **income**, either run the following syntax: DESCRIPTIVES VARIABLES=income /STATISTICS=MEAN. , or click on Analyze, Descriptive Statistics, Descriptives, select **income** from the variables list and paste it into the Variable(s) box by clicking the ▶ button, click on Options to choose which summary statistics you want to include, click Continue, and Paste. Once you have the sample standard deviation, mean and sample size, you can enter them into the macro syntax commands introduced earlier in this chapter.

In fact, there are advantages to sticking with the macro-command method even when you have the original data because the canned SPSS routines we are about to explore do not tell you whether you are using the most appropriate technique for the data you want to analyse. It is possible to find out the precise formulae being used by SPSS for each and every test, but this is not straightforward. You will need to go to the SPSS website and navigate your way through their reference documents, and even then you will not be certain what the data requirements are for the particular formula being employed unless you have a degree in statistics!

4.6.1 Using 'Explore'

The simplest way to compute confidence intervals for means of variables in your sample is to use the EXAMINE VARIABLES syntax, which can be typed directly (e.g. EXAMINE VARIABLES = income.) or obtained from the point-and-click menu options. To use the menu method, click on Analyze, Descriptive Statistics, and Explore. The first thing you need to do is select the variables you want to analyse. If you then click on the Statistics button, you will see it gives you the option (amongst other things) to select the desired confidence interval for the mean. Once you've done this, select Continue and then choose whether you want to display the plots as well as the statistics. You can then either click OK or Paste. The latter is recommended as you can edit the syntax more quickly and keep a record of what you have done.

As you will see from the output there is a whole bundle of statistics that you get from the Explore function, much of which is superfluous to our present requirements.

Exercise 4.6 Using SPSS to Calculate Confidence Intervals when you have the original data:

1. Open up the data on house prices and run the following EXAMINE syntax on purchase price (note the **/PLOT NONE /CINTERVAL 95** qualifiers which suppress the graph output and specify the confidence level respectively):

   EXAMINE VARIABLES = sellingprice /PLOT NONE /CINTERVAL 95 .

   Notice the confidence interval listed in the Descriptives output box copied below.

Descriptives

			Statistic	Std. Error
sellingprice	Mean		109229.5	1040.527
	95% Confidence Interval for Mean	Lower Bound	107189.4	
		Upper Bound	111269.5	
	5% Trimmed Mean		102971.4	
	Median		90000.00	
	Variance		4.0E+09	
	Std. Deviation		63557.35	
	Minimum		13000.00	
	Maximum		497250.0	
	Range		484250.0	
	Interquartile Range		67769.00	
	Skewness		1.830	.040
	Kurtosis		4.794	.080

   Now let's check how this interval compares to that obtained using our macro method. Make a note of the mean, sample size, and standard deviation which you have just obtained using the EXAMINE command. Then use this information to run the macro syntax for confidence intervals based on the t-distribution, copied below (note that although the sample size is large the t-distribution can be used since it tends towards the normal distribution as the sample size increases – in statistical parlance we would say that the t-distribution is *asymptotically normal*).

   CI_S1M n = (3731) x_bar = (109,229.5) s = (63557.35) c = (0.95).

   You should obtain the following confidence interval which is identical to that produced by the EXAMINE command:

```
Small sample confidence interval for the population mean
        n       x_bar          TiL         SE        err       Lower       Upper
 3731.00000 109229.500   -1.96060 1040.52653 2040.05650 107189.443 111269.557
```

   Unfortunately, the canned SPSS routine will not fair so well if you want to compute the confidence interval of a proportion, as we shall see in the next example.

2. You have a sample of 83 observations on income as listed in the **income.sav** data file (which you should have copied into your C:\STATISTICS folder from the Downloads page of www.geebeejey.co.uk). Compute (a) a 90% confidence interval for income; and (b) a 90% confidence interval for the proportion of households with incomes of £80,000 and over.

Answers to question 2.:

(a) First open the data set and then run the EXAMINE VARIABLES syntax on income:

   GET FILE='C:\STATISTICS\income.sav'.
   EXAMINE VARIABLES = income /PLOT NONE /CINTERVAL 90 .

   This results in the following output which tells us that we are 90% sure that the average income in the population lies between £32,699.38 and £39,075.06.

Descriptives

			Statistic	Std. Error
income	Mean		35887.22	1916.171
	90% Confidence Interval for Mean	Lower Bound	32699.38	
		Upper Bound	39075.06	
	5% Trimmed Mean		35011.68	
	Median		33333.33	
	Variance		3.0E+08	
	Std. Deviation		17457.15	
	Minimum		5000.00	
	Maximum		83333.33	
	Range		78333.33	
	Interquartile Range		23666.67	
	Skewness		.764	.264
	Kurtosis		.063	.523

We could alternatively obtain the confidence interval using the following macro syntax:

CI_S1M n = (83) x_bar = (35887.22) s = (17457.15) c = (0.90).

which would produce an identical confidence interval, as listed in the following output :

```
Small sample confidence interval for the population mean
          n      x_bar         TiL          SE        err       Lower      Upper
   83.00000 35887.2200   -1.66365 1916.17115 3187.83657 32699.3834 39075.0566
```

(b) We first need to create a *dummy variable* for incomes of £80,000 or more. This is simply a dummy variable equal to 1 if income is greater than or equal to £80,000, and equals zero otherwise. To achieve this we can run the following syntax to create a new variable called **incover80K**:

```
GET FILE='C:\STATISTICS\income.sav'.

RECODE income (Lowest thru 79999.9999=0) (80000 thru Highest=1) (ELSE=SYSMIS) INTO incover80K.
VARIABLE LABELS incover80K 'Income over 80K'.
EXECUTE .
```

Note that we had to use **GET FILE** to re-open our income.sav file. This is because we had previously run the **CI_S1M** macro command which, like many of the other macro commands, automatically closes the file you had open. We have now created our dummy variable **incover80K**, so we can run EXAMINE VARIABLES on this new variable to get the confidence interval:

```
EXAMINE VARIABLES = incover80K /PLOT NONE /CINTERVAL 90 .
```

Descriptives

			Statistic	Std. Error
Income over 80K	Mean		.0120	.01205
	95% Confidence Interval for Mean	Lower Bound	-.0119	
		Upper Bound	.0360	
	5% Trimmed Mean		.0000	
	Median		.0000	
	Variance		.012	
	Std. Deviation		.10976	
	Minimum		.00	
	Maximum		1.00	
	Range		1.00	
	Interquartile Range		.00	
	Skewness		9.110	.264
	Kurtosis		83.000	.523

There is clearly a problem here. The lower bound on the confidence interval is negative! To say that we are 95% certain that the proportion of households in the population with an income over £80,000 lies between –1.19% and 3.6% is meaningless since we know that a proportion cannot be negative.

This spurious result arises because SPSS does not know that you are dealing with a proportion rather than a mean and therefore does not apply the correct formula for calculating the confidence interval. A more meaningful result is achieved if we run frequencies on our dummy variable to find the number of households in our sample with incomes of at least £80,000,

```
FREQUENCIES VARIABLES=incover80K .
```

Income over 80K

		Frequency	Percent	Valid Percent	Cumulative Percent
Valid	.00	82	98.8	98.8	98.8
	1.00	1	1.2	1.2	100.0
	Total	83	100.0	100.0	

and then use the appropriate macro syntax to compute a 90% confidence interval for a proportion:

CI_L1P n=(83) x=(1) c=(.90).

```
Traditional Large sample CI for one proportion
      ptrad       zstar     se_trad       etrad    low_trad     up_trad
    .012048   -1.644854     .011975     .019698    -.007650     .031746

Wilson Large sample CI for one proportion
      pwlsn       zstar     se_wlsn       ewlsn    low_wlsn     up_wlsn
    .034483   -1.644854     .019562     .032177     .002306     .066660
```

The Wilson large sample confidence interval estimate gives us the correct result: we are 90% certain that between 0.2% and 6.7% of the population have incomes of at least £80,000.

4.7 Graphical Representation of Confidence Intervals for Data

An appealing way to represent confidence intervals is to use the Error Bar graphing facility in SPSS. For the reasons explained above, SPSS does not know whether you are looking for a confidence interval for a mean or for a proportion, so you should be aware that the Error Bar facility explained below should only be used if you are comparing several means (rather than proportions). Note also that the facility only works if you have the original data.

To use the Error Bar facility, click on Graphs, then Error Bar, and you will see that you have the option of either comparing several variables (such as purchase price vs valuation in the exercise below) or groups of cases of the same variable (such as whether the average auction price is different in Cumberland to the average auction price in Durham). You can also choose to do both on the same graph by choosing Clustered which allows you to plot confidence intervals for groups of cases for different variables. Each of these options will represent the confidence interval for the population mean as a vertical line with the sample mean in the middle. It is a nice way of representing the range of possible values of the population mean around the known sample mean and is particularly convenient for comparing the confidence intervals when you have lots of means to compare. Notice that in both the Simple and Clustered windows you can also opt to consider the confidence interval for the *standard error of the mean* (rather than the mean), and you can also insert titles.

Exercise 4.7 Using the GRAPH / ERRORBAR command to compare confidence intervals

1. Open the **auction.sav** data set. The file records the estimated and final sale prices of 100 items entered for auction at venues in Cumberland and Durham. Use the EXAMINE VARIABLES command to compare the 95% confidence intervals of the auctioneer's estimated value (**value**) and the actual purchase price (**purchase**). Now compare the two variables using the GRAPH /ERRORBAR command. Does the graph confirm what you found from using the 'Explore' function? What happens if you change the confidence level to 80%? Explain your findings.

Answer:

Attempt the question yourself before referring to the answer below.

First we need to open the **auction.sav** data and run the EXAMINE VARIABLES command on the **value** and **purchase** variables:

```
GET FILE='C:\STATISTICS\auction.sav'.
EXAMINE VARIABLES = purchase value /PLOT NONE /CINTERVAL 95 .
```

This produces the following output:

Descriptives

			Statistic	Std. Error
Actual final purchase price	Mean		869.9500	240.3828
	95% Confidence Interval for Mean	Lower Bound	392.9783	
		Upper Bound	1346.922	
	5% Trimmed Mean		447.2222	
	Median		165.0000	
	Variance		5778390	
	Std. Deviation		2403.828	
	Minimum		5.00	
	Maximum		19190.00	
	Range		19185.00	
	Interquartile Range		555.00	
	Skewness		5.484	.241
	Kurtosis		36.131	.478
Auctioneer's estimated valuation	Mean		861.3000	232.0542
	95% Confidence Interval for Mean	Lower Bound	400.8540	
		Upper Bound	1321.746	
	5% Trimmed Mean		454.3111	
	Median		200.0000	
	Variance		5384917	
	Std. Deviation		2320.542	
	Minimum		5.00	
	Maximum		19200.00	
	Range		19195.00	
	Interquartile Range		635.00	
	Skewness		5.724	.241
	Kurtosis		40.363	.478

Notice that you can enter more than one variable at a time in the EXAMINE VARIABLES command. Notice also that the confidence intervals for the two variables overlap. Next, graph the error bars:

```
GRAPH   /ERRORBAR( CI 95 )=purchase value .
```

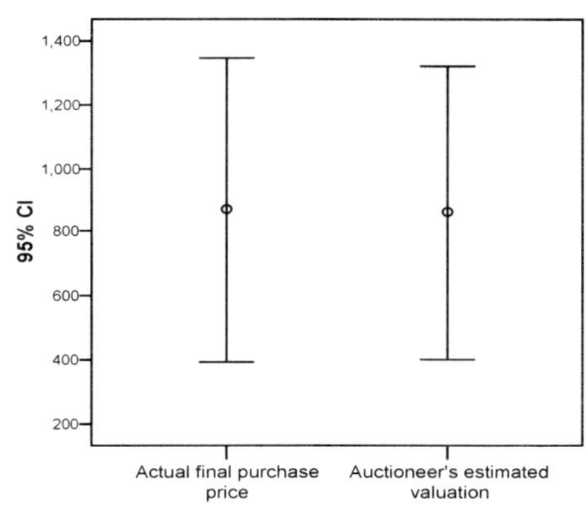

It is clear that although the means of the two variables are slightly different, the confidence intervals almost entirely overlap. In fact, the confidence interval for the population mean of auctioneer's estimates (£393 to £1,347) lies entirely within that of the confidence interval for the population mean final purchase price (£401 to £1,322). The fact that the confidence intervals overlap means that we cannot distinguish between the population means of the two variables (that is, we cannot say with any certainty that if we had data on all valuations and all purchase prices that the averages of the two variables would be different). So it seems that although the auctioneer may not perfectly predict the sale price of each item, our sample data suggests that on average his estimates are pretty reliable. There is certainly no evidence that he is systematically *over-* or *under-*predicting the auction price of items for sale.

To obtain the 80% confidence intervals you would simply re-run the syntax changing only the confidence level:

```
GET FILE='C:\STATISTICS\auction.sav'.
EXAMINE VARIABLES = purchase value /PLOT NONE /CINTERVAL 80 .
GRAPH   /ERRORBAR( CI 80 )=purchase value .
```

To save space we have not reproduced the output, but as you might expect, the confidence intervals for both variables are narrower, yet still overlap.

Exercise 4.7 Continued:

2. Compare the 95% confidence intervals for the purchase price of lots entered in Durham vs those entered in Cumberland. What do your results tell you?

Answer

Attempt the question yourself before referring to the answer below.

Notice that the two means we want to compare are contained within the same variable, **purchase**. We can compare confidence intervals across groups by running the following syntax:

```
GRAPH /ERRORBAR( CI 95 )=purchase BY zcounty /MISSING=REPORT.
```

which results in the following graph:

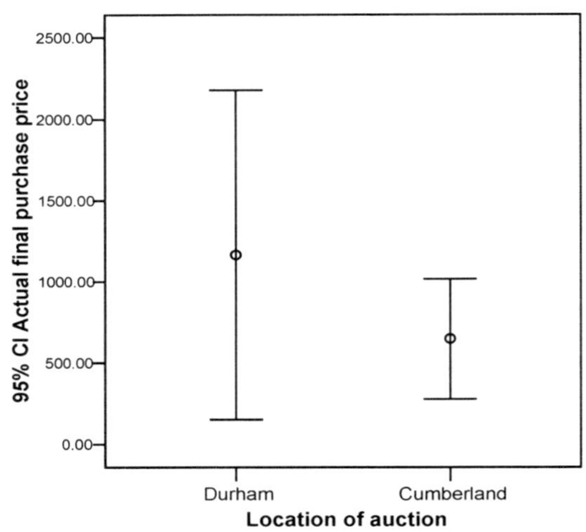

Although the confidence intervals still overlap, they do so to a lesser extent than for the comparison between purchase and value. Nevertheless, the fact that the intervals do overlap means that, at the 95% level of confidence, we cannot identify any significant difference between the average purchase price at Durham auctions compared with those at Cumberland. This is perhaps surprising given that the mean prices appear to be quite different. The uncertainty arises from the large variation in prices at Durham (note how the standard deviation in the table below is much larger for Durham than for Cumberland) which causes the confidence interval to be much wider.

To compare descriptive statistics and confidence intervals between groups you again make use of the EXAMINE VARIABLES command but simply insert BY between your continuous variable (**purchase**) and your grouping variable (**zcounty**). In the syntax below we reduce the confidence level to 80%, but the confidence intervals still overlap:

```
GRAPH /ERRORBAR( CI 80 )=purchase BY zcounty /MISSING=REPORT.
EXAMINE VARIABLES=purchase BY zcounty /PLOT NONE /CINTERVAL 80 .
```

Descriptives

	Location of auction			Statistic	Std. Error
Actual final purchase price	Durham	Mean		1165.349	502.8289
		80% Confidence Interval for Mean	Lower Bound	510.6477	
			Upper Bound	1820.050	
		5% Trimmed Mean		532.5452	
		Median		130.0000	
		Variance		1.1E+07	
		Std. Deviation		3297.270	
		Minimum		5.00	
		Maximum		19190.00	
		Range		19185.00	
		Interquartile Range		440.00	
		Skewness		4.525	.361
		Kurtosis		22.557	.709
	Cumberland	Mean		647.1053	184.6678
		80% Confidence Interval for Mean	Lower Bound	407.6183	
			Upper Bound	886.5922	
		5% Trimmed Mean		383.1189	
		Median		170.0000	
		Variance		1943826	
		Std. Deviation		1394.212	
		Minimum		10.00	
		Maximum		7960.00	
		Range		7950.00	
		Interquartile Range		605.00	
		Skewness		3.841	.316
		Kurtosis		15.940	.623

Note that you can compare variables and groups all on the same graph. For example,

```
GRAPH /ERRORBAR( CI 95 )=purchase value BY zcounty
 /TITLE= 'Comparison of Confidence Intervals for the Mean' 'Purchase price and valuation'
 /SUBTITLE= 'Cumberland and Durham compared'
 /FOOTNOTE= 'Source: Acme Auction Data'.
```

Comparison of Confidence Intervals for the Mean

Purchase price and valuation

Cumberland and Durham compared

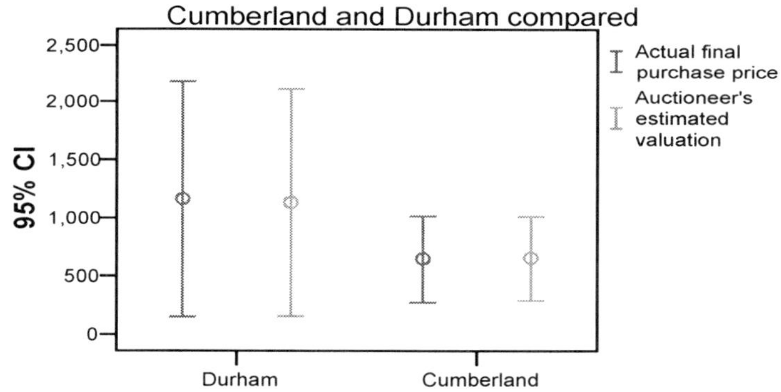

Source: Acme Auction Data

Thus, we have managed to display on one graph what the two previous graphs showed separately: that although the confidence intervals still overlap for the two areas, they do so to a lesser extent than for the comparison between areas than for the comparison between purchase and value.

4.8 Sample Size Determination

4.8.1 Sample Size for Desired Margin of Error for a Mean

Suppose you want to estimate the average weight of 5 year olds with a margin of error e of 2 pounds when you apply a 95% confidence interval. The sample size necessary for estimating the population *mean* with the desired accuracy will be given by:

$$n = \frac{z_i^2 \sigma^2}{e^2}$$

e	=	2 lbs
c	=	0.95
z_i	=	?
s.d.	=	guess at 14 lbs

We can either compute this by hand, using zi gl zp to compute the value of z_i such that Prob($-z_i < z < z_i$),

```
Value of zi such that Prob(-zi < z < zi) = PROB, when PROB is given
     ZIL        ZIU       PROB
  -1.95996   1.95996    .95000
```

n = (1.96*1.96*14*14)/4 = 188.23

or we can use the following macro syntax command:

N_L1M — **N_L1M** computes the sample size for desired margin of error for one mean. The command requires three inputs, e, c and s. For example,

```
N_L1M   e=(2)  c=(0.95)  s=(14) .
```

results in the following output:

```
n_hat = estimated sample size needed to achieve an error of size e given c
      E         C        ZIL        ZIU      N_HAT
   2.00000   .95000  -1.95996   1.95996  188.23148
```

So, we would need a sample of around 188 to derive a reasonably accurate confidence interval on average weight.

4.8.2 Sample Size for Desired Margin of Error for a Proportion

Suppose, however, your variable is categorical and you want to estimate the population *proportion*. The sample size necessary for estimating the population proportion with a desired level of accuracy would be:

$$n = \frac{z^{*2} \pi^* (1 - \pi^*)}{e^2}$$

Exercise 4.8.2: Sample size determination

For your PhD, you want to estimate the mean hourly wage rate of unskilled labour in Easterhouse within ±£0.10 at the 99% confidence level. A 1987 study (large sample size) by the Department of Employment resulted in a standard deviation of £0.85. Using this as an approximation for σ, compute the necessary sample size to arrive at the desired level of accuracy.

Answer:

First summarise the information provided in the question:

e	=	£0.10
c	=	0.99
z_i	=	?
s	=	£0.85

Then enter the details into the appropriate syntax command:

```
N_L1M   e=(0.1)  c=(0.99)  s=(0.85) .
```

which results in the following output:

```
n_hat = estimated sample size needed to achieve an error of size e given c
      E        C       ZIL      ZIU     N_HAT
  .10000   .99000  -2.57583  2.57583  479.37128
```

These results suggest that a sample size of 480 is needed to achieve the desired level of accuracy.

4.9 Conclusion

In this chapter we have introduced one of the most useful techniques available to empirical researchers. Confidence intervals allow us to take account of our sample size and the variability of our sample data to approximate the likely range of values of the population mean. We considered three steps of interval estimation: First, you need to decide on the appropriate formula and the desired confidence level. Second, you need to calculate the value of z associated with your desired level of confidence. Third, you must compute the confidence interval by plugging in the known values from our sample into the formula we have identified.

We considered also how to deal with situations when we only have a small sample (use the t-distribution), how to compute a confidence interval for a proportion (rather than a mean), and how to make use of SPSS's in-built facilities for calculating confidence intervals when we have the original data (we also identified limitations in these facilities, particularly when we want to compute the confidence interval on a proportion). Finally, we considered a technique for helping us approximate the size of sample needed to achieve a desired margin of error in our final estimates.

We now move on to the second major strand of introductory statistics: hypothesis testing.

5 Introduction to Hypothesis Testing

Aim:
The purpose of this chapter is to introduce a common framework for hypothesis testing that the reader will be able to apply to the great majority of statistical tests most commonly used by social scientists.

Objectives:
By the end of this chapter you should be able to understand the meaning of statistical significance and run a hypothesis test on the value of the population mean using summary data on a large sample. You should also be fully familiar with the four steps of hypothesis testing and the **H_L1M** and **H_S1M** commands for small and large sample hypothesis testing respectively. You should also understand the difference between a one-tail and a two-tail test and be able to run either sort of test both manually and using the SPSS output.

Further Reading:
D. S. Moore and G. P. McCabe, *Introduction to the Practice of Statistics,* 4th Ed., Freeman, New York, pp. 444-447 and pp. 496-501.

Plan:

5.1 Introduction

In Chapter 2 we learnt how the sampling distribution of the mean (the histogram of means from repeated samples of the same size) is always normal provided the sample size is large. This law of nature is known as the *Central Limit Theorem* and holds true even if the distribution of the variable we are interested in does not have a bell-shaped distribution.

In Chapter 3 we practised calculating areas under the standard normal curve (also called the z-distribution). We learnt that this is a useful skill because these areas correspond to probabilities. Also, any normal distribution can be transformed into the z-curve using a simple conversion formula, which means that we can convert any value of a normally distributed variable into a z-score. This fact, combined with the Central Limit Theorem, means that we can compute z-scores (and associated probabilities) for the sampling distribution of *any* variable, provided our sample size is reasonably large. If sample sizes are small, we can employ the t-distribution, which is in fact a family of distributions, one for each sample size. For large sample sizes, the t-distribution becomes indistinguishable from the z-distribution. The corollary of this is that statisticians often use the t-distribution to solve statistical problems whether or not the sample size is small – if the sample size is large, the t-distribution gives the same results as the z-curve anyway.

Knowing that the sampling distribution of the mean is normal, and that the mean of sample means equals the population mean, allows us to compute *confidence intervals*, and this was the subject of Chapter 4. For any given sample mean, and predetermined level of confidence, we learnt how to calculate the upper and lower limits of the likely range of values of the population mean. For example, if we want to compute a and b so that we are 95% confident that the population mean lies between a and b, the normality of the sampling distribution allows us to compute these bounds. Our calculation would run as follows: first we would take advantage of the fact that all normal distributions are related and that all points on a particular sampling distribution can be converted into equivalent points on the standard normal curve – the *z*-distribution. The flip-side of this fact is that any point on the *z*-distribution can be translated onto any sampling distribution. This means that once we have computed z_a and z_b, the lower and upper bounds of the central 95% of the standard normal curve, we can translate these values onto particular sampling distribution, such as that associated with the income of single parent households. In other words we can find the values of income, *a* and *b*, that correspond to z_a and z_b, and hence identify where the central 95% of all sample mean incomes lie. Given that the central point of our sampling distribution is always the mean-of-means – which we know equals the population mean – we can be 95% sure that the population mean income lies between income *a* and income *b*.

In this chapter, we learn how to do *hypothesis tests*. Here we are concerned with the extent to which our sample is *atypical*. To do this we translate the mean of our data onto the *z*-distribution to work out the probability that we could randomly select a sample with an average at least as far away from the *assumed* value of the population mean as our observed sample mean. You will see that our calculations still make use of the standard normal and t-distributions, but that our calculations run the opposite way to confidence interval estimation. In confidence interval estimation we first calculate the bounds of the central 95% of the *z*-distribution, find the corresponding z-scores, and then translate these values onto our particular sampling distribution. In hypothesis testing we start with our observed sample mean, convert it to a *z*-score, and exploit the properties of the standard normal curve to work out the proportion of all possible samples that have a sample mean at least as far away as our sample mean from the assumed population mean.

Crucial to hypothesis testing is the concept of statistical significance. It is very important to be clear in our minds what statisticians mean when they talk of *significance*, and so our first step will be to consider the meaning of this term and how it is used in hypothesis testing. We shall then introduce the four steps of hypothesis testing.

The terminology and structure of hypothesis tests can seem obscure to the newly initiated, but when you have become familiar with the jargon and procedure, you will find that once you can do one hypothesis test you can do them all. Indeed, there are many different sorts of hypothesis tests. Thousands, possibly hundreds-of-thousands, of tests have been developed by statisticians to deal with different empirical problems, but they all conform to the same pattern. In this chapter, we learn how to conduct two tests: the *large* sample hypothesis test on one mean, and the *small* sample hypothesis test on one mean. As you might expect, the two tests are identical, other than the fact that the first uses the z-distribution to calculate the desired probabilities, and the second uses the *t*-distribution.

5.2 Significance and Significance Levels

For statisticians, *significance* has nothing to do with *importance*, which is the most common meaning of the word. When statisticians talk of significance they are referring to something specific to inference. They sometimes define *significance* as *real differences in fact* between our observed sample mean and our assumption about the population mean, which means simply that any difference between our sample summary measure and the assumed population value is not due simply to random sampling variation. In other words, if our sample mean differs from the assumed population mean, then that difference can be described as *significant* if it is unlikely to be because we have randomly selected an atypical sample.

Another important term used by statisticians, is the *level of significance*. The term is confusing because it sounds very similar to significance but has come to mean almost the exact opposite. The significance level is in fact an estimate of the chances of our observed sample mean occurring, given that our assumption about the population (denoted by "H_0") is true. So if we find that this probability is small, it might lead us to question our assumption about the population mean as specified in H_0. The significance level is the *probability of false rejection of our assumption about the population mean.* The greater the *significance level*, the less *significant* the difference between our sample mean and assumed population mean. The converse is also true: the smaller the *significance level* the more *significant* the difference between our sample mean and the assumed population mean. It sounds bizarre, but this is the terminology which has rather inconveniently emerged in statistical analysis.

If our sample mean is a long way from our assumed population mean then it is either a freak sample, or our assumption about the population mean is wrong. If we draw the conclusion that it is our assumption that is wrong and reject H_0 then we have to bear in mind that there is a chance that H_0 was in fact true. In other words, on average, every twenty times we reject H_0 when $P = 0.05$, then on one of those occasions we would have rejected H_0 when it was in fact true.

Obviously, as the sample mean moves further away from our assumption (H_0) about the population mean, we have stronger evidence that H_0 is false. If P is very small, say 0.001, then there is only one chance in a thousand of our observed sample mean occurring if H_0 is true. This also means that if we reject H_0, also called the *null hypothesis*, when $P = 0.001$, then there is only a one in a thousand chance that we have made a mistake. This probability is the significance level, it is the probability that we have *falsely rejected the null hypothesis* and been guilty of what statisticians call a "**Type I error**".

There is a tradition (initiated by English scientist R. A. Fisher 1860-1962) of rejecting H_0 if the probability of incorrectly rejecting it is ≤ 0.05 (that is, we reject the null hypothesis if there is no more than a one in twenty chance of false rejection).

- If $P \leq 0.05$ then we say that, "H_0 can be rejected at the 5% significance level".
- If $P > 0.05$, then, argued Fisher, the chances of incorrectly rejecting H_0 are too high to allow us to do so. In this event, we say that, "We cannot reject H_0 at the 5% significance level". In other words, we conclude that H_0 is true, although statisticians are reluctant to say this in the positive!

To recap, the significance level (often abbreviated to "sig." and designated by P in the notes below) is the probability of a sample mean at least as extreme as our observed value occurring, given our assumption about the population mean. The size of this probability will depend not only on the difference between our sample mean and our assumption about the population mean, but also on the variability of our data (measured using the standard deviation) and the number of observations in our sample.

5.2.1 Lower-, Upper- and Two-Tail Tests

Conducting a Hypothesis Test: An Example of an Upper-Tail Test

When you conduct a hypothesis test, you must first state the *null hypothesis*, written as simply H_0, which is often (but not always) a *straw-man* that we would actually prefer to reject. Suppose, for example, that football clubs work on the assumption that on average players will retire at the age of 36, but you believe the average retirement age has in fact been rising in recent years, so this assumption is unlikely still to be valid. You obtain a random sample of recent retirement records. You want to use this sample to prove that the population mean retirement age of footballers is in fact greater than 36.

The first thing you would need to do to conduct a hypothesis test is state your null hypothesis. In this case, the null hypothesis is that "the population mean *equals* 36". Note that, whatever the test being carried out, the null is *always* stated in terms of *something equals something*. Since the population mean is abbreviated using μ (the Greek letter for 'm'), we can use the following shorthand for this particular null hypothesis:

H_0: $\mu = 36$ (null hypothesis)

We test this hypothesis against the *alternative hypothesis*, denoted by H_1, which is usually what we think the outcome is going to be. In this case, we think that the population mean may be greater than 36, so we write our alternative hypothesis as:

H_1: $\mu > 36$ (alternative hypothesis)

To calculate the *significance level* (the probability of falsely rejecting the null hypothesis) we calculate the probability that we could observe a sample mean at least as large as that of our current sample when the population mean is assumed to be 36 years. If our sample mean is a long way from our assumption regarding the population mean, then this may lead us to doubt our assumption about the population mean.

Suppose that the mean retirement age in your sample turns out to be 42 years. This seems to support your suspicions, but how do you know that you do not have an atypical sample? In this case the significance level would be the probability of observing a sample with mean retirement age of 42 given that the population mean retirement age is 36. Because sample means have a normal distribution provided the sample size is large, the significance level will equal the area highlighted in the right tail of the diagram below.

Note that this is *not* a graph of the standard normal curve, but a hypothetical plot of the sampling distribution of mean retirement ages (i.e. a stylised histogram of means from repeated samples of recently retired footballers). We know that the mean-of-means (the line of symmetry of this distribution) will equal the population mean. Hence, we have drawn the graph such that the centre of the distribution occurs at 36 years (i.e. the graph is drawn assuming the null hypothesis about the population mean retirement age is correct).

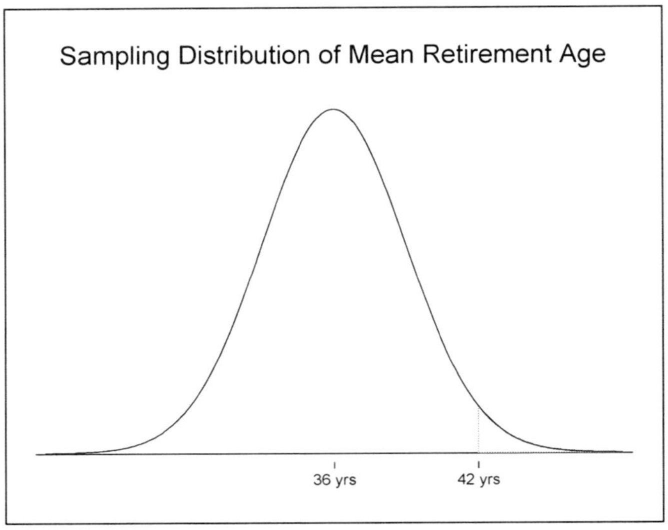

To compute the chances of observing a sample at least as extreme as ours (assuming the null is true), we need to convert our mean age into a *z*-score. We considered the formula to compute z_i in Chapter 3. The formula is copied below, and requires us to know the standard error of the mean (i.e. the standard deviation of sample means from repeated samples).

$$z_i = \frac{\bar{x}_i - \mu}{\sigma_{\bar{x}}}$$

where :

μ = population mean

$\bar{x}_i$ = sample mean

$\sigma_{\bar{x}}$ = standard deviation of all the sample means, called the standard error of the mean

z_i = z - score

Suppose we know that the standard error of the mean is 3 years. If we did not know the standard error of the mean, we could always approximate it by dividing our sample standard deviation by the square root of the sample size. The resulting statistic would have an approximately normal distribution if the sample size is large. We can compute z_i as follows:

$z_i = (42 - 36)/3 \quad = 2.00$

We have therefore translated our sample mean of 42 years onto the standard normal curve as illustrated below. All we need to do now is calculate the area to the right of 2.00 under the standard normal curve.

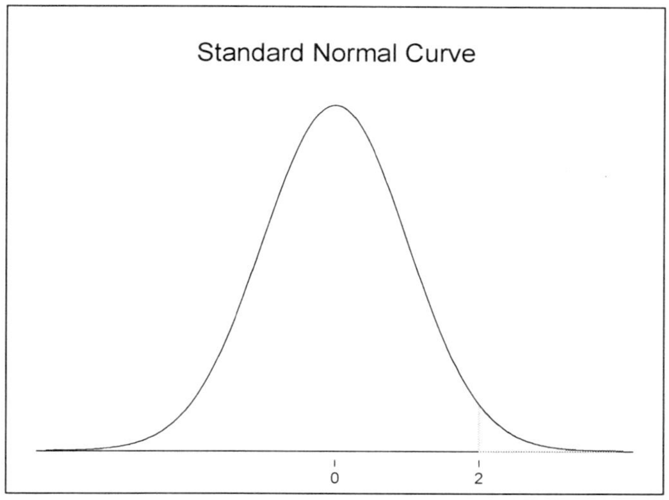

We can easily compute this area using either Table A at the back of the book, or by using the macro syntax introduced in Chapter 3 for computing the probability that z is greater than a particular value:

pz_gt_zi (2.0).

This results in the output below which calculates Pr(z > 2.00) to be 0.023.

```
Prob(z > zi) for a given zi
      zi          Prob
   2.00000       .02275
```

We conclude that the probability of observing a sample with a mean retirement age at least as large as 42 years (given an assumed population mean of 36 years) is only 2.3%. Such a small probability would in fact lead us to question the null assumption about the population mean. If we reject the null hypothesis that the mean retirement age of footballers is 36 then we have only a 2.3% chance that our decision to reject H_0 has been incorrect. Given Fisher's recommendation that we use 5% as our threshold for rejection, we would have to reject the null hypothesis in favour of our alternative hypothesis that the mean retirement age is greater than 36. We can now confidently say that the average retirement age of footballers is significantly greater than 36.

Lower-Tail Test

How we calculate the significance level – the probability of false rejection of the null hypothesis – depends on whether we want to conduct an upper-, lower- or two-tail test. The example above was in fact an illustration of an *upper-tail test* because our alternative hypothesis was that the population mean was *greater than* the assumed 36 year average retirement age, and so the significance level we were trying to estimate corresponded to the area under the standard normal curve in the upper-tail (or right tail) of the *z*-distribution as illustrated in the figure above.

When our alternative hypothesis is that the population mean is *less than* the value assumed in our null hypothesis, we conduct what is called a *lower-tail test.* Here the probability of observing a sample mean at least as *small* as our own is called the *lower-tail* significance test. This is because the significance level we are trying to estimate corresponds to the area under the standard normal curve in the *lower*-tail (or left tail) of the *z*-distribution.

Two-tail Test

If our alternative hypothesis is simply that the actual population mean is *different* to the assumed value of the population mean (that is, either less than or greater than the assumed value) then we need to do a two-tail significance test. The two-tail significance is the probability of observing a sample mean at least as extreme – in either direction – as that observed in our sample given the assumed value of the population mean. As such, we add together the sum of areas in the two-tails of the standard normal curve.

Calculating the Significance Level

If you are computing the significance levels using Table A, the following rules will help you:

For Upper-tail Tests:	H_1: $\mu > \mu_0$ then $P = \text{Prob}(z > z_i)$
For Lower-tail Tests:	H_1: $\mu < \mu_0$ then $P = \text{Prob}(z < z_i)$
For Two-tail Tests:	H_1: $\mu \neq \mu_0$ then $P = 2\text{xProb}(z > \lvert z_i \rvert)$

Where P is the significance level, and $|z_i|$ is the absolute value of z_i.

5.3 The Four Steps of Hypothesis Testing

In the previous chapter we looked at *confidence interval* estimation. Confidence intervals allow us to establish the range of values of the population mean for a given level of confidence. We can say, for example, that we are 90% confident that population mean age of heads of households in repossessed dwellings in the Great Depression lay between 32.17 and 36.83 years, based on a sample of 200 with mean = 34.5 years. To calculate such confidence intervals we used a three-step recipe.

It is useful to adopt a similarly systematic approach when conducting hypothesis tests. The recipe we suggest requires four steps, as outlined in the table below:

Confidence Interval	Hypothesis Tests
Find the 90% confidence interval of the population mean age	Test the hypothesis that the population mean age = 30 using a significance level of 0.1
	1. Specify null and alternative hypothesis: H_0: $\mu = 30$ H_1: $\mu \neq 30$
1. Choose the appropriate test statistic: $z_i = \dfrac{\bar{x}_i - \mu}{s/\sqrt{n}} \Rightarrow \mu = \bar{x}_i \pm z^* \dfrac{s}{\sqrt{n}}$	**2. Specify the level of significance and the test statistic** Significance level: α = likelihood of Type I error that you are prepared to tolerate = Prob(Reject H_0 when it is true) = 0.1 Test Statistic: n > 30, therefore we can us z: $z_c = \dfrac{\bar{x}_i - \mu}{s/\sqrt{n}} = z_c = \dfrac{\bar{x}_i - 30}{s/\sqrt{n}}$ i.e. we write the z_c formula assuming that H_0 is correct
2. Establish the value of z*: Prob(-z*<z<z*) = 0.9 Area of tails = (0.1)/2 = 0.05 ⇒ <u>**z* = 1.65**</u>	**3. Specify the decision rule:** Reject H_0 iff P (the calculated level of Type I error) is no greater than the tolerated level: i.e. Reject H_0 iff $P \leq \alpha$ (the smaller is P, the less risk involved in rejecting H_0)
3. Calculate the confidence interval: $\mu = 34.5 \pm 1.65 \dfrac{20}{\sqrt{200}} = 45.5 \pm 2.33$	**4. Compute *P* and state your conclusion:** $z_c = 3.18$; $P = 2(1 - \text{Prob}(z < 3.18)) = 0.0014$ Since $P < \alpha$ (i.e. < 0.1), its safe to reject H_0

The next table compares the steps required for lower-tail and upper-tail tests:

Lower Tail Hypothesis Tests	Upper Tail Hypothesis Tests
Test the hypothesis that the population mean age < ? using a significance level of α	Test the hypothesis that the population mean age > ? using a significance level of 0.1
1. Specify null and alternative hypothesis: H_0: $\mu = ?$ H_1: $\mu < ?$	**1. Specify null and alternative hypothesis:** H_0: $\mu = ?$ H_1: $\mu > ?$
2. **Specify the level of significance and the test statistic** Significance level: α = likelihood of Type I error that you are prepared to tolerate = Prob(Reject H_0 when it is true) Test Statistic: If n > 30, we can us z: $z_c = \frac{\bar{x}_i - \mu}{s/\sqrt{n}} = z_c = \frac{\bar{x}_i - ?}{s/\sqrt{n}}$ i.e. we write the z_c formula assuming that H_0 is correct	2. **Specify the level of significance and the test statistic** Significance level: α = likelihood of Type I error that you are prepared to tolerate = Prob(Reject H_0 when it is true) Test Statistic: If n > 30, we can us z: $z_c = \frac{\bar{x}_i - \mu}{s/\sqrt{n}} = z_c = \frac{\bar{x}_i - ?}{s/\sqrt{n}}$ i.e. we write the z_c formula assuming that H_0 is correct
3. Specify the decision rule: Reject H_0 iff P (the calculated level of Type I error) is no greater than the tolerated level: i.e. Reject H_0 iff $P \le \alpha$	**3. Specify the decision rule:** Reject H_0 iff P (the calculated level of Type I error) is no greater than the tolerated level: i.e. Reject H_0 iff $P \le \alpha$
4. Compute *P* and state your conclusion: $P = \text{Prob}(z < z_c) = ??$ Note that z_c will be negative if $\bar{x} < \mu$	**4. Compute *P* and state your conclusion:** $P = \text{Prob}(z > z_c)) = ??$ Note that z_c will be positive if $\mu < \bar{x}$

5.4 Large Sample Hypothesis Test on One Mean

As an alternative to computing the result by hand and looking up the significance level in the tables, you can use the following macro syntax which calculates the large sample significance test for a single population mean:

H_L1M H_L1M calculates the large sample significance test on one mean. The arguments for this command are entered as follows:

H_L1M n=(?) x_bar=(?) m=(?) s=(?).

For example, if sample size is 107, sample mean = 10.92, hypothesised population mean = 11, and sample standard deviation = 0.28, then we would enter:

```
H_L1M   n=(107)  x_bar=(10.92)  m=(11)  s=(0.28).
```

which results in the following output:

```
Large sample sig. test for one mean
         N      X_BAR        SE          ZI    SIGZ_2TL   SIGZ_LTL   SIGZ_UTL
 107.00000   10.92000    .02707    -2.95545      .00312     .00156     .99844
```

where `N` is sample size, `X_BAR` is the sample mean, `SE` is the standard error of the mean (that is, the standard deviation of the sampling distribution of the mean), `ZI` is the z-score you wish to calculate in order to establish the significance level, `SIGZ_2TL` is the two-tail significance associated with z_i, `SIGZ_LTL` is the lower-tail significance associated with z_i, and `SIGZ_UTL` is the upper-tail significance associated with z_i.

Exercise 5.4: Large Sample Hypothesis Test on One Mean:

Suppose your area of research is the disappearance of thousands of civil servants and other workers during Joseph Stalin's Great Purge in Soviet Russia 1936-38. One of the questions you are interested in is the average age of the workers when they disappeared. Your thesis is that Stalin felt most threatened by older, more established 'enemies', and so you anticipate their average age to be over 50. Unfortunately, you only have access to 506 records on the age of individuals when they disappeared.

You have calculated the average age in this sample to be 56.2 years, which would appear to confirm your thesis. The standard deviation of your sample was found to be 14.7 years. Assuming that your 506 records constitute a random sample from the population of those who disappeared (a questionable assumption?), test your theory about the average age of the Disappeared.

Answer:

n = 506
$\bar{x}$ = 56.2
μ_0 = 50
s = 14.7

(1) Specify hypotheses:

H_0: $\mu = 50$ years
H_1: $\mu > 50$ years

(2) Specify sig. and the test statistic:

Sig. = P = probability of Type I error
= P(reject H_0 when in fact true) = 0.05

n is relatively large so we could justify using the standard normal curve:

$$z_c = \frac{\bar{x}-\mu}{s/\sqrt{n}} = \frac{\bar{x}-50}{s/\sqrt{n}}$$ i.e. we write the z formula assuming H_0 is correct.

(3) Specify the decision rule:

Reject H_0 iff the probability of rejecting H_0 when it is in fact true is less than 5%.

(4) Compute sig. and state your conclusion:

$$z_c = \frac{\bar{x}-50}{s/\sqrt{n}} = \frac{56.2-50}{14.7/\sqrt{506}} = \frac{6.2}{0.654} = 9.487$$

Upper-tail test:

H_1: $\mu > \mu_0$ then P = Prob($z > z_i$)

Sig. = Prob(z > 9.487)
= 1- Prob(z < -9.487)
= 0.0000

This probability is well below our specified threshold for the probability of Type I error of 0.05 and so we can confidently reject H_0.

We could even reject H_0 if we had set the tolerance level at 0.01 or even 0.0001 since our estimated significance level suggests that there is less than a 1 in 1000 chance that we are wrong about rejecting the null hypothesis. Your thesis about the seniority of those Stalin eliminated would appear to hold true.

Now let's do the same test, but this time we'll use the macro syntax:

H_L1M n=(506) x_bar=(56.2) m=(50) s=(14.7).

```
Large sample sig. test for one mean
         N        X_BAR           SE          ZI    SIGZ_2TL    SIGZ_LTL    SIGZ_UTL
  506.00000    56.20000       .65349     9.48745      .00000     1.00000      .00000
```

This corroborates the finding in the last chapter that the confidence interval is very narrow because of your large sample size and because of the small standard deviation in your sample:

```
Large sample confidence interval for the population mean
         N       X_BAR          ZI          SE         ERR       LOWER       UPPER
  506.00000   56.20000     1.96039      .65349     1.28111    54.91889    57.48111
```

5.5 Small Sample Hypothesis Test on One Mean

If we have small samples, the hypothesis testing procedure remains essentially the same, except that we use the t-distribution to calculate the significance level:

$$t_i = \frac{\bar{x} - \mu}{s/\sqrt{n}}, df = n-1$$

If you want to compute the significance levels based on the t-distribution you can use the **TCDF(ti,df)** function built into SPSS as standard which calculates the probability that t is less than t_i, where t_i is the value of t you've calculated, where df = degrees of freedom = n-1. If you want to avoid having to calculate t_i or work out the separate significance levels for lower-, upper- and two-tail tests, then you may prefer to use the following macro command written specifically for this book:

H_S1M H_S1M calculates a small sample significance test for one mean. The arguments for this command are entered as follows:

H_L1M n=(?) x_bar=(?) m=(?) s=(?).

Exercise 5.5: Hypothesis Tests on One Mean

1. A machine used to fill pre-packaged emergency insulin injections is correctly adjusted if the average net weight of insulin is 11 ounces per syringe. A random sample of 107 syringes had an average fill of 10.92 ounces and standard deviation of 0.28 ounces. Is the machine adjusted properly? Test at the 5% significance level.

Answer:

First set out the information you need to answer the question:

n = 107
$\bar{x}$ = 10.92
μ_0 = 11
s = 0.28

(1) Specify hypotheses:

H_0: μ = 11 ounces
H_1: $\mu \neq$ 11 ounces

(2) Specify sig. and the test statistic:

Sig. = probability of Type I error = P(reject H_0 when in fact true) = 0.05
n is relatively large so we could justify using the standard normal curve:

$$z_c = \frac{\bar{x} - \mu}{s/\sqrt{n}} = \frac{\bar{x} - 11}{s/\sqrt{n}}$$ i.e. we write the z formula assuming H_0 is correct.

(3) Specify the decision rule:

Reject H_0 iff the probability of rejecting H_0 when it is in fact true is less than 5%.

(4) Compute sig. and state your conclusion:

$$z_c = \frac{\bar{x}-11}{s/\sqrt{n}} = \frac{10.92-11}{0.28/\sqrt{107}} = \frac{-0.08}{0.027} = -2.963$$

Because this is a two-tail test, the significance level is equal to the sum of the areas in the two-tails of the z-distribution, highlighted in the diagram below:

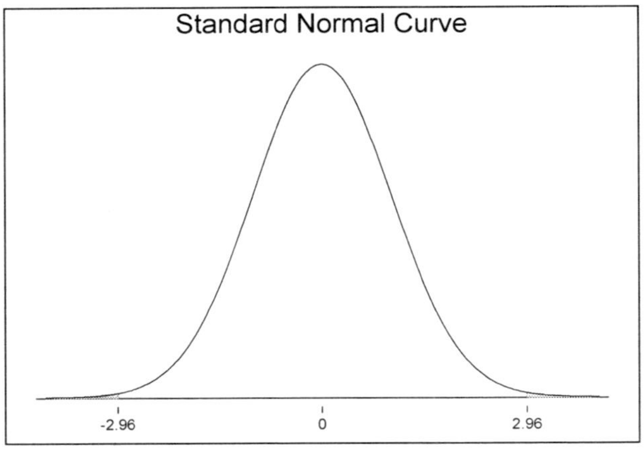

Sig. = 2(1-Prob(z < $|z_c|$))
= 2(1-Prob(z < 2.963))
= 2(1- 0.9985)
= 2(0.0015)
= 0.003

Somewhat worryingly, we have to reject the hypothesis that the syringe-filling machine is operating correctly. There is only a 3 in 1000 chance that we are wrong about rejecting the null hypothesis. We can confirm this using the SPSS command:

H_L1M n=(107) x_bar=(10.92) m=(11) s=(0.28).

```
Large sample sig. test for one mean
         N       X_BAR          SE          ZI    SIGZ_2TL    SIGZ_LTL    SIGZ_UTL
 107.00000    10.92000      .02707    -2.95545      .00312      .00156      .99844
```

We could alternatively do a lower-tail test: that the syringes are being under-filled. This leads to an even lower significance level, making it even less likely that our sample is a freak sample.

Interestingly, if we run a *t*-test on the same hypothesis we get a slightly more cautious estimate of the significance level, but the result is essentially the same. This is because, as the sample size gets larger, the *t*-distribution estimates of the significance level will tend toward the *z*-distribution estimates. In this case the sample size is fairly large so you'd expect the *z* and *t* estimates of *P* to be similar.

H_S1M n=(107) x_bar=(10.92) m=(11) s=(0.28).

```
Small sample sig. test for one mean
         N       X_BAR          SE          TI    SIGT_2TL    SIGT_LTL    SIGT_UTL
 107.00000    10.92000      .02707    -2.95545      .00385      .00192      .99808
```

Exercise 5.5 Continued:

2. A newspaper has claimed that the average time GPs spend with patients in a particular session has fallen to an all-time low of 3.6 minutes. A report from the Scottish Executive disagrees, contending that the health service has met New Labour's manifesto target of 4 minutes average consultation time, and that the data used by the newspaper was based on a freak sample. The newspaper's survey was based on a random sample of 80 doctors with a mean of 3.60 minutes and a standard deviation of 1.80 minutes. Is the government bluffing or is there a good chance that this is indeed a freak sample? Perform the appropriate hypothesis test using a significance level of 0.05.

Answer:

The null hypothesis is that the average time patients spent with doctors is 4 minutes (the Government's claim). The alternative hypothesis is that this is a freak sample with an unusual average time of less than 4 minutes. If the true average time is indeed 4 minutes, how unlikely is a sample to be drawn with an average time of 3.6 minutes or less? This is obviously a lower-tail test. If such a sample is very unlikely (i.e. if the significance level is low), then this might lead us to call into question the null hypothesis. If we then reject the null hypothesis, the significance level will tell us how likely we are to have made an incorrect decision:

(1) Specify hypotheses:

H_0: $\mu = 4$ mins

H_1: $\mu < 4$ mins

(2) Specify sig. and the test statistic:

Sig. = probability of Type I error = P(reject H_0 when in fact true) = 0.05

n is relatively large so we could justify using the standard normal curve:

$$z_c = \frac{\bar{x} - \mu}{s/\sqrt{n}} = \frac{\bar{x} - 4}{s/\sqrt{n}}$$ i.e. we write the *z* formula assuming H_0 is correct.

(3) Specify the decision rule:

Reject H_0 iff the probability of rejecting H_0 when it is in fact true is less than 5%. That is, reject the government's claim that the average time spent with a patient is 4 minutes if, and only if, the significance level is less than 0.05 (i.e. if the chances of the newspaper's sample being a freak sample is 1 in 20).

(4) Compute sig. and state your conclusion:

$$z_c = \frac{\bar{x} - 4}{s/\sqrt{n}} = \frac{3.6 - 4}{1.8/\sqrt{80}} = \frac{-0.4}{0.201} = -1.988$$

Because this is a lower-tail test, the significance level is equal to the area in the left tail of –1.988 in the z-distribution below:

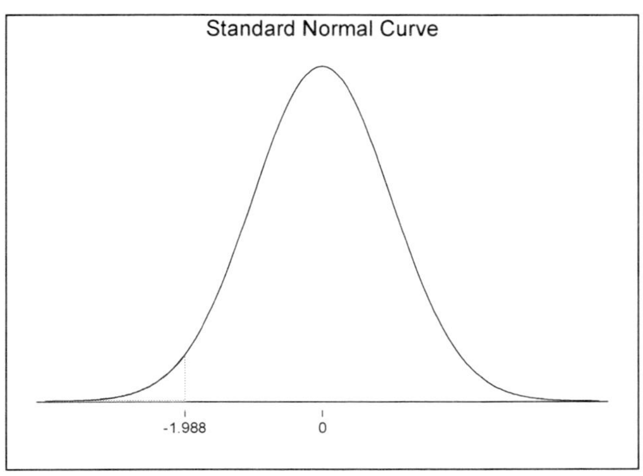

For a lower-tail test, we use the following procedure for calculating *P* from Table A:

H_1: $\mu < \mu_0$ then P = Prob($z < z_i$)

Sig. = Prob($z < |z_c|$)
= Prob($z < -1.988$) = **0.023**

If we reject the government's claim, there is only a 2.3% chance that we have done so incorrectly. We reject New Labour's claim.

Alternatively we could use the syntax (but make sure you understand the output!):

H_L1M n=(80) x_bar=(3.6) m=(4.0) s=(1.8).

```
Large sample sig. test for one mean
       N        X_BAR          SE          ZI    SIGZ_2TL    SIGZ_LTL    SIGZ_UTL
80.00000      3.60000      .20125    -1.98762      .04685      .02343      .97657
```

Exercise 5.5 Continued:

3. For your PhD, you want to estimate the number of times an American phrase or pronunciation occurs in a typical 5 minute conversation between teenage youths in Liverpool. Because of the time taken to build up sufficient rapport with such youths for them to speak in a relaxed way, you only manage to observe 23 such conversations. The average number of Americanisms in 5 minute conversations amongst your small sample is 137.71, with a standard deviation of 69.56. The last study that was done demonstrated that the average was 128.2 words per 5 minute conversation and this has become the accepted wisdom in the literature. Do a hypothesis test to establish whether the average has in fact increased at the 5% significance level. Also do a two-tail test for whether there has been any change at all. Compare your answer with the 95% confidence interval estimated in the previous set of lab exercises.

Answer:

If we use the large sample syntax (i.e. use the z-distribution to calculate the probability of the sample being atypical) then we end up with the following output:

H_L1M n=(23) x_bar=(137.71) m=(128.2) s=(69.56).

```
Large sample sig. test for one mean
  N        X_BAR         SE         ZI       SIGZ_2TL    SIGZ_LTL    SIGZ_UTL
23.00000  137.71000   14.50426    .65567      .51204      .74398      25602
```

Note, however, that the sample size is only 23, and so one should really use the t-distribution:

H_S1M n=(23) x_bar=(137.71) m=(128.2) s=(69.56).

```
Small sample sig. test for one mean
      N       X_BAR         SE            TI        SIGT_2TL    SIGT_LTL    SIGT_UTL
 23.00000  137.71000   14.50426       .65567       .51884      .74058      .25942
```

The significance level for the upper-tail test was found to be 0.259 (slightly higher than that derived using the *z*-distribution, reflecting the slightly flatter shape of the *t*-distribution i.e. more area in the tails). This suggests that if we reject the null hypothesis (that the average number of Americanisms amongst Liverpool youth is still 128.2) in favour of the alternative hypothesis (that average has risen) based on your PhD sample, then there is a 26% chance that we are wrong. This is too high a risk to take and so we cannot reject the null hypothesis. In other words, we cannot say that the average number of Americanisms has risen.

If we do a two-tail test, we find that the chances of our sample being a freak sample is more than 50% (sig. = 0.519) and so we have even less of a basis to reject the null hypothesis.

This result should not surprise us since the 95% confidence interval based on your PhD sample was found to be 108 Americanisms to 168 Americanisms (compare the output below for small and large sample confidence interval estimation):

C1_L1M n = (23) x_bar = (137.71) s = (69.56) c = (0.95).

```
Large sample confidence interval for the population mean
        N      X_BAR        ZIL        SE        ERR       LOWER      UPPER
 23.00000  137.71000   -1.95996  14.50426   28.42783  109.28217  166.13783
```

C2_S1M n = (23) x_bar = (137.71) s = (69.56) c = (0.95).

```
Small sample confidence interval for the population mean
        N      X_BAR        TIL        SE        ERR       LOWER      UPPER
 23.00000  137.71000   -2.07387  14.50426   30.08000  107.63000  167.79000
```

Exercise 5.5 Continued:

4. As part of your research you seek to analyse the policy of using the planning system to encourage the building of residential properties on brownfield sites (i.e. recycled industrial land), rather than greenfield sites (i.e. former agricultural or park land). One of your concerns is that brownfield land is more likely to be contaminated, and the methods for surveying the level of contamination do not preclude the possibility that a site may be declared safe when it is not. Surveys gauge contamination by taking bore-extracts every 100m. The land is declared safe for residential construction if the average level of toxicity is no more than 1g per extract. In your case study area, the former steelworks site in Cambuslang, Glasgow, you find that a random sample of 64 bores has been taken yielding an average of 0.88g with standard deviation of 0.79g. The average is below the safety threshold but do you think the Local Authority should grant this site residential planning permission?

Answer:

First set out the information you need to answer the question:

n = 64
$\overline{x}$ = 0.88
μ_0 = 1.0
s = 0.79

H_L1M n=(64) x_bar=(0.88) m=(1) s=(0.79).

Large sample sig. test for one mean

N	X_BAR	SE	ZI	SIGZ_2TL	SIGZ_LTL	SIGZ_UTL
64.00000	.88000	.09875	-1.21519	.22429	.11215	.88785

The SIGZ_LTL figure is the probability of observing a value of z smaller than -1.215. If we reject the null that the mean level of contamination in extracts is = 1g in favour of the alternative hypothesis that it is less than 1g, there is more than a one in ten chance that we have rejected the null incorrectly.

If we reject the null in favour of the alternative hypothesis, that it is *greater* than 1g, we can only be 88% sure that we will have rejected the null incorrectly.

Exercise 5.5 Continued:

5. As part of your research into the contamination levels experienced by workers in the Cambuslang steel industry in the first half of the twentieth century, you examine 273 random medical checks on workers which reveal an average contamination level of 92.7 units with a standard deviation of 39.7 units. The legal threshold for exposure is that the average should not exceed 94 units and so the steel industry always claimed on the basis of this sample that their workers were safe. How sure can you be that this conclusion is valid?

Answer:

First set out the information you need to answer the question:

n = 273
$\overline{x}$ = 92.7
μ_0 = 94
s = 39.7

The question, of course, is whether when we take into account random sampling variation the population mean is likely to be below the legal threshold. Let's do an upper-tail test to see if the population mean is likely to be above the legal limit:

$H_0: \mu$ = 94
$H_1: \mu$ > 94

H_L1M n=(273) x_bar=(92.7) m=(94) s=(39.7).

Large sample sig. test for one mean

N	X_BAR	SE	ZI	SIGZ_2TL	SIGZ_LTL	SIGZ_UTL
273.00000	92.70000	2.40275	-.54105	.58848	.29424	.70576

These results show that, because of the large standard deviation in the sample, we cannot reject the null hypothesis that the mean exposure score in the population of workers equals 94 units, whether the alternative hypothesis is upper-, lower- or two-tail. If we look at the confidence interval, this result is not surprising since the upper limit on the 95% confidence interval is 97.4 units. In short, we cannot be sure on the basis of this sample that the population mean is not well above the legal threshold.

C1_L1M n=(273) x_bar=(92.7) s=(39.7) c=(0.95).

```
Large sample confidence interval for the population mean
         N        X_BAR          ZIL          SE         ERR       LOWER       UPPER
 273.00000     92.70000     -1.95996     2.40275     4.70931    87.99069    97.40931
```

Exercise 5.5 Continued:

6. You are a research assistant on a project investigating sectarian attitudes amongst Rangers supporters, you interview 24 supporters in pubs after a football match at Ibrox. You find that the average age of supporters with sectarian attitudes is 22.7 years (s.d. = 9.2 years) which is well below the most recent estimate published five years ago which said that the average age of this group was around 30 years. Run a lower-tail *t*-test to see if this difference between estimates is statistically significant and reflect on the robustness of your method.

First set out the information you need to answer the question:

n = 24

$\bar{x}$ = 22.7

μ_0 = 30

s = 9.2

H_0: μ = 30

H_1: μ < 30

H_S1M n=(24) x_bar=(22.7) m=(30) s=(9.2).

```
Small sample sig. test for one mean
        N      X_BAR         SE          TI    SIGT_2TL    SIGT_LTL    SIGT_UTL
 24.00000   22.70000    1.87794    -3.88723      .00074      .00037      .99963
```

This result tells us that, despite your small sample, you can be pretty confident of rejecting the null hypothesis (that the average age of sectarian Rangers supporters equals 30) in favour of the alternative hypothesis that the average age is less than 30 years. There is less than a one in a thousand chance that your rejection of the null is incorrect.

Note, however, that the t-test assumes a normally distributed variable (i.e. that the age of sectarian Rangers supporters is normally distributed) but this may well not be the case. If the normality assumption fails and you have a small sample, then non-parametric methods should be used. If you have a large sample, then the normality assumption does not matter since the Central Limit Theorem will start to kick in (this says that the sampling distribution of the mean is normal even if the variable itself is not normal, provided the sample sizes used in the repeated samples are large).

The *t*-test (and z-test and confidence interval estimates and any other form of inference) also assumes that your sample is randomly selected from all sectarian Rangers supporters, but this might not be the case. Older supporters, for example, may be less likely to attend the match (rather than watch on television) and may be less likely to stay around for a drink at the pub. The type of sample may also be affected by the outcome of the match, as may your measurement of sectarianism. All these lead to what is known as *sample selection bias*. Such bias undermines our ability to make inferences about the population from a particular sample.

5.6 Conclusion

In this chapter we have learnt how to conduct a simple hypothesis test on a mean when (a) the sample is large; and (b) the sample is small (the macro commands are **H_L1M** and **H_S1M** respectively). More important than the two specific tests we have been looking at is the *general hypothesis testing process*. The four steps we have introduced here will be applicable to every hypothesis test you will ever come across. It is therefore a very useful framework. The biggest obstacle to learning how to do hypothesis testing is not the calculations themselves, but familiarising yourself with this process and the rather bizarre terminology that has come to be associated with the subject. In particular, the use of the words *significance* and *significance levels* to mean diametrically opposed things is very confusing. But if you can get over this, and work within the prescribed framework, you will find that any hypothesis test will be within your grasp.

6 Hypothesis Testing for All Occasions

Aim:
The aim of this chapter is to introduce a selection of hypothesis tests for means and proportions and, in the process, further familiarise the reader with the general technique of hypothesis testing.

Objectives:
By the end of this chapter you should be able to run hypothesis tests on the equality of two means (both from independent samples and from matched pairs), and on proportions (both from single and double populations).

Further Reading:
D. S. Moore and G. P. McCabe (2003) *Introduction to the Practice of Statistics,* 4th Ed., Freeman, New York, sections 7.2, 7.3, 8.1 and 8.2.

Plan:

6.1 Introduction

In the last chapter we learnt the four steps of hypothesis testing and the associated terminology. We applied this procedure to hypothesis tests on a single mean when we have (a) a large sample; and (b) a small sample. Suppose, however, that we want to compare means from separate populations? For example, we might want to compare average earnings of ethnic minorities with the average earnings of whites. Or suppose we want to conduct a hypothesis test, not on a mean, but on a proportion? (To test, for example, the hypothesis that one in ten men are impotent). How does the hypothesis testing procedure change?

Well the answer is, very little. As arduous and arcane as hypothesis testing terminology is, there is some consolation in knowing that all hypothesis tests follow a similar pattern. The only thing that changes is the formula used to derive the significance level. For some types of test, these formulae become horrendously complicated and so it makes sense to use the macro syntax commands where possible. As a result, we shall devote little time in this chapter to computing results using statistical tables and manual calculations, and focus instead on using the following macro commands and associated concepts:

Hypothesis tests

Command	Definition
H_L1M	Large sample significance test on one mean
H_S1M	Small sample significance test on one mean
H_S2MP	Small independent samples significance test for equality of 2 means (pooled variance)
H_S2MD	Small independent samples significance test for equality of 2 means (different variances)
H_L1P	Large sample significance test on one proportion
H_L2P	Large samples significance test on two proportions
H_S2VF	Simple small sample F-test on equality of two variances (see also Levene's test in the SPSS help menu for more sophisticated test of homogenous variances).

6.2 Recap: Significance Tests on One Mean

In the last chapter we looked at two tests using the following macro commands:

H_L1M = Large sample significance test on one mean

H_S1M = Small sample significance test on one mean

The small sample test followed the same basic procedure as the large sample test except that we use the *t*-distribution rather than the z-distribution. Remember that to use the t-distribution our original variable has to be approximately normal. If we have a small sample and our variable is very non-normal, then we have to use *non-parametric tests*, which are not covered in this text (except for the Chi-square test for independence – see Chapter 7).

We now go on to consider a range of hypothesis tests to tackle situations of more than one population and where our data are categorical rather than continuous (that is, when we are interested in the proportion rather than the mean).

6.3 Significance Test for the Equality of Two Means

Note that any small sample test that uses the *t*-distribution (as in the tests that follow) works equally well on large samples because the *t* distribution becomes indistinguishable from the z-distribution when sample sizes are large. So in effect, most statisticians use *t*-values to calculate significance levels for both large and small sample hypothesis tests. As we emphasised above, however, in small samples it is important that the variable in question is itself normally distributed, otherwise the *t*-distribution does not apply. With this caveat in mind, we examine below only formulae based on the *t*-distribution.

6.3.1 Two Independent Samples

These tests are applicable to situations where we are trying to compare the means of two independent populations. The test is applicable to randomised comparative trials where the researcher randomly divides the subjects into two groups and exposes each group to a different treatment, but is equally applicable to comparison of subgroups, such as male and female earnings from a survey based on a random sample. The two samples are assumed to be independent. This is distinct from situations where the researcher observes the same person before and after a treatment (for such experiments we use the *Paired Samples* t-test – see SPSS help function for details and section 6.4 below).

There are two formulae for calculating the appropriate test statistic for comparing two population means: one assumes equal (or *homogeneous*) variances across the two populations, and the other assumes unequal (or *heterogeneous*) variances across the two populations.

6.3.2 Equal variances:

If we believe the variances in our two samples are similar, then we use the following formula to calculate the test statistic, t_c:

$$t_c = \frac{(\bar{x}_1 - \bar{x}_2) - (\mu_1 - \mu_2)}{s_p \sqrt{\frac{1}{n_1} + \frac{1}{n_2}}}$$

$$df = n_1 + n_2 - 2$$

where s_p is the pooled standard deviation calculated as follows:

$$s_p = \sqrt{\frac{(n_1 - 1)s_1^2 + (n_2 - 1)s_2^2}{n_1 + n_2 - 2}}$$

This is quite a complex set of computations, so it's a good idea to check your answers using the following syntax:

H_S2Mp **H_S2MP** calculates the small independent samples significance test for equality of 2 means (*pooled* variances – see *Moore and McCabe 2003 pp.537-542*). The inputs to the command are entered as follows:

H_S2Mp n1=(?) n2=(?) x_bar1=(?) x_bar2=(?) s1=(?) s2=(?).

Example 6.3.2 Pooled Variance Independent Samples t Test

Suppose you are interested in testing the view put forward by some feminist sociologists, that in the porn movie-making world, women play a controlling rather than subordinate role. This claim is apparently substantiated by the higher salaries of female porn stars as compared to their male counterparts. You aim to test this hypothesis by sending an anonymous postal survey to a sample of male and female porn stars. Your 39 male respondents report a mean income of £156,452 per annum (s.d. = £46,198) whereas your 42 female respondents report a mean income of £179,231 per annum (s.d. = £46,125). What can you conclude from your survey results?

Answer:

First you should consider whether your sample is truly random. Non-response is often non-random, which can result in what is known as sample selection bias. It may be, for example, that highly-paid male stars are less likely to respond to your survey than their female counterparts, or vice versa. Second you should consider whether the incomes of both groups are approximately normal since the sample sizes are not very large and *t*-tests require normality in the underlying variable.

With these caveats in mind, you can work through the four steps of hypothesis testing:

Step 1: Specify the Null and Alternative Hypotheses:

H_0: $\mu_1 = \mu_2$

H_1: $\mu_1 < \mu_2$

where μ_1 is the population mean earnings of male porn stars, and μ_2 is the population mean earnings of female porn stars.

Step 2: Specify the Threshold Level of Significance and the Test Statistic

Although the question does not specify it, we shall adopt 5% as the tolerable threshold for the risk of false rejection. The formula for computing the test statistic *t* is given above.

Step 3: Specify the Decision Rule

Reject H_0 if $P < 5\%$.

Step 4: Compute *P* and State Your Conclusion:
We shall use the following SPSS macro command to compute *P*:

H_S2Mp n1=(39) n2=(42) x_bar1=(156452) x_bar2=(179231) s1=(46198) s2=(46125).

Entering this syntax results in the following output:

```
Equal vars Indep samples t-test for equality of means (H0:pop1ave = pop2ave)
        DF     X1B_X2B          SE          TI    SIGT_2TL    SIGT_LTL    SIGT_UTL
  79.00000 -22779.000 10264.8491    -2.21913      .02935      .01467      .98533
```

where DF = degrees of freedom; x1B_x2B = x_bar1 - x_bar2 = the difference in sample means; SE = standard error; TI = estimated t-value; SIG_2TL = two-tail significance level; SIGT_LTL = lower-tail significance level; and SIG_UTL = upper-tail significance level.

Note that we have labelled the male stars as sample 1 and the female stars as sample 2. Our alternative hypothesis of males earning less than females will therefore be phrased as *the mean of population 1 being lower than the mean of population 2*. This requires a *lower-tail* test. If we had labelled the two samples the other way round, then we would need to do an *upper-tail* test (see the caveat below). Anyhow, the lower-tail significance, SIGT_LTL, is 0.015 which says that there is a 1.5% chance of incorrectly rejecting H_0. Most social scientists would agree that this is a sufficiently low probability of false rejection to refute the null hypothesis that male and female porn stars earn equal amounts.

NB: there is a general caveat to be observed in the above example: that if you are doing one-tail tests on two populations (i.e. one has a larger mean than the other) then you need to think carefully about which mean sample is labelled as '1' and which is labelled as '2' as this will obviously affect how the upper and lower-tail results are interpreted. This is particularly true when you use the SPSS canned routine (considered later in this chapter) which automatically assigns the ordering of your two groups.

6.3.3 Unequal Variances

The formula for computing the test statistic when variances between the two groups are unequal is given below:

$$t_c = \frac{(\bar{x}_1 - \bar{x}_2) - (\mu_1 - \mu_2)}{\sqrt{\frac{s_1^2}{n_1} + \frac{s_2^2}{n_2}}}$$

$$df \approx \min[n_1 - 1, n_2 - 1]$$

where s_1^2 and s_2^2 are the sample variances from independent simple random samples of sizes n_1 and n_2, and $\bar{x}_1$ and $\bar{x}_2$ are the sample means. Rather than working through the formula by hand, you may prefer to use the following syntax:

H_S2Md

H_S2Md computes the small independent samples significance test for equality of 2 means assuming *different* variances (see *Moore & McCabe pp.529-532*). The arguments for **H_S2Md** are entered as follows:

H_S2Md n1=(?) n2=(?) x_bar1=(?) x_bar2=(?) s1=(?) s2=(?).

If we run this test on the porn star example above,

H_S2Md n1=(39) n2=(42) x_bar1=(156452) x_bar2=(179231) s1=(46198) s2=(46125).

we obtain the following output,

```
Uneq vars Indep samples t-test for equality of means (H0:pop1ave = pop2ave)
        DF     X1B_X2B          SE          TI    SIGT_2TL    SIGT_LTL    SIGT_UTL
 38.000000 -22779.000 10265.4579   -2.218995     .032534     .016267     .983733
```

You will see that the results are virtually identical. This is because the variances of the two samples are very similar.

The two calculations will diverge a little, however, as the variances diverge, particularly in small samples and/or samples of different sizes. Try running the same two SPSS commands but increase the standard deviation of female stars to £190,000 and reduce the sample sizes to 56 and 12 respectively and you will see how this is borne out in practice:

H_S2Mp n1=(56) n2=(12) x_bar1=(156452) x_bar2=(179231) s1=(46198) s2=(190000).

```
Equal vars Indep samples t-test for equality of means (H0:pop1ave = pop2ave)
         DF     X1B_X2B          SE         TI   SIGT_2TL   SIGT_LTL   SIGT_UTL
   66.00000 -22779.000 28085.6063    -.81106     .42025     .21012     .78988
```

H_S2Md n1=(56) n2=(12) x_bar1=(156452) x_bar2=(179231) s1=(46198) s2=(190000).

```
Uneq vars Indep samples t-test for equality of means (H0:pop1ave = pop2ave)
         DF     X1B_X2B          SE         TI   SIGT_2TL   SIGT_LTL   SIGT_UTL
  10.000000 -22779.000 55194.6105   -.412703    .688533    .344267    .655733
```

The difference in the degrees of freedom is particularly noticeable and also the estimate of the standard error (affected in part by the sample sizes, as you can see from the formulae presented above).

Note that the null hypothesis in both the equal variance and unequal variance tests is that the population means are equal:

$H_0: \mu_1 = \mu_2$

The alternative hypothesis can be one of the following three:

$H_1: \mu_1 > \mu_2$
$H_1: \mu_1 < \mu_2$
$H_1: \mu_1 \neq \mu_2$

The significance level, P, associated with each is calculated as follows:

Upper-Tail Test:	$H_1: \mu_1 > \mu_2$	then $P = \text{Prob}(t > t_i)$
Lower-Tail Test:	$H_1: \mu_1 < \mu_2$	then $P = \text{Prob}(t < t_i)$
Two-Tail Test:	$H_1: \mu_1 \neq \mu_2$	then $P = 2\text{xProb}(t > \|t_i\|)$

These rules are already incorporated into the calculations that lie behind the **H_S2Mp** and **H_S2Md** commands, but they are worth learning if you are going to do the tests manually.

6.3.4 The Test for Equality of Variances

How do you decide whether variances are equal or not? Do we just make an arbitrary decision based on whether we think the standard deviations are similar or not? Often we can get away with doing this, particularly if the differences in variance seem very large or very small (it is the intermediate cases, as always, that pose difficulty).

However, one must remember that what we really want to know is whether the *sampling distributions* of the two populations have similar or different *standard errors*. Since we only have the variance of one sample from each population to base our estimate on, we must remember that the difference between the two sample variances is just one of many possible differences (because our two samples are just two of many possible samples) and so we should ask whether the one difference in variances we are able to observe is likely to be typical. This again depends on the sample size. If our two samples are small, we may be less certain of our estimate of the variance of all samples, and because it is the estimate of that variance which is used to estimate the standard error of the sampling distribution, we will also be less certain of whether the standard error of the two sampling distributions are different. Once more, therefore, we need a hypothesis test based on sound rules of inference. A simple test for the equality of variances uses following formula (see p. 554 of Moore and McCabe):

$F = s_1^2 / s_2^2$

This basically says that the ratio of variances has an F-distribution with the *denominator degrees of freedom* calculated as $n_1 - 1$ and the *numerator degrees of freedom* calculated as $n_2 - 1$. Because the critical values for the F-distribution are only calculated at the upper end, if the F-value you are have calculated is less than one, you need to invert it (i.e. swap around the numerator and denominator). F-tests are structured so that you only ever do an upper-tail test even though the alternative hypothesis is *always* that the variances are not equal,

$$H_0: \sigma_1^2 = \sigma_2^2$$
$$H_1: \sigma_1^2 \neq \sigma_2^2$$

and so if the significance level is small (less than 0.05, for example) we reject the assumption of equal variances and use the *Unequal Variances* t-test above. If the significance level is large, we use the *Equal Variances* t-test.

Once you have computed the value of F, you can make use of the following built-in SPSS function to calculate the associated probability: **CDF.F(q, df1, df2)** . This function returns the cumulative probability that a value from the F-distribution, with degrees of freedom **df1** and **df2**, will be less than **q** . Note that **q** is the value of F you have calculated from $F = s_1^2 / s_2^2$. Since we want to know the upper-tail area, we have to take the result of this command away from 1. If we want the result to have more than the default number of decimal places we must also specify FORMATS. So the full syntax would be:

```
COMPUTE Fsig = 1 - CDF.F(q, df1, df2) .
FORMATS Fsig (F5.4).
EXECUTE.
```

If you run this syntax (which only works if you have at least one cell of numerical data in your Data View), a new variable will be created called **Fsig**, all the values of which will equal the probability you are trying to calculate.

6.3.5 Macro Syntax for Equality of Variance Test

The following macro syntax will run this simple equality of variance test for you (the syntax works out which values should go in the numerator and which in the denominator) and compute the significance level:

H_S2VF

H_S2VF computes the simple small sample F-test on equality of two variances (see Levene's test in SPSS for more sophisticated test of homogenous variances). The necessary arguments are entered as follows:

```
H_S2VF   n1=(?)  n2=(?)  s1(?)  s2(?)
```

where n1 = sample size of sample one; n2 = sample size of sample two; s1 = standard deviation of sample one; and s2 = standard deviation of sample two.

Using our initial values for the sample sizes and standard deviations of the two groups of film stars in the example above, we enter the following syntax and obtain the following output:

```
H_S2VF   n1=(39)  n2=(42)  s1=(46198)  s2=(46125).
```

```
F-Test for equality of variance (H0: V_nmrtor = V_dnmtor)
   V_NMRTOR    V_DNMTOR    DF_NMRTOR    DF_DNMTOR       FC       SIGF_UTL
 2134255204 2127515625    38.00000     41.00000     1.00317      .49445
```

where V_NMRTOR and V_DNMTOR are the variances of the numerator and denominator respectively, DF_NMRTOR and DF_DNMTOR are the numerator and denominator degrees of freedom respectively, FC is the F-value that you have calculated and SIGF_UTL is the upper-tail degrees of freedom. The very high significance level tells us that if we reject the null of equal variances there is virtually a 50% chance of false rejection. In other words, we cannot be at all sure that any differences between our two sample variances are not due entirely to sampling variation within each of the two populations.

Compare this with the output for the second set of values for the sample sizes and standard deviations assumed in the example above,

H_S2VF n1=(56) n2=(12) s1=(46198) s2=(190000).

```
F-Test for equality of variance (H: V_nmrtor = V_dnmtor)
 V_NMRTOR   V_DNMTOR    DF_NMRTOR    DF_DNMTOR          FC    SIGF_UTL
 3.610E+10 2134255204    11.00000     55.00000    16.91457      .00000
```

which shows that the chances of false rejection of H_0 are now incredibly small (not surprising given that the sample two variance is now four times that of the sample one variance). Note how the program has swapped around which sample is entered in the numerator and which is entered in the denominator – it has done this to ensure that the ratio of variances is greater than or equal to one.

6.3.6 The Levene Test

Whilst the above method of testing for differences between variances is usually adequate, a more robust method of comparing the equality of variances is the "Levene Test" which is based on a very complex formula that weights each case of the sample with a unique group weight, so you need access to the original data. Fortunately, SPSS will calculate this for you if you have the original data (you cannot calculate it simply from summary statistics like the means and standard deviations of your two samples). Given the complexity of the calculation, it is not recommended that you attempt to calculate it by hand, so there is not much point considering the formula here. We shall, however, consider how to use the Levene's test as part of SPSS's canned Independent Samples T-Test procedure.

6.4 Testing Equality of Means when you have the Original Data

If you have the original observations (and not just summary statistics on the data) you can use the built-in facility in SPSS to test for equality of means between two independent samples. Simply click on Analyze, then Compare Means, then Independent Samples T Test.

The Grouping Variable option allows you to compare means across two categories of your Test Variable. You can alternatively use the T-TEST standard SPSS syntax explained in the following example.

Example 6.4 Testing for equality of Means in Independent Samples when you have the Original Data

Use the auction.sav data to compare the mean purchase price of auction sales in Cumberland and Durham.

Answer:

Step 1: Specify the Null and Alternative Hypotheses:

H0: $\mu_1 = \mu_2$

H1: $\mu_1 \neq \mu_2$

where: μ_1 is the population mean purchase price of auction sales in Durham, and μ_2 is the population mean purchase price of auction sales in Cumberland.

Step 2: Specify the Threshold Level of Significance and the Test Statistic
Although the question does not specify it, we shall adopt 5% as the tolerable threshold for the risk of false rejection. The formula for computing the test statistic *t* is as given earlier.

Step 3: Specify the Decision Rule
Reject H_0 if $P < 5\%$.

Step 4: Compute *P* and State Your Conclusion:
First open the data,

```
GET FILE = 'C:\STATISTICS\auction.sav'.
```

and then run the **T-TEST** SPSS syntax. The ordering of the groups is specified in brackets after the grouping variable, which in this case is **zcounty**. Durham is coded as **zcounty** = 1 and Cumberland is coded as **zcounty** = 2 so we must enter them in this order in the brackets following **zcounty** if SPSS is to follow the specification of our alternative hypothesis as set out in Step 1 above. The syntax should be entered as follows:

```
T-TEST  GROUPS = zcounty(1 2)  /VARIABLES = purchase.
```

Two tables emerge from this test, the first is simply a table of descriptives:

Group Statistics

	Location of auction	N	Mean	Std. Deviation	Std. Error Mean
Actual final purchase price	Durham	43	1165.349	3297.270	502.8289
	Cumberland	57	647.1053	1394.212	184.6678

Looking at the means, there seems to be a very considerable difference between them, so we are expecting the null of equal means to be rejected. Note also that the standard deviations look very different (indicating heterogeneous variances).

The second is a very wide table which is really in three parts. The first part, is the Levene's Test for equality of variances:

		Levene's Test for Equality of Variances	
		F	Sig.
Actual final purchase price	Equal variances assumed	4.757	.032
	Equal variances not assumed		

The null hypothesis (as always) is that the variances are equal. If the significance level is small (less than 0.05) then we can reject this hypothesis in favour of the alternative hypothesis of different variances. The outcome of this part of the table will determine which *t*-test result you need to look at on the right side of the table.

In the above example, the significance level is very small (3.2%) and so we can reject the null hypothesis of homogenous variances. As a result, we would read along to the second row of the "Sig. (2-tail)" significance level column which tells us the significance level associated with the ***unequal** variances t-test*. This is found to be 0.993, which is incredibly high (only if it were less than 0.05 would we reject the null hypothesis of equal mean floorarea).

If the Levene's test had suggested that we could indeed reject the assumption of equal variances, we would read along to the *second* row of the "Sig. (2-tail)" significance level column which tells us the significance level associated with the *Unequal Variances t-test*. Thus, the relevant t-test significance value is 0.338.

		Levene's Test for Equality of Variances		t-test for Equality of Means		
		F	Sig.	Sig. (2-tailed)	Mean Difference	Std. Error Difference
Actual final purchase price	Equal variances assumed	4.757	.032	.288	518.24357	485.20255
	Equal variances not assumed			.338	518.24357	535.66702

In this instance, both the pooled-variances and heterogeneous-variances *t*-tests yield similar significance levels (0.288 and 0.338) neither of which allow us to reject the null of equal means. This is perhaps a surprising result given the large difference in sample means between the two locations. However, the sample sizes are not very large and, more importantly, the sample standard deviations are huge, which severely hampers our ability to make precise inferences about the population values.

The third part of the table (on the far right) presents the 95% confidence intervals associated with the difference between the two population means.

		Levene's Test for Equality of Variances	
		F	Sig.
Actual final purchase price	Equal variances assumed	4.757	.032
	Equal variances not assumed		

95% Confidence Interval of the Difference	
Lower	Upper
-444.625	1481.112
-555.997	1592.484

The full, un-dissected table is copied below:

Independent Samples Test

		Levene's Test for Equality of Variances		t-test for Equality of Means						
									95% Confidence Interval of the Difference	
		F	Sig.	t	df	Sig. (2-tailed)	Mean Difference	Std. Error Difference	Lower	Upper
Actual final purchase price	Equal variances assumed	4.757	.032	1.068	98	.288	518.24357	485.20255	-444.625	1481.112
	Equal variances not assumed			.967	53.366	.338	518.24357	535.66702	-555.997	1592.484

6.4.1 A Drawback of the Built-in SPSS Procedure

You will notice from the output of the canned SPSS output that it only provides the 2-tail significance level for the t-tests. You can of course work out what the correct upper- or lower-tail significance should be, but this can be very confusing, particularly since the output does not make it clear which sample is being considered as 'sample 1' and which sample is being counted as 'sample 2' in the computations. If you want to take advantage of the (marginal) increase in robustness derived from applying the Levene's test (rather than the simple ratio-of-variances test of homogenous variance executed by **H_S2VF**), then you should do the following if you have the original data to play with and you want to do a one-tail *t*-test for the equality of means:

1. **Use the Levene's test to decide on the equality of variances**
   Note that in the Levene's test it doesn't matter which sample is being considered as sample 1 and which is being considered as sample 2. The problem only arises when we come to do one-tail t-tests.

2. **Use the H_S2Mp or H_S2Md syntax** (depending on whether the variances can be pooled or whether they are different) to do the t-test since this gives you the upper- and lower-tail significance levels (be careful, though, to make sure you have correctly specified the ordering of samples, and whether the test you are interested in is lower- or upper-tail).

Exercise 6.4 Testing for Equality of Means

1. As part of your PhD research, you want to test whether the new "Fun Phonics" reading method is better than the "Letterland" method. You examine the reading ability of six year old children from two similar schools. The first used the FP method and you found that this produced an average reading proficiency score of 53.7 (based on a sample of 22 children; s.d. = 11.5). The second school used the Letterland method and you found that this produced an average reading proficiency score of 42.51 (sample = 24; s.d. = 16.9). Test whether the FP method produces higher results at the 1% significance level.

Answer:

The data can be summarised as follows:

$$\bar{x}_{FP} = 53.7, n_{FP} = 22, s_{FP} = 11.5$$
$$\bar{x}_L = 42.51, n_L = 24, s_L = 16.9$$

First we need to test for equality of variances:

$F = s_{FP}^2/s_L^2 = 132.25 / 285.61 = 0.463$

with $n_1 - 1$ and $n_2 - 1$ degrees of freedom: $df_{FP} = 21$ and $df_L = 23$. Because the critical values for the *F*-distribution are only calculated at the upper end, if the *F* value you are have calculated is less than one, you need to invert it (i.e. swap round the numerator and denominator). So in this case, the test becomes:

$F = s_L^2/ s_{FP}^2 = 285.61 / 132.25 = 2.1596$

and the numerator and denominator degrees of freedom become 23 and 21 respectively. If you prefer not to use the macro syntax, you can make use of the built-in SPSS function:

CDF.F(q, df1, df2)

which returns the cumulative probability that a value from the *F*-distribution with degrees of freedom df1, df2, will be less than q. Since we want to know the upper-tail area, we have to take the result of this command away from 1. If we want the result to have more than the default number of decimal places we must also specify FORMATS:

```
COMPUTE Fsig = 1 - CDF.F(2.1596 ,23,21) .
FORMATS Fsig (F5.4).
EXECUTE.
```

If you run this syntax (which only works if you have at least one cell of numerical data in your Data View), a new variable will be created called **Fsig**, all the values of which will equal 0.0404 (go to your Data View window to check this). Because this significance level is small (less than 0.05), we can reject the null of equal variances and use the *Unequal Variances t-test.*

Alternatively, we could use the macro syntax outlined above for doing the same equality of variances test:

```
H_S2VF    n1=(22)  n2=(24)  s1=(11.5)  s2=(16.9).
```

which results in the following output:

```
F-Test for equality of variance (H0: V_nmrtor = V_dnmtor)
V_NMRTOR     V_DNMTOR     DF_NMRTOR     DF_DNMTOR          FC          SIGF_UTL
285.61000  132.25000   23.00000    21.00000     2.15962      .04040
```

Now that we have found that the variances are different, we can apply the *Unequal Variances* t test. We again follow the four steps of hypothesis testing:

(1) H_0: $\mu_{FP} = \mu_L$
H_1: $\mu_{FP} > \mu_L$

(2) $\alpha = 0.01$ (implies critical t value of 2.528),

$$t_c = \frac{\bar{x}_1 - \bar{x}_2}{\sqrt{\frac{s_1^2}{n_1} + \frac{s_2^2}{n_2}}} = \frac{53.7 - 42.51}{\sqrt{\frac{132.25}{22} + \frac{285.61}{24}}} = 2.644$$

$$df = \min[n_1 - 1, n_2 - 1] = 21$$

(3) Reject H_0 iff $P < \alpha$, I.e. if $P < 0.01$

(4) P = Prob(t > 2.644) = 0.0076, so reject H_0

– (SPSS syntax: **COMPUTE probt = CDF.T(-2.644,21).**)

We can confidently reject the null hypothesis of equal mean reading scores in favour of the alternative hypothesis that the FP method produces a higher mean reading proficiency score.

Alternatively, we could use the macro syntax for different variances,

```
H_S2Md   n1=(22)  n2=(24)  x_bar1=(53.7)  x_bar2=(42.51)  s1=(11.5)  s2=(16.9).
```

to obtain the following output:

```
Uneq vars Indep samples t-test for equality of means (H0:pop1ave = pop2ave)
       DF      X1B_X2B          SE          TI    SIGT_2TL    SIGT_LTL    SIGT_UTL
21.000000  11.190000   4.232231   2.643995     .015176     .992412     .007588
```

which confirms our rejection of the null of equal mean reading scores in favour of the alternative hypothesis that the FP method produces a higher mean reading proficiency score (upper-tail significance = SIGT_UTL = 0.007588).

6.5 Matched Pairs Significance Test for Equality of Two Means

As with the confidence interval for matched pairs, we simply compute the mean difference between pre and post scores, and then treat this as a *single sample* hypothesis test (**H_S1M**) where the null hypothesis is that the mean difference in pre and post scores equals zero.

6.6 Large Sample Significance Test on One Proportion

Sometimes the variable we are interested in is categorical. For example, we might be interested in whether a household does or doesn't have mortgage payment protection insurance; whether person is homosexual or not homosexual; whether a person has Aids or does not have Aids. In such cases, what we are usually interested in is the *proportion* of cases that fall into a particular category (e.g. the *proportion* of households with insurance; or the *proportion* of people who are homosexual; or the *proportion* of people with Aids).

To calculate the proportion, we first denote the number of cases with the attribute of interest (e.g. the *number of* households with insurance) as x. We denote the sample size as n. The *proportion* of cases in our sample with the attribute of interest is then simply:

$$p = x / n$$

We said in previous sessions that the Central Limit Theorem allows us to calculate probabilities associated with the likelihood of selecting our sample because it says that the means from repeated samples will be normally distributed and we know the probabilities associated with every part of the normal distribution. So the question we want to ask now is, 'Does the Central Limit Theorem apply to sample proportions?'

In short, the answer is, 'Yes'. The sample proportion p has an approximately normal distribution if the samples are randomly selected and are sufficiently large. We denote the population proportion that we are trying to estimate as π. To carry out a hypothesis test on the population proportion, we can use the following z statistic:

$$z_i = \frac{p - \pi}{\sqrt{\frac{\pi(1-\pi)}{n}}}$$

NB Hypothesis tests on proportions using *small* samples are not recommended. The above test statistic should only be applied when the expected number of successes ($n\pi$) and the expected number of failures ($n(1-\pi)$) are both greater than 10.

P-values for one and two-tail tests are calculated as follows:

Upper-tail Test: H_1: $\pi > \pi_0$ then $P = \text{Prob}(z > z_i)$
Lower-tail Test: H_1: $\pi < \pi_0$ then $P = \text{Prob}(z < z_i)$
Two-tail Test: H_1: $\pi \neq \pi_0$ then $P = 2\text{xProb}(z > |z_i|)$

Alternatively, the following macro syntax can be used:

H_L1P H_L1P computes the large sample significance test for a single proportion (see Moore & McCabe, 2003, pp. 575-577) where the arguments are entered as follows:

```
H_L1P   n=(?)   x=(?)   pi=(?).
```

Example 6.6 Large Sample Hypothesis Test on One Proportion

As a historian, you want to find the proportion of citizens in medieval Scotland that contracted the plague. From a sample of 400 parish records, you find that 22 died of the plague. Until your study was done, the assumption in the literature was that 10% of the population had died. Test whether this assumption was valid using a 2% tolerance level for Type I errors and use both one- and two-tail tests.

Answer:

First make the calculation by hand:

(1) Specify the null and alternative hypotheses:

H_0: $\pi = 10\%$
H_1: $\pi \neq 10\%$ ($\Rightarrow$ 2-tail test)

(2) Specify the test statistic and the threshold significance level:

$\alpha = 0.02$

$$z_i = \frac{p - \pi}{\sqrt{\frac{\pi(1-\pi)}{n}}}$$

where,

π	=	the population proportion
p	=	the sample proportion = x/n
x	=	the no. of items in sample with the attribute of interest
n	=	the sample size.

$$z_c = \frac{0.055 - 0.1}{\sqrt{\frac{0.1(1-0.1)}{400}}} = \frac{-.045}{\sqrt{\frac{0.09}{400}}} = \frac{-.045}{0.015} = -3.00$$

(3) Reject H_0 iff P < α where α = 0.02

This will happen if $z_c < -2.33$ or if $z_c > 2.33$, where 2.33 is the z-value associated with $\alpha = 0.02$. Since $z_c = -3.0$, we know we can safely reject H_0.

(4) Compute P = 2x(Prob(z < -3))

= 2x 0.0013 = 0.0026

Since P < 0.02 we can reject H_0.

I.e. the chances of observing p (our sample proportion) assuming H_0 (π = 10%) to be true are so small that we are forced to question this assumption.

You could alternatively use the **H_L1P** macro syntax as follows:

H_L1P n=(400) x=(22) pi=(0.1).

This syntax results in the following output:

```
Large sample sig. test for one proportion
           N          P        SE_PI          Z    SIGZ_2TL   SIGZ_LTL   SIGZ_UTL
   400.00000     .05500       .01500   -3.00000      .00270     .00135     .99865
```

H_L1P therefore estimates the significance level for the two-tail test to be 0.00270, confirming our decision to reject the null that the population proportion equals 10%. If we carry out a lower-tail test (i.e. where the alternative hypothesis is H_1: $\pi < \pi_0$) then the probability of a Type I error is even smaller (0.00135) and so we can say with confidence that the proportion of citizens in medieval Scotland that contracted the plague is less than the received wisdom of 10%.

6.6.1 Using the Syntax When You Only Have p and n:

Sometimes you only have p, the sample proportion, and you don't have x. You can of course calculate x by multiplying n by p. So in the above example, if you were only told that $p = 0.055$ and that $n = 400$, you would calculate $x = 0.055 \times 400 = 22$, and enter the arguments accordingly into the **H_L1P n=(?) x=(?) pi=(?).** command.

Exercise 6.6.1a Hypothesis Tests:

In your dissertation sample of 59 nurses, 29 had performed a manual bowel evacuation. You want to test the hypothesis that, as part of the general broadening in the range of tasks performed by nurses, more nurses are performing manual bowel evacuations compared with 10 years ago when only 40% of nurses had performed the procedure. Also test whether there has been any change since 5 years ago when the proportion was 45%. Compare your answer with the 90% confidence interval.

Answer:

Only the macro syntax results are presented below, but you should attempt to work through each of the four steps of the hypothesis testing procedure. Your results should match those presented below:

H_L1P n=(59) x=(29) pi=(40).

Large sample sig. test for one proportion

N	P	SE_PI	Z	SIGZ_2TL	SIGZ_LTL	SIGZ_UTL
59.00000	.49153	.06378	1.43503	.15128	.92436	.07564

If the null hypothesis is that the population proportion of nurses performing manual bowel evacuations (MBE) is greater than 0.40, then the results for the upper-tail test show that we can reject the null hypothesis at the 10% significance level (i.e. probability of a type one error on the upper-tail test is 0.08 and so is less than 0.1) but not at the 5% significance level. So we can reject the null hypothesis that there has been no increase in the proportion of nurses performing MBEs from 10 years ago. However, if we do a two-tail test, we cannot reject the null. However, if we re-run the test assuming the population proportion is 0.45, we find that the significance level associated with the upper-tail test has risen to 0.26 (i.e. there is a 26% chance that if we reject the null, we do so incorrectly).

H_L1P n=(59) x=(29) pi=(0.45).

Large sample sig. test for one proportion

N	P	SE_PI	Z	SIGZ_2TL	SIGZ_LTL	SIGZ_UTL
59.00000	.49153	.06477	.64114	.52143	.73928	.26072

Now let's look at the 90% **confidence interval** for the proportion of nurses performing MBEs, calculated using the **CI_L1P** syntax introduced in Chapter 4:

CI_L1P n=(59) x=(29) c=(.90).

Confidence Interval for a Single Population Proportion (TRADITIONAL method):

N	X	CONFID	PTRAD	ZSTAR	SE_TRAD	ETRAD	LOW_TRAD	UP_TRAD
59.00000	29.00000	.900000	.491525	-1.64485	.065085	.107055	.384470	.598581

Confidence Interval for a Single Population Proportion (WILSON method):

N	X	CONFID	PWLSN	ZSTAR	SE_WLSN	EWLSN	LOW_WLSN	UP_WLSN
59.00000	29.00000	.900000	.492063	-1.64485	.062986	.103603	.388461	.595666

The Wilson estimate (which in this case is almost identical to the result from the traditional method) tells us that we are 90% sure that the proportion of nurses performing MBEs lies between 39% and 60%. This is a very wide interval which incorporates both the proportion estimated 5 years ago and even the proportion estimated 10 years ago. It is not surprising, therefore, that we cannot reject either of the null hypotheses when using a two-tail test. If we had a larger sample we would be able to narrow this CI considerably.

Exercise 6.6.1b Hypothesis Tests:

For your PhD you interview 102 drug users in Glasgow and find that 70 had shoplifted to support their habit. Before the advent of "Big Issue" magazine, it was estimated that 78% of drug users in Glasgow shoplifted to support their habit. Test the hypothesis that the shoplifting rate is now lower amongst drug users. What would be the effect on your results if you had a smaller sample (e.g. 35, of whom 25 had shoplifted)? Compare your answer with the 95% confidence interval.

Answer:

Only the macro syntax results are presented below, but you should attempt to work through each of the four steps of the hypothesis testing procedure.

H_L1P n=(102) x=(70) pi=(0.78).

Large sample sig. test for one proportion

N	P	SE_PI	Z	SIGZ_2TL	SIGZ_LTL	SIGZ_UTL
102.00000	.68627	.04102	-2.28507	.02231	.01115	.98885

The lower-tail significance level is 0.01115 which is relatively low (if we reject H_0 there would be a 1% chance that we had done so incorrectly). So we can reject the hypothesis that shoplifting rates have remained the same since the advent of the Big Issue in favour of the alternative hypothesis that shoplifting rates amongst the drug addicts have fallen.

Comparing this result with the 95% Wilson confidence interval:

CI_L1P n=(102) x=(70) c=(.95).

Confidence Interval for a Single Population Proportion (WILSON method):

N	X	CONFID	PWLSN	ZSTAR	SE_WLSN	EWLSN	LOW_WLSN	UP_WLSN
102.0000	70.00000	.950000	.679245	-1.95996	.045336	.088858	.590388	.768103

we find that the pre-Big Issue shoplifting rate of 78% lies outside of the interval based on your recent sample, and so the difference between the proportion estimated in your sample and that in the pre-Big Issue study is unlikely to be due to random sample variation alone.

However, note that unless the earlier estimate was based on the full population of drug addicts people (unlikely) then there would be a random error due to sampling variability associated with the earlier estimate also (see below for the hypothesis test for comparing two proportions).

Exercise 6.6.1c Hypothesis Tests:

From the newspaper article below, compute a confidence interval for the proportion of the Metro survey who voted for The Bard. Also, conduct a hypothesis test at the 5% level of significance that The Bard won more than 18% of the vote. Do a second hypothesis test that he gained more than 16% of the vote.

Sorry, Winston, the Bard's Best

One was a political giant who saved Britain in its darkest hour, the other a literary giant whose influence is still prominent after 400 years. Among Metro readers, cultural heritage appears to outweigh the protection of civilisation – after William Shakespeare beat Winston Churchill in our own survey to find the greatest Briton. The Bard was backed by 19 percent of readers, pushing the World War II leader into second place on 18 percent. Charles Darwin was third, with 16 percent. Support for Shakespeare in Metro's Urban Life study was highest in Manchester (23 percent) and London (21 percent), and greater among women (23 percent) than men (16 percent). Results of the survey of 3,000 readers aged 18 to 44 were at odds with the BBC's Great Britons poll on Sunday, in which Churchill came top and Shakespeare was fifth.

(Metro newspaper, Nov 26, 2002, page 3)

Answer:

Only the macro syntax results are presented below, but you should attempt to work through each of the four steps of the hypothesis testing procedure.

The confidence interval for The Bard vote is obtained using the following syntax:

CI_L1P n=(3000) x=(570) c=(.95).

which results in the following output:

Confidence Interval for a Single Population Proportion (WILSON method):

N	X	CONFID	PWLSN	ZSTAR	SE_WLSN	EWLSN	LOW_WLSN	UP_WLSN
3000.000	570.0000	.950000	.190413	-1.95996	.007164	.014040	.176372	.204453

So we are 95% certain that the proportion of all Metro Readers who voted for Shakespeare lies between 17.6% and 20.4%. The lower bound of this range is lower than the vote for Churchill at 18% so we cannot say that The Bard is more popular than Churchill. This is confirmed by the hypothesis test where we assume x = 0.19 x 3000 = 570; and π = 18:

H_L1P n=(3000) x=(570) pi=(0.18).

Large sample sig. test for one proportion

N	P	SE_PI	Z	SIGZ_2TL	SIGZ_LTL	SIGZ_UTL
3000.00000	.19000	.00701	1.42566	.15397	.92302	.07698

The upper-tail significance level is 0.08 which means that we cannot say that the proportion of all Metro Readers who voted for the Bard is significantly greater than 18% (at the 5% significance level).

When we run the same test, but this time against the null hypothesis of 16%, we find a very low probability of a Type I error: the upper significance level is 0.000004, suggesting that if we reject the null hypothesis (that the proportion of all readers who voted for the Bard equals 16%) in favour of the alternative hypothesis (that the proportion of all readers who voted for the Bard is greater than 16%) there is less than a one in a hundred thousand chance of doing so incorrectly.

H_L1P n=(3000) x=(570) pi=(0.16).

Large sample sig. test for one proportion

N	P	SE_PI	Z	SIGZ_2TL	SIGZ_LTL	SIGZ_UTL
3000.00000	.19000	.00669	4.48211	.00001	1.00000	.00000

However, this does not mean that we can say that more voted for Shakespeare than for Darwin, because the Darwin estimate of 16% will also be subject to sampling variability. We would need to run a confidence interval on the Darwin vote and see if it overlaps with the Shakespeare vote. As the following table shows, the Darwin confidence interval (0.147, 0.173) does not in fact overlap with the Shakespeare confidence interval:

Confidence interval for the Darwin vote:
CI_L1P n=(3000) x=(480) c=(.95).

Confidence Interval for a Single Population Proportion (WILSON method):

N	X	CONFID	PWLSN	ZSTAR	SE_WLSN	EWLSN	LOW_WLSN	UP_WLSN
3000.000	480.0000	.950000	.160453	-1.95996	.006696	.013125	.147328	.173578

Our job would be made simpler, of course, if there were a *two-proportion* hypothesis test, and this is objective of our next and final hypothesis test to be considered in this chapter.

6.7 Large Sample Significance Test on Two Proportions

We follow the same established logic as applied in the tests considered above only we use the following formula to compute the z score:

$$z = \frac{(p_1 - p_2)}{SE_{Dp}}$$

where, $SE_{Dp} = \sqrt{p(1-p)\left(\frac{1}{n_1} + \frac{1}{n2}\right)}$ and, $p = \frac{x_1 + x_2}{n_1 + n_2}$

You can alternatively use the following macro syntax to run the test:

H_L2P H_L2P calculates the large sample significance test for the equality of two proportions (see *Moore & McCabe, 2003, pp. 591-592*). The arguments enter the syntax in the following way:

```
H_L2P   n1=(?)  n2=(?)  x1=(?)  x2=(?).
```

Example 6.7 Hypothesis Tests on Two Proportions:

Suppose 1,630 out of a random sample of 7,180 black males have experienced stop-and-search procedures from the police in London, compared with 1,684 out of a sample of 9,916 white males. You want to test whether the difference in the proportions was due to sampling variation or due to a genuine difference in the incidence of stop-and-search across the two populations.

Answer:

The null hypothesis would of course be that the proportion stopped-and-searched in the black population of males is the same as the proportion stopped-and-searched in the population of white males. The following syntax treats black males as *population one*, and white males as *population two*. We want to conduct an upper-tail test because our alternative hypothesis is that the proportion of black males is greater than the proportion of white males stopped by the police. We also want to run a two-tail test where the alternative hypothesis is simply that the two proportions are different.

Running the following syntax will give the results of both the two-tail and upper-tail tests:

```
H_L2P   n1=(7180)  n2=(9916)  x1=(1630)  x2=(1684).
```

P1	P2	SE	Z	SIGZ_2TL	SIGZ_LTL	SIGZ_UTL
.22702	.16983	.00613	9.33658	.00000	1.00000	.00000

You can see from the output that both the two-tail hypothesis and the upper-tail hypothesis are conclusively rejected. The chance of false rejection is so small in either case that five decimal places of accuracy are insufficient to detect it.

Exercise 6.7 Hypothesis Tests on Two Proportions:

1. Re-do the Metro survey question from the previous set of exercises using the two-proportions t-test. How do your results compare with your previous answer?

2. Two surveys of mortgage payment protection insurance (MPPI) are carried out, one on single parents with 1 child and one on single parents with 3 children. Amongst the first group, 67 out of a sample of 300 were found to have taken out MPPI, compared with 15 out of a sample of 101 in the second group. Is take-up significantly lower amongst the households with three children?

   Answer:

   Only the macro syntax results are presented below, but you should attempt to work through each of the four steps of the hypothesis testing procedure.

   Let sample one be 1 child families and sample two be 3 child families. The summary data are then entered into the **H_L2P** syntax as follows:

   H_L2P n1=(300) n2=(101) x1=(67) x2=(15).

P1	P2	SE	Z	SIGZ_2TL	SIGZ_LTL	SIGZ_UTL
.22333	.14851	.04640	1.61250	.10685	.94657	.05343

   The question of whether take-up is lower amongst the second sample (i.e. 3 child families) can be answered using an upper-tail test (i.e. where the alternative hypothesis is H_1: □$_1$ > □$_2$). The upper-tail test reveals a chance of false rejection of H_0 of just over 5%, which is just about enough for us to be confident that our alternative hypothesis holds true in the populations.

6.8 Conclusion

We have considered a range of hypothesis tests in this chapter, including test for equality of two means assuming homogenous variances, and also a test for equality of two means assuming different variances (**H_S2Mp** and **H_S1Md** respectively). We found that the simple *F*-ratio test for equality of variances is a very approximate measure that should only be used if we do not have the original data (the Levene's test is much more precise than the simple *F*-ratio test performed by the **H_S2VF** macro command, but requires you to have access to the full set of observations rather than simply the summary statistics). We also learned how to run hypothesis tests on one and two proportions using the **H_L1P** and **H_L2P** macro commands.

7 Relationships Between Variables

Aim:
This chapter introduces methods of examining relationships between variables.

Objectives:
By the end of this section, the you should be able to understand how to examine relationships between categorical variables using *two-way tables* (also known as contingency tables or cross-tabs) and the *Chi-square test for independence*. You should also have a sound grasp of regression terminology, understand the meaning of the *BLUE* acronym, and be able to run and interpret regression procedures run on real data using SPSS.

Further Reading:
D. S. Moore and G. P. McCabe (2003) *Introduction to the Practice of Statistics,* 4th Ed., Freeman, New York, Chapter 9, and Chapters 2, 10 and 11.
Kennedy, P. (1994) *A Guide to Econometrics,* MIT Press, Cambridge, MA
Pryce, G. (2006) *Advanced Regression in SPSS*

Plan:

7.1 Introduction

Often the questions of greatest interest to social science and business researchers are concerned with relationships between variables:

- *Is employee loyalty related to length of tenure?*
- *Is entrepreneurial ability related to academic achievement?*
- *Is social class related to political allegiance?*
- *Is income related to education?*
- *Is work alienation related to job monotony?*
- *Does the social class of parents determine the class of their children?*

We are also often interested in the direction of causation, but this is more difficult to prove empirically – usually we have to assume a particular direction of causation based on our theory. Limited methods for testing for causation do exist (such as the Granger Causality test) but are only applicable to time-series variables, which require a specialist set of techniques to analyse and are therefore beyond the scope of this book.

The first half of this chapter will consider how to test for the existence of a relationship between two variables when they are both categorical. The easiest way to represent relationships between categorical variables is to use *contingency tables*, also called *cross-tabs* or *two-way tables*. They show the number of observations (or % of observations) in particular categories and naturally lead to a test of independence which has a Chi-square (or "$\chi 2$") distribution.

The second half of the chapter is devoted to analysing the relationship between a continuous dependent variable and multiple independent variables.

7.2 Relationships Between Categorical Variables

How does one test for the existence of a relationship between two categorical variables? For example, suppose we are interested in whether there is a relationship between social class and access to higher education. Neither of these variables are easily measured as a continuum, and most measures place households and/or individuals into a set of ordered categories. For example, education might be coded as follows:

6 if has PhD,
5 if has Masters,
4 if has Degree,
3 if has Highers,
2 if has Standard Grades,
1 if no qualifications

We have attached the value 4 to individuals with a university degree, and a value of 3 to those who have only Highers. However, these scores are arbitrary. We might more reasonably attach 4 to those with Highers, and ascribe a value of 10 to those with degrees, 15 to those with Masters degrees and so on.

For social class, we might have a similar ordered classification system (underclass, working class, lower middle class, upper middle class) and a similar problem of arbitrary scoring. Some variables, like voting preferences, are inherently categorical (you either voted for a particular party, or you didn't) while others could feasibly be measured as a continuous variable, but are often broken into categories, usually in the hope of increasing questionnaire response rates (most people would prefer to specify their income bracket rather than their precise earnings, for example).

All of these variables are categorical but nevertheless have an intrinsic order to the categories. For other categorical variables this is not the case. Country of origin, for example, may have no meaningful ordering in your analysis, but nevertheless be of interest.

The simplest way of testing for a relationship between categorical variables is to use contingency tables and corresponding tests for independence. Since these tests are rather long-winded to compute by hand, it is recommended that you use SPSS's easy to follow built-in facilities, which we shall now explain.

7.2.1 Contingency Tables and Chi-Square Test for Independence

To run contingency tables in SPSS, go to the data edit window, click Analyse, Descriptive Statistics, and Crosstabs. Once in the **Crosstabs** window you can transfer variables from your variable list into the Row box and Column box. You can also specify which statistics you want SPSS to report by clicking on the Statistics button at the bottom of the Crosstabs screen, and you can specify the information that is to be reported in each cell of the table by clicking on the Cells button. There are also a range of formatting options that can be accessed by clicking on the Format button.

Example 7.2.1: Relationship Between Social Class and Voting Preferences

Suppose you have collected data on voting preferences and social class. Your data were collected using a simple telephone questionnaire which achieved 556 responses. Your survey consisted of two simple questions: *(1) Do you consider yourself to be working class?* and *(2) Did you vote New Labour at the last general election?*

Everyone who responded answered either yes or no to both of these questions. You entered your data into an SPSS file and saved it as **votes.sav.** How would you establish whether there was a relationship between whether someone described themselves as working class and whether they voted New Labour?

Answer:

First open up the **votes.sav** dataset:

```
GET FILE='C:\STATISTICS\votes.sav'.
```

Go to the Variable View window and look at how the variables have been coded. Then run a simple contingency table (known as *cross-tab* in SPSS) by selecting Analyse, Descriptive Statistics, and Crosstabs. Then enter the **workingclass** variable in the Row(s) box, enter **votedlabour** in the Column(s) box and click OK. (or click Paste if you want the syntax to be pasted to your syntax window). Alternatively you can enter the following syntax:

```
CROSSTABS /TABLES=workingclass BY votedlabour.
```

This will produce the most basic cross-tab which lists simply the count in each category:

workingclass * votedlabour Crosstabulation

Count

		votedlabour		
		Voted New Labour	Did not vote New Labour	Total
workingclass	Working Class	203	154	357
	Not working Class	104	95	199
Total		307	249	556

You can add % in each category by returning to the cross-tabs window, selecting the Cells button, and choosing which percentages you want. You can also choose to include Observed as well as (or instead of) Expected counts in each category, and you can select Row, Column, and Total percentages.

Suppose you believe that social class determines voting preference. More precisely, you believe that working class people are more likely to vote New Labour. If this is true you would expect the proportion that voted New Labour to be higher among those who described themselves as working class. It would be logical, therefore, to look at the incidence of New Labour votes among those who are working class and compare this percentage with those who described themselves as not being working class.

In terms of the contingency table, you need to request the row percentages, which you can either do using the menu system (click Analyse, Descriptive Statistics, Crosstabs, Cells, Row, Continue and OK), or by amending your syntax:

```
CROSSTABS /TABLES=workingclass BY votedlabour /CELLS= COUNT ROW.
```

This will produce the following table:

workingclass * votedlabour Crosstabulation

			votedlabour		
			Voted New Labour	Did not vote New Labour	Total
workingclass	Working Class	Count	203	154	357
		% within workingclass	56.9%	43.1%	100.0%
	Not working Class	Count	104	95	199
		% within workingclass	52.3%	47.7%	100.0%
Total		Count	307	249	556
		% within workingclass	55.2%	44.8%	100.0%

We can now see that, of those who described themselves as working class, 56.9% voted New Labour (and 43.1% did not), whereas only 52.3% of those said they were *not* working class voted New Labour. This seems to confirm your theory, but how do you know that these findings are not due to random sampling variation? You need to find a way of formally testing whether these two variables are not contingent on each other (i.e. independent).

7.2.2 Chi-Square Test for Independence

Note that this test is *non-parametric*. That is, it makes no assumptions regarding the distribution of variables you are analysing. The test is rather involved if computed by hand but simple to run in SPSS. If you click on the Statistics button in the Crosstabs window, you will be presented with a range of statistical options, most of which are not covered in this text. The only one we are interested here is the Chi-square statistic in the top left corner. If you check the Chi-square option, or simply add /STATISTIC=CHISQ to your CROSSTABS command, as in the following syntax,

```
CROSSTABS /TABLES=workingclass BY votedlabour /CELLS= COUNT ROW /STATISTIC=CHISQ.
```

you will obtain the following output in addition to your contingency table:

Chi-Square Tests

	Value	df	Asymp. Sig. (2-sided)	Exact Sig. (2-sided)	Exact Sig. (1-sided)
Pearson Chi-Square	1.094[b]	1	.296		
Continuity Correction[a]	.916	1	.339		
Likelihood Ratio	1.093	1	.296		
Fisher's Exact Test				.328	.169
Linear-by-Linear Association	1.092	1	.296		
N of Valid Cases	556				

a. Computed only for a 2x2 table

The only figure you are interested is the *Pearson Chi-square.* This statistic is the result of a test of the null hypothesis that the two variables are independent. If the *P* value (found in the third column of figures under "Asymp. Sig (2-sided)" is small (e.g. less than 0.05) then you can reject the null hypothesis in favour of the alternative hypothesis that there is indeed some level of relationship between the two variables. In the above example, *P* is 0.296, so there is a 29.6% chance that if we reject H_0, it would in fact be true). It would therefore be too risky to reject the null hypothesis that social class and voting preference are independent. In other words, we have no conclusive proof that there is a relationship between these two variables.

Before we move on to consider relationships between continuous variables, we should really try to understand how the Chi-square test works. To do this, we need to revisit the rules of probability discussed in Chapter 2 and so you would do well to review that chapter before progressing.

7.2.3 How the Chi-Square Test for Independence is Calculated

In Chapter 2 we demonstrated how we can use the independence and contingent events probability rules to test for independence. We said that if A and B are *independent*, then the probability of events A and B simultaneously occurring is simply equal to the product of the two events occurring:

$$\Pr(A \cap B) = \Pr(A) \times \Pr(B)$$

However, if A and B are not independent, in other words they are *contingent*, then the probability of them both occurring is equal to the probability of one event multiplied by the contingent probability of the other event (e.g. probability of B given that A has happened):

$$\Pr(A \cap B) = \Pr(A) \times \Pr(B \text{ given } A)$$

We can use the difference between these two rules to test whether events are independent. The basic rationale of this test is to ask whether the distribution of *observed* outcomes resembles the random distribution we would get if events were truly independent. In other words, if we assume independence and calculate the *expected* number of cases in each category of combined outcome, do these figures correspond fairly closely to the actual distribution of outcomes found in our data?

Example 7.2.3a Relationship Between Class and Higher Education

In Chapter 2 we outlined the following scenario: suppose we are interested in whether there is a relationship between social class and access to higher education. We said that one way of testing whether the two are connected is to look at the following categories in our data: working class, middle class, attend University, do not attend University. Suppose we have 300 observations in our data distributed across these categories as follows:

		A	B
		Working Class	**Middle Class**
1	**Go to university**	18	84
2	**Do not go to university**	162	36

To test for independence we need to compare *expected* number of observations in each cell in the above table with the *observed* number of observations in each cell. Given that we already know the observed counts in each cell (given in the table above), the next step is to calculate e_i, the expected number of observations in category *i*. How do we do this? First of all we need to understand what it is we are actually trying to calculate. The "expected number of observations" is, in fact, the number of cases expected in cell *i* assuming that the variables are independent. The formula for e_i is derived by multiplying the probability of an observation falling into category *i* (assuming independence between class and education) by the total number of observations in our entire sample:

$$e_i = \text{expected number of cases in cell } i = \text{Pr(observation being in cell } i) \times n$$

where *n* is the total sample size = 300.

How do we calculate Pr(observation being in cell i)? We use the *independence* probability formula. For example, to compute the probability of an observation in our sample being in cell **A1** of our table, assuming independence, means using the following formula:

$$\Pr(WC \cap Uni) = \Pr(Uni) \times \Pr(WC)$$

Similarly, the probability of an observation in our sample being in cell **A2** is given by:

$$\Pr(WC \cap no\ Uni) = \Pr(no\ Uni) \times \Pr(WC)$$

The probability of an observation in our sample being in cell **B1** is given by:

$$\Pr(MC \cap Uni) = \Pr(Uni) \times \Pr(MC)$$

The probability of an observation in our sample being in cell **B2** is given by:

$$\Pr(MC \cap no\ Uni) = \Pr(no\ Uni) \times \Pr(MC)$$

But how do we work out Pr(Uni), Pr(WC), Pr(*no* Uni), and Pr(MC): the probabilities needed to calculate the above equations? The answer is simple. Because we are assuming for the sake of argument that class and education are independent, we can estimate these probabilities by dividing the total observations in our sample by the total number in the headline category. So, for example, Pr(Uni) assuming independence is given by:

$$\Pr(Uni) = \text{Total no. observations that go to university} \div n = (18 + 84) / 300 = \mathbf{0.34}$$

So the expected number of observations in cell A1 will be given by:

$$\Pr(WC \cap Uni) = \Pr(Uni) \times \Pr(WC)$$

The full workings of computing expected cell counts, e_i, for each cell are given in the table below:

		A **Working Class**	B **Middle Class**
1	**Go to university**	e_{A1} = Pr(Uni) × Pr(WC) × n = (no. at Uni ÷ n) × (no. WC ÷ n) × n = (102 / 300) × (180 /300) × 300 = 0.34 × 0.6 x 300 = **61.2**	e_{B1} = Pr(Uni) × Pr(MC) × n = (no. at Uni ÷ n) × (no. MC ÷ n) × n = (102 / 300) × (120 /300) × 300 = 0.34 × 0.4 × 300 = **40.8**
2	**Do not go to university**	e_{A2} = Pr(no Uni) × Pr(WC) × n = (no. not at Uni ÷ n) × (no. WC ÷ n) × n = (198 / 300) × (180 /300) × 300 = 0.66 × 0.6 × 300 = **118.8**	e_{B2} = Pr(no Uni) × Pr(MC) × n = (no. not at Uni ÷ n) × (no. MC ÷ n) × n = (198 / 300) × (120 /300) × 300 = 0.66 × 0.4 × 300 = **79.2**

We can now compare our observed counts for each cell with the expected counts based on an assumption of independence:

		A Working Class	B Middle Class
1 **Go to university**	*Observed:*	18	84
	Expected:	61.2	40.8
2 **Do not go to university**	*Observed:*	162	36
	Expected:	118.8	79.2

If we had the original data, we could very easily obtain this type of table in SPSS by clicking on Analyse, Descriptive Statistics, Crosstabs, Cells, and selecting Expected count.

If the expected and observed cell counts are similar, then we can reasonably conclude that the two variables – education and class – are *independent*. This is because our observed cell counts would be what we would expect if the variables are truly independent.

In the above example, the differences between observed and expected cell counts are fairly large. If class and education were indeed independent we would expect three times as many people from working class backgrounds to go to university than we observe in our sample. This means that it is very unlikely that class and education are independent.

The hypothetical data we have used here show very large differences between expected and observed cell counts. However, sometimes the differences are much smaller and our conclusions more ambiguous. We would like, therefore, to state what the *probability* is that the two variables are independent. This is where the Pearson Chi-square hypothesis test comes in. The test works as follows:

(1) H_0: *x* and *y* are independent

I.e. Prob(*x*) is ***not*** affected by whether or not *y* occurs

H_1: *x* and *y* are *not* independent

I.e. Prob(*x*) ***is*** affected by *y* occurring.

(2) $\alpha = 0.05$

$$\chi^2 = \sum_{i=1}^{k}\left(\frac{(o_i - e_i)^2}{e_i}\right) \qquad df = (r-1)(c-1)$$

where:

- k = no. of categories
- e_i = expected (given H_0) no. of sample observations in the ith category
- o_i = actual no. of sample observations in the ith category
- df = degrees of freedom = no. of parameters that have to be estimated from the sample data.
- r = no. of rows in table
- c = no. of columns in table

(3) Reject H_0 iff $P < \alpha$

(4) Calculate *P* and decide.

The tricky bit, if you are doing the calculation by hand, is step (4): computing the Chi-square value needed to derive the significance level *P*. We know from our first table,

		A Working Class	B Middle Class
1	**Go to university**	18	84
2	**Do not go to university**	162	36

that there are four cells (so $k = 4$) and we know the values of o_i, the actual number of sample observations in each category, so let's enter these into the formula to make it easier to follow where the numbers have come from:

$$\chi^2 = \sum_{i=1}^{k}\left(\frac{(o_i - e_i)^2}{e_i}\right) = \left(\frac{(18 - e_i)^2}{e_i}\right) + \left(\frac{(84 - e_i)^2}{e_i}\right) + \left(\frac{(162 - e_i)^2}{e_i}\right) + \left(\frac{(136 - e_i)^2}{e_i}\right)$$

In our third and final table,

		A Working Class	B Middle Class
1 **Go to university**	*Observed:*	18	84
	Expected:	61.2	40.8
2 **Do not go to university**	*Observed:*	162	36
	Expected:	118.8	79.2

we worked out the expected number of observations in each cell assuming the two variables are independent, so we can now insert the values for e_i into our formula:

$$\chi^2 = \sum_{i=1}^{k}\left(\frac{(o_i - e_i)^2}{e_i}\right) = \left(\frac{(18-61.2)^2}{61.2}\right) + \left(\frac{(84-40.8)^2}{40.8}\right) + \left(\frac{(162-118.8)^2}{118.8}\right) + \left(\frac{(136-79.2)^2}{79.2}\right)$$

Now let's compute the values in the parentheses in each numerator:

$$\chi^2 = \sum_{i=1}^{k}\left(\frac{(o_i - e_i)^2}{e_i}\right) = \left(\frac{(-43.2)^2}{61.2}\right) + \left(\frac{(43.2)^2}{40.8}\right) + \left(\frac{(43.2)^2}{118.8}\right) + \left(\frac{(56.8)^2}{79.2}\right)$$

then work out the value of each fraction and the overall sum:

$$\chi^2 = \sum_{i=1}^{k}\left(\frac{(o_i - e_i)^2}{e_i}\right) = (30.494) + (45.741) + (15.709) + (40.735) = 132.679$$

Degrees of freedom are calculated as follows:

$df = (r\text{-}1)(c\text{-}1) = (2\text{-}1)(2\text{-}1) = 1$

If you are computing the Chi-square statistic by hand, and you want to use SPSS to compute probability associated with your test statistic, then you can use the following function as part of the COMPUTE command: CDF.CHISQ(c2c,df) calculates Prob(c2 < c2c) with df degrees of freedom. (Like the *t*-distribution, the shape of the Chi-square distribution – and hence the probabilities associated with the regions under the curve – changes with the number of degrees of freedom). You would use this function as part of a command to create a new variable, as in the following syntax:

```
COMPUTE chi_prob = 1 - CDF.CHISQ(c2c,df).
EXECUTE.
```

In this case, the Chi-square statistic is computed as 1.094 with 1 degree of freedom, so we would run the following syntax (note that we have included the FORMATS command to obtain a different number of decimal places on our new variable than that of the default setting):

```
COMPUTE chi2sig = 1 - CDF.CHISQ(132.679,1).
FORMATS chi2sig (F5.4).
EXECUTE.
```

This results in a new variable chi2sig set equal to 0.0000 for all observations. In other words, the chances of false rejection of the null of independence are very small indeed, and so we can confidently assert that there is evidence of a relationship between social class and attendance at university.

However, although we have established that there is a relationship between the two variables, we cannot say from the data alone which variable *causes* the other. This is where social science theory (rather than statistical theory) is crucial. Because class background precedes going to university it is very unlikely indeed that attending university determines class background (even if you wanted to, you could not change the social class of your parents – that is determined long before you go to university). So in this case, the direction of causation is pretty clear.

Example 7.2.3b Relationship Between First Time Buyer and Location

Is there a relationship between whether a borrower is a first time buyer (FTB) and whether they live in Durham (D) or Cumberland (C)? The only difficult concept to grasp in the Chi-square test is how we calculate e_i the expected number of observations in category *i*? We calculate this as the number of cases expected in category *i* assuming the null hypothesis of independence of the two variables. The formula for e_i is the probability of an observation falling into category *i* multiplied by the total number of observations:

$$e_i = \Pr(x \text{ and y occur assuming } H_0) \times n$$

Probability theory states that:

if *x* and *y* are ***independent***, then the probability of events *x* and *y* simultaneously occurring is simply equal to the product of the two events occurring:

$$\text{Prob}(x \cap y) = \text{Prob}(x) \times \text{Prob}(y)$$

if *x* and *y* are not independent, then the last term of the above formula changes to include a conditional probability term:

$$\text{Prob}(x \cap y) = \text{Prob}(x) \times \text{Prob}(y \text{ given that } x \text{ has occurred})$$

So, if $FTB_{Y \text{ or } N}$ and $County_{D \text{ or } C}$ are independent (i.e. assuming H_0) then:

Prob(FTB_Y Ç $County_D$) = Prob(FTB_Y)´Prob($County_D$)

where *Y* stands for *yes*, and *N* stands for *no*. So FTB_Y indicates that the purchaser was a first time buyer, whereas FTB_N means that he/she was not. The expected number of cases for each of the four mutually exclusive categories are as follows:

	$County_C$	$County_D$
FTB_N	$\Pr(FTB_N) \times \Pr(County_C) \times n$	$\Pr(FTB_N) \times \Pr(County_D) \times n$
FTB_Y	$\Pr(FTB_Y) \times \Pr(County_C) \times n$	$\Pr(FTB_Y) \times \Pr(County_D) \times n$

Note that,

Prob(FTB_N) = Total no. cases FTB_N ÷ All observations

which we can substitute into the cell formulae used in the previous table:

	$County_C$	$County_D$
FTB_N	$\left(\frac{\text{Total}FTB_N}{n}\right) \times \left(\frac{\text{Total}County_C}{n}\right) \times n$	$\left(\frac{\text{Total}FTB_N}{n}\right) \times \left(\frac{\text{Total}County_D}{n}\right) \times n$
FTB_Y	$\left(\frac{\text{Total}FTB_Y}{n}\right) \times \left(\frac{\text{Total}County_C}{n}\right) \times n$	$\left(\frac{\text{Total}FTB_Y}{n}\right) \times \left(\frac{\text{Total}County_D}{n}\right) \times n$

We can see how this works if we apply it to the following first time buyer (FTB) data:

Count

		House County from Postcode		
		Cumber	Durham	Total
first time buyer y=2 n=1	N	203	154	357
	Y	104	95	199
Total		307	249	556

To see how these figures enter our calculation of the expected counts, we have circled the relevant figures:

	$County_C$	$County_D$
FTB_N	$\left(\frac{357}{556}\right) \times \left(\frac{307}{556}\right) \times n$	$\left(\frac{357}{556}\right) \times \left(\frac{249}{556}\right) \times n$
FTB_Y	$\left(\frac{199}{556}\right) \times \left(\frac{307}{556}\right) \times n$	$\left(\frac{199}{556}\right) \times \left(\frac{249}{556}\right) \times n$

Working through the calculations gives us the following expected count:

first time buyer y=2 n=1 * House County from Postcode Crosstabulation

Expected Count

		House County from Postcode		
		Cumber	Durham	Total
first time buyer y=2 n=1	N	197.1	159.9	357.0
	Y	109.9	89.1	199.0
Total		307.0	249.0	556.0

To obtain this table in SPSS, go to Analyse, Descriptive Statistics, Crosstabs, Cells, and choose *expected count* rather than *observed.*

We are now ready to calculate our Chi-square value:

$$\chi^2 = \sum_{i=1}^{k}\left(\frac{(o_i - e_i)^2}{e_i}\right)$$

All the data we need for this formula is included in the following table:

first time buyer y=2 n=1 * House County from Postcode Crosstabulation

			House County from Postcode		
			Cumber	Durham	Total
first time buyer y=2 n=1	N	Count	203	154	357
		Expected Count	197.1	159.9	357.0
	Y	Count	104	95	199
		Expected Count	109.9	89.1	199.0
Total		Count	307	249	556
		Expected Count	307.0	249.0	556.0

which are entered into the formula as follows:

$$\chi^2 = \sum_{i=1}^{k}\left(\frac{(o_i - e_i)^2}{e_i}\right)$$

$$= \left(\frac{(203-197.1)^2}{197.1}\right) + \left(\frac{(154-159.9)^2}{159.9}\right) + \left(\frac{(104-109.9)^2}{109.9}\right) + \left(\frac{(95-89.1)^2}{89.1}\right)$$

$$= 1.094071$$

We can work out the appropriate significance level using the following syntax:

```
COMPUTE chi2sig = 1 - CDF.CHISQ(1.094,1).
FORMATS chi2sig (F5.4).
EXECUTE.
```

which yields a significance level of 0.2956.

Each step of the test is summarised below:

(1) H_0: FTB and County are independent
H_1: there is some relationship

(2) $\alpha = 0.05$

$$\chi^2 = \sum_{i=1}^{k}\left(\frac{(o_i - e_i)^2}{e_i}\right) = 1.094071 \qquad df = (r-1)(c-1) = (2-1)(2-1) = 1$$

(3) Reject H_0 iff $P < \alpha$

(4) Calculate the significance level (i.e. proabability of false rejection)

$P = \text{Prob}(\chi^2 > \chi^2_c) = \mathbf{0.29557}$ **Do *not* reject H_0**

I.e. if we were to reject H_0, there would be a 1 in 3 chance of us rejecting it incorrectly, and so we cannot do so. In other words, FTB and County are independent.

We cannot, therefore, reject the null of independence. Notice that the figures used in this example are exactly the same as those used in our fist example (class background and voting preference), so you can refer back to that example to see how the SPSS output was derived.

7.3 Regression Analysis

Regression is used when we want to estimate the relationship between a dependent variable and two or more explanatory variables, where those variables are all scale variables (i.e. continuous rather than categorical). Regression (in its simplest form) employs a technique called 'Ordinary Least Squares' of which any student of statistics should have a basic understanding.

Consider two variables, *X* and *Y*. You believe *Y* to be determined by *X*; that is, you hypothesise that *X* is an "independent" variable (ie not determined by *Y*), and *Y* is a "dependent" variable (ie dependent on *X*). Now imagine a scatter plot of a sample of *Y* observations, such as in the figure below. You can obtain a scatter plot of any two variables in your data by clicking on Graphs, Scatter, Simple, Define, and then select which variables you want to plot, and click OK or Paste. Alternatively you could use the following syntax,

```
GRAPH /SCATTERPLOT(BIVAR)= Y WITH X .
```

where Y is the name of the variable you want to put on the vertical axis (usually the dependent variable) and X is the name of the variable to be plotted on the horizontal axis (usually the independent variable).

A Scatter Plot of *Y* observations on *X*.

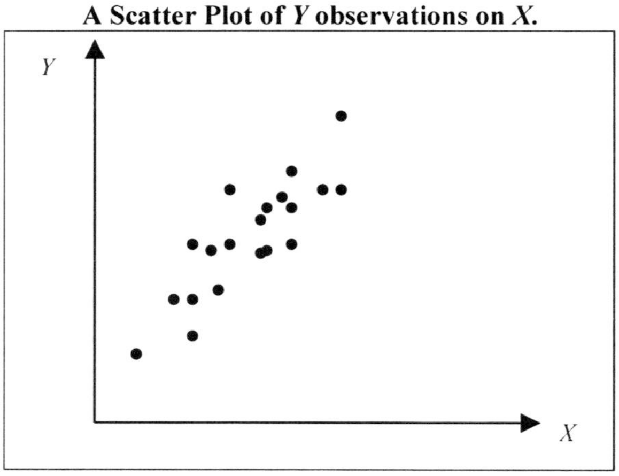

We can see from the scatter of points on this particular plot that there may be some relationship between the two variables, possibly a linear (i.e. "straight line") relationship. We could guesstimate the nature of this relationship by using a ruler to draw what looks to be the line of best fit.

Alternatively, we could use a simple mathematical formula called OLS (ordinary least squares). This draws the line that minimises the sum of squared deviations from the line to each scatter point above and below it. In SPSS, you can add a line of best fit by double clicking on the scatter plot you have created using the syntax described above, then right-clicking on the scatter-points in the body of the graph, and selecting Add Fit Line at Total, selecting Linear, Apply, Close, then closing the graph itself.

As with any linear relationship, the equation of the computed line will comprise of a *Y intercept* (also called "the constant") denoted by α, and a *slope coefficient* donated by β:

$$Y = \alpha + \beta X$$

If this is the "true" or "underlying" relationship between Y and X that we would observe from the population, we use OLS to *estimate* values for α and β (usually denoted α-hat and β-hat respectively). However, because any straight line we draw through the scatter points will rarely fit exactly (i.e. deviations will not be zero), even when run on the population, we have to include an error term, ε. Thus:

$$Y_i = \alpha + \beta X_i + \varepsilon_i,$$

where i is the ith observation of Y and X. Note that once we have estimated the straight line relationship between Y and X, we can use that estimated relationship to tell us what we would predict the value of Y to be for any value of X. So, suppose we only have 80 observations on X and Y and we want to estimate what the value of Y would be if X was 23.7. Of the 80 observations on X, none of them equal 23.7. Now, once we have estimated the values of α and β, we can use them to give us a predicted value for Y given that X = 23.7:

$$Y_i = \alpha + \beta \times 23.7 + \varepsilon_i$$

Ignoring the error term for now, let's assume that our estimates of α and β, come out as 3.6 and 7.4 respectively, then the value of Y when X is 23.7 is calculated as follows:

$$Y_i = 3.6 + 7.4 \times 23.7$$

$$= \mathbf{178.98}$$

7.3.1 OLS Estimates are BLUE

One of the major attractions of using OLS (Ordinary Least Squares) is that, given certain assumptions, the OLS estimates for α and β (α-hat and β-hat) are **BLUE** (**B**est **L**inear **U**nbiased **E**stimators). They are *best* in that they have the minimum variance compared with other estimators (i.e. given repeated samples, the OLS estimates for α and β vary less between samples than any other sample estimates for α and β). In other words, if we use OLS to estimate β, the standard error of the sampling distribution for these estimates will be as small as it can possibly be.

OLS estimates are also *linear* in the sense that a straight line relationship is assumed. They are *unbiased* because, in repeated samples, the mean of all the estimates achieved will tend towards the population values for α and β. In other words, the mean of the sampling distribution of the OLS estimate of β will equal the true population value of β. If this were not the case, we would say that the estimates were *biased*, and we would measure the bias as the difference between the true population value of the coefficient we are trying to estimate and the average value achieved from running the regression on repeated samples.

And they are *estimates* in that the true values of α and β cannot be known, and so we are using statistical techniques to arrive at the best possible assessment of their values, given the information available.

For estimates to be BLUE, however, certain assumptions have to be met. These assumptions, and what happens when they fail, are considered below. First, however, it should be noted that we have so far only considered the case of one RHS (right-hand side) variable. When we only have one RHS variable, our regression is called *simple regression.* When we have more than one explanatory variable, (eg $Y_i = \alpha + \beta_1 X_{1i} + \beta_2 X_{2i} + \varepsilon_i$) the analysis becomes that of *multiple regression.*

Usually Xs are assumed to be variables that influence Y (Y is said to be dependent on the Xs). It should also be noted that there are several alternative terms used in the literature for Y and $X_1, X_2 \ldots X_k$. This is often confusing to someone new to the subject, so I have reproduced the following table from Maddala (1992, p61).

Classification of Variables in Regression Analysis

Y	$X_1, X_2 \ldots X_k$
(a) Predictand	Predictors
(b) Regressand	Regressors
(c) Explained variable	Explanatory variables
(d) Dependent variable	Independent variables
(e) Effect variable	Causal variables
(f) Endogenous variable	Exogenous variables
(g) Target variable	Control variables

Each of the terms in the table is relevant for a particular view of regression analysis. Terminology (a) is used if the purpose is prediction. For instance, sales might be the *predictand* and advertising expenditures the *predictor*. The terminology in (b), (c) and (d) is used by different people in their discussion of regression models and is largely equivalent. Terminology (e) is used in studies of causation. Terminology (f) is specific to time-series econometrics and should be used with great care (Engle, Hendry and Richard, 1983, "Exogeneity", *Econometrica*, Vol 51, for example, argue that exogeneity should be redefined in terms of weak, strong and super exogeneity). Finally, terminology (g) is used in control problems. For instance, our objective might be to achieve a certain level of sales (target variable) and we would like to determine the level of advertising expenditures (control variable) required to achieve that objective.

7.3.2 Doing Regression Analysis in SPSS

To run regression analysis in SPSS, click on Analyse, Regression, Linear. You will then need to select your dependent (i.e. 'explained') variable and independent (i.e. 'explanatory') variables. If you click OK once you've entered your variables, you will end up with a series of output tables including a **Model Summary** (details on the overall goodness of fit as measured by R square), **ANOVA** (Analysis of Variance), and **Coefficients** (the estimates of the slope and intercept terms).

Example 7.3.2 Building an Automatic Valuation Model

Suppose you have been commissioned by Her Majesty's Valuation Office to construct an automatic valuation model (AVM) of residential dwellings. The model will be used to help with the forthcoming Council Tax revaluation when a reliable and up-to-date valuation will be needed of every residential property in England and Wales. Sending out Chartered Surveyors to each and every property was deemed infeasible, and so a cheaper computer-based system is being sought. You have been given a sample of house price data – avmdata.sav – with which to build your model. You start off by exploring the relationship between purchase price and the floor area of a house. You reason that the larger the floor area, the more valuable the property, which suggests the following relationship (assumed to be linear) between house price and floor area:

House price = $\alpha + \beta$ Floor area + ε

If we run this regression in SPSS using the data provided,

```
GET FILE='C:\STATISTICS\avmdata.sav'.
REGRESSION /DEPENDENT purchase /METHOD=ENTER floorare .
```

we would get the following Model Summary output:

Model Summary

Model	R	R Square	Adjusted R Square	Std. Error of the Estimate
1	.721[a]	.519	.519	26925.177

a. Predictors: (Constant), Floor Area (sq meters)

The Model Summary table includes the *R Square*, which tells you the proportion of the dependent variable that your independent variables explain (in this case = 0.519 = 51.9%). If you have more than one explanatory variable you should use the *Adjusted R Square* which controls for the fact that the R-square will rise each time you add an additional variable, even if there is no real gain in the explanatory power of the model.

The second table produced by the regression procedure is the Analysis of Variance (ANOVA) table:

ANOVA[b]

Model		Sum of Squares	df	Mean Square	F	Sig.
1	Regression	4.3E+11	1	4.341E+11	598.724	.000[a]
	Residual	4.0E+11	554	724965158.6		
	Total	8.4E+11	555			

a. Predictors: (Constant), Floor Area (sq meters)

b. Dependent Variable: Purchase Price

The most useful information in the ANOVA table at this stage is the *F-statistic*. This tests the H_0 that all slope coefficients are jointly equal to zero. It is another summary test of the whole model and is related to the R Square measure. If "Sig" is small, you can confidently reject the null. Also useful is the *total degrees of freedom* which tells you at a glance how many observations were included in the model (in this case 555+1).

The third and most important table in the output is the Coefficients table:

Coefficients[a]

Model		Unstandardized Coefficients B	Unstandardized Coefficients Std. Error	Standardized Coefficients Beta	t	Sig.
1	(Constant)	-10029.0	3242.545		-3.093	.002
	Floor Area (sq meters)	638.825	26.108	.721	24.469	.000

a. Dependent Variable: Purchase Price

This table tells you the estimated value of the intercept – labelled *Constant* in SPSS output – and of the slope coefficient – in this case we only have one independent variable and so only one slope coefficient is produced (for Floor Area). The estimated values of the intercept and slope coefficient are listed under the column headed *B* in the table. The t statistic tests the hypothesis that B = zero and is calculated by dividing B by the Standard Error of B, which is listed in column three. If Sig. is small – less than 0.05 say – then you can confidently reject the null that B = 0.

While the Constant term is occasionally of interest, it is usually the slope coefficient(s) that we are most interested in. In the above example, the coefficient on Floor Area equals 638.8, which tells us that as the floor area of a house rises by one square metre, the value of the house rises by £638.8. So the slope coefficient is measured and interpreted in terms of the scale used for the dependent variable (which in this case is pounds sterling). Because the t value is large for the slope coefficient (resulting in a small significance level = 0.000), we can reject the null hypothesis that the slope coefficient = 0 (i.e. that there is no relationship between house price and floor area). Similarly, the *t* value is large for the intercept term, and so we can reject the null hypothesis that the slope coefficient is zero.

Exercise 7.3.2 Regression Analysis

1. Using data from **avmdata.sav**, do a scatter plot of the relationship between purchase price and floor area. Comment on the plot and then insert a linear line of best-fit. How well do you think the regression line fits the data? Use the **REGRESSION /DEPENDENT purchase /METHOD=ENTER floorare.** syntax to run a linear regression to obtain the numerical values of the relationship. What does the statistical output tell you about the relationship?

2. Run a 3-D Scatter plot with floor spikes using the following menu sequence: Graphs, Scatter, Simple, and Define. Place purchase price on the Y axis, floorarea on the X axis and number of bathrooms on the Z axis,

then click OK or Paste. Alternatively you can use the following syntax: **GRAPH /SCATTERPLOT(XYZ)=floorare WITH purchase WITH bathroom.**

To include the floor spikes, double click on the graph, then right-click on the data points in the body of the graph, select Properties Window, select Spikes, Floor, Apply and Close.

Now try viewing the graph from different angles by using the 3-D rotation facility. To rotate the graph in, right-click on the data points in the graph, and select Properties Window, and 3-D Rotation. Try changing the horizontal view (move the slider and click Apply). Comment on the graph and run a regression equation with the second explanatory variable included. Has the inclusion of the extra variable added anything to the explanatory power of the model? Try replacing it with number of bedrooms and comment on your results.

3. Experiment with a number of 2-explanatory variable models, comparing the 3-D scatter plot with the regression output. Then experiment with more than 2 explanatory variables.

7.3.3 Confidence Intervals for Regression Coefficients

Suppose we want to compute confidence intervals for α and β (i.e. the intercept and slope coefficient). You will recall from the work we did on inference for a single variable that the confidence intervals for the population mean are calculated as follows.

To find the *K* percent confidence interval estimate of the population mean using the *t*-distribution, first find a value t_i such that Prob($-t_i < t < t_i$) = *K*, with degrees of freedom = $n-1$. Then calculate the confidence interval using the following formula:

$$\mu = \bar{x} \pm t_i \frac{s}{\sqrt{n}}$$

where

$\bar{x}$	=	the sample mean
s	=	the sample standard deviation
n	=	the sample size.
t_I	=	critical value of t such that, Prob($-t_i < t < t_i$) = *K*, where *K* is the desired confidence level (e.g. 0.95).

You will also remember that $s/\sqrt{n}$ was simply an approximation for the standard error of the sample mean, $SE_{\bar{x}}$, which is the name we give to the standard deviation of means from repeated samples (we don't usually know the standard deviation of the sampling distribution of the mean and so we used $s/\sqrt{n}$ to approximate it).

More generally, we can write:

Population parameter we are trying to estimate = estimate ± $SE_{estimate}$

The population parameter we are trying to estimate might be the mean or a proportion of a single variable, or it might be the *slope coefficient* in a regression model. It follows, then, that you can calculate the confidence interval for the population value of β using the following formula:

$$\beta = b \pm t_i SE_b$$

where:

b	=	*B* in SPSS notation = sample estimate of the population value of the slope coefficient β
SE_b	=	standard error of *b*.
t_i	=	critical value of t such that that Prob($-t_i < t < t_i$) = *K*, where *K* is the desired confidence level (e.g. 0.95), with degrees of freedom = $n-1$.

The calculation of the SE_b is quite complicated (particularly when there is more than one explanatory variable), but thankfully we rarely need to compute this by hand as SPSS churns this out in its standard output (see Moore and McCabe, 2003, section 10.2 if you want to know the basic formula).

Rule of Thumb:
Provided your sample size is reasonably large (say more than 25) you can use $t = 2$ as a rough guess for the value of t_i associated with the 95% confidence interval. You will notice from the tables that as n increases it converges to the z value for the 95% confidence interval, which is 1.96. Below a sample size of 25, you will notice the critical value for t for the 95% confidence interval rises to about 2.1 for 20 observations, 2.3 for 10 observations, and 2.8 for 5 observations. So, a useful rule of thumb for reasonably large samples is to say that:

We are 95% sure that the population value of the slope coefficient is roughly equal to the sample estimate of the slope plus or minus twice the standard error:

$$\beta \approx b \pm 2 \times SE_b$$

Example 7.3.3 Applying the Rule of Thumb for Confidence Interval Estimation on b

Below is the output from a regression of floor area on number of bathrooms:

Coefficients[a]

Model		Unstandardized Coefficients		Standardized Coefficients	t	Sig.
		B	Std. Error	Beta		
1	(Constant)	40.928	4.700		8.708	.000
	Number of Bathrooms	64.622	3.819	.584	16.920	.000

a. Dependent Variable: Floor Area (sq meters)

We can calculate the confidence interval on the slope coefficient using our *rule of thumb* as follows:

$$\beta = 64.6 \pm 2 \times 3.8$$
$$= 64.6 \pm 7.6$$

In other words, the 95% confidence interval for the population slope coefficient is (57, 72).

7.3.4 Confidence Intervals in SPSS

We can check this using the built-in facility in SPSS to compute confidence intervals for slope coefficients. In the linear regression window (Analyse, Regression, Linear), click on Statistics and select Confidence intervals. Then click Continue and (assuming you have already selected your dependent and independent variables) finally click OK

Alternatively, you could use the following syntax:

```
REGRESSION /STATISTICS COEFF OUTS CI R ANOVA /DEPENDENT floorare
/METHOD=ENTER bathroom.
```

The regression output should now include an augmented Coefficients table with the lower and upper bounds of the confidence interval in the final two columns. As you can see from the table below our approximation of the interval using our rule of thumb was fairly accurate. SPSS finds the 95% interterval for the slope coefficient on bathrooms to be 57.120 to 72.123. That is to say, we are 95% sure that a regression run on the population of house sales would find that an extra bathroom raises the floorarea of a house by between 57.12 m^2 and 72.123m^2.

This sounds implausible at first – few of us have bathrooms quite so large! But think carefully what this coefficient is telling us. Houses with two bathrooms tend to be larger overall. And houses with three bathrooms larger still. So this coefficient is not telling us the average size of bathroom, but how much larger the *overall* house size tends to be when there is an additional bathroom. We need to be careful when interpreting coefficients!

Coefficients[a]

Model		Unstandardized Coefficients B	Unstandardized Coefficients Std. Error	Standardized Coefficients Beta	t	Sig.	95% Confidence Interval for B Lower Bound	95% Confidence Interval for B Upper Bound
1	(Constant)	40.928	4.700		8.708	.000	31.697	50.160
	Number of Bathrooms	64.622	3.819	.584	16.920	.000	57.120	72.123

a. Dependent Variable: Floor Area (sq meters)

Note that if you wish to suppress the ANOVA table or the Model Summary table, or any of the STATISTICS options, you simply delete it from the above syntax. For example, if you run the following syntax,

```
REGRESSION /STATISTICS CI /DEPENDENT floorare /METHOD=ENTER bathroom.
```

you end up with a rather more manageable table:

Coefficients[a]

Model		95% Confidence Interval for B Lower Bound	95% Confidence Interval for B Upper Bound
1	(Constant)	31.697	50.160
	Number of Bathrooms	57.120	72.123

a. Dependent Variable: Floor Area (sq meters)

We could also apply our rule of thumb to the intercept term (labelled the 'Constant' in SPSS output):

$$\begin{aligned} \alpha &= a && \pm 2 \times SE_a \\ &= 40.9 && \pm 2 \times 4.7 \\ &= 40.9 && \pm 9.4 \end{aligned}$$

which gives the 95% confidence interval for the intercept as (31.5, 50.3), which is again confirmed when we compare it to the SPSS estimate of the interval: (31.697, 50.160).

Exercise 7.3.4 Comparing SPSS Confidence Intervals with those Derived from the Rule of Thumb

1. Use the rule of thumb to calculate the 95% confidence interval for the slope and intercept terms in the regression of purchase price on floor area. Confirm your results by comparing them with the SPSS estimates of the confidence intervals.

2. Run a regression of purchase price on two explanatory variables: floor area and number of bathrooms. Comment on the meaning of the intercept and slope estimates and calculate the 95% confidence intervals.

7.3.5 OLS Assumptions (also called the Gauss-Markov theorem)

In order for the OLS estimates of α and β to be BLUE, a number of conditions have to be met. Below we list the conditions and we also state briefly what happens when these conditions are not met. See an econometrics text such as Peter Kennedy's (1994) *A Guide to Econometrics* (Cambridge, MA: MIT Press), or Gwilym Pryce's (2006) *Advanced Regression in SPSS* (GeeBeeJey Publishing, Glasgow), for a more detailed explanation of what happens when these conditions fail.

i) *Equation is Correctly Specified*

That is, the equation:
a) Is linear (Failure implies *functional form misspecification*)
b) Contains all relevant variables
c) Contains no irrelevant variables
d) Contains only variables that are measured without error

Failure to correctly specify the regression equation can make the estimates for α and β biased and *inconsistent* (estimates are only *consistent* if, as the sample size increases, the variance tends to zero and the means of the repeated estimates tend towards the population values for α and β).

ii) *Error Term has Zero Mean*

That is, the long run average (called the *expected value*) of the error term equals zero:
$E(\varepsilon_i) = 0$ for all i.
(Failure implies non zero mean)

iii) *Error Term has Constant Variance (Homoscedasticity)*

That is, Var $(\varepsilon_i) = \sigma^2$, where σ^2 is constant for all i.
(Failure implies Heteroscedasticity).

If heteroscedasticity exists, the OLS estimates of α and β will remain unbiased and consistent (provided the other OLS conditions are met), but the estimated standard errors of the coefficients (see below) and F statistic will be biased. This will distort the computation of the t and F statistics. Heteroscedasticity can be caused by a non-constant coefficient (eg $\beta_i = \beta + \varepsilon_i$), omitted variables, or the aggregation methods used for certain variables.

There are a number of detection tests for heteroscedasticity (eg Glejser, Goldfield Quandt, Breusch Pagan), each one detecting a different form of heteroscedasticity. The G-Q (Goldfield Quandt) test, for example, tests for heteroscedasticity of the form:

σ^2 *is monotonically related to variable* Z_i

To run the G-Q test, first order all observations of all variables in the regression according to Z_i, and omit p central observations. Then fit separate regressions to both lower (n_1) and upper (n_2) sets of observations. The test statistic G is then calculated from RSS_2 / RSS_1 (assuming σ^2_i is positively related to variable Z_i) which has an F distribution of the form F [((n-p)/2-k), ((n-p)/2-k)]. If G is greater than the critical value (chosen from the tables) for F, then the null hypothesis of no heteroscedasticity is rejected.

iv) *No Autocorrelation*

This assumption is necessary if we are using time series data. The condition requires the current period's error term to be uncorrelated with error terms from previous periods.

v) *Explanatory Variables are Fixed Regressors*

That is, $X_1, X_2 \ldots X_k$ are non-random (ie they are fixed in repeated samples as in an experiment). Failing this, we can do the regression analysis conditional on the regressors. This allows the regressors to be stochastic, but assumes that they are uncorrelated with the error term. If this assumption breaks down we have the problem of *simultaneity*, which implies that the estimates of α and β are not consistent.

vi) *Data Matrix has Full Rank*

That is, there is no linear dependence between the RHS variables. Failure implies perfect multicolinearity which means that OLS is not possible. More common is imperfect multicolinearity, which results in estimates being unstable across sample sizes.

More specialist texts, such as Gwilym Pryce's (2006) *Advanced Regression in SPSS*, consider in more detail what happens when these assumptions fail, how to test whether they have failed, and what remedies (if any) are available. Full treatment of these topics is beyond the scope of the current textbook, so why raise them here? We have included the above summary of regression assumptions as a caveat; to remind ourselves that the reliability of any regression we estimate, rests on the extent to which these assumptions are met. Regression results should be treated with a degree of caution, therefore, if you cannot verify that your data do indeed meet these requirements.

7.4 Guide to Regression Terms

Even the basic regression facility in SPSS churns out a plethora of outputs, and offers a rather bewildering array of options. In this final section on regression analysis we briefly summarise the meaning of the key terms used in the options windows and output tables.

What follows is not intended to be a comprehensive account, but a basic reference source to help you find your way around the rudimentary regression facilities that SPSS has to offer (it also offers lots of sophisticated facilities and techniques that are beyond our current remit). Combined with the Help facilities built into SPSS, these descriptions should be sufficient to help you reach a reasonable understanding of your regression output though, as we have already indicated, you need to refer to a more specialised text if you want to take things further.

i) Listwise Deletion of Missing Data

Missing values can be dealt with using the listwise method of deletion; cases that have missing values for any of the variables named are omitted from the analysis, therefore the regression uses only the cases with valid values for all variables.

Alternative methods of dealing with missing values include: **pairwise deletion of missing data** (ie SPSS calculates each correlation coefficient using all the cases with valid values for the two variables being correlated) and **replace with mean** (SPSS substitutes the mean value of the variable for missing values).

ii) Blocks

One can control the entry of independent variables into the analysis in two ways: 1] by grouping them in **blocks**; and 2] by choosing the **method** by which the variables in each block are processed (see iii) below). Concerning the former, one can divide the construction of a final regression model into blocks. Each block starts with the final model of the previous block, if there was one, and adds or removes independent variables according to the specified method. The final model becomes the starting point for the next block, if there is one.

iii) Method:

a) ENTER Method.
This is the standard (and simplest) method for estimating a regression equation. All variables for the block are added as a group for the equation. If ENTER is used in a subsequent block, the variables for that block are added as a group for the final model for the preceding block.

b) *REMOVE Method.*
REMOVE is a method which takes variables out of a regression analysis. It is used in a block after the first. The variables for the remove block, as a group, are taken out of the final model for the preceding block.

c) *STEPWISE Method.*
This method adds and removes individual variables according to the criteria chosen until a model is reached in which no more variables are eligible for entry or removal. Two different sets of criteria can be used, either,

1) Probability of F. This is the default method. A variable is entered if the significance level of its F-to-enter is less than the entry value, and is removed if the significance level is greater than the removal value. You can change the entry and removal thresholds with the proviso that the entry value must be less than the removal value.

Or,

2) *F*-Value. A variable is entered if its *F*-value is greater than the entry value, and is removed if the *F*-value is less than the removal value. The entry must be greater than the removal value.

d) *BACKWARD Method.*
This method removes individual variables according to the criteria for removal (see note on c) above) until a model is reached in which no more variables are eligible for removal. (If no variables are in the equation from a previous block, they are entered as a group and then removed individually).

e) *FORWARD Method.*
This method adds individual variables, according to the criteria set for entry (see note on c) above), until a model is reached in which no more variables are eligible for entry.

iv) Multiple R

The correlation coefficient between the observed and predicted values of the dependent variable. It ranges in value from 0 to 1. A small value indicates that there is little or no linear relationship between the dependent variable and the independent variables.

v) R-Squared

A measure of the goodness of fit of a linear model. It is sometimes called the *coefficient of determination*. It is the proportion of the variation in the dependent variable explained by the regression model. It is the square of the multiple R, the correlation of the observed and predicted values of the dependent variable. R^2 can also be calculated from ESS/TSS, where ESS is the explained sum of squares (also called the Regression sum of squares) and TSS is the total sum of squares (TSS = ESS + RSS; where RSS is the residual sum of squares). These terms are explained below under "Analysis of Variance". R^2 can range in value from 0 to 1. Small values indicate that the model does not fit the data well, and *vice versa*.

vi) Adjusted R-Squared

One of the problems of R-squared is that it tends to increase as the number of regressors increases. Consider the regression equation: $Y = \alpha + \beta X_1$ and assume that we only have three observations for X_1 and Y. Applying OLS will calculate the straight line of best fit between these three points on the scatter diagram. Assume that this estimated line has an R^2 of 0.8.

Now consider what happens if we add another explanatory variable, X_2 which also has only three observations. In adding another variable to the equation, we are effectively adding a third dimension to our graphical representation (imagine a scatter plot in 3-D). Note that we still only have three scatter points on our scatter diagram. Now OLS will fit the *plane* of best fit to the observations attained. But with only three observations for each variable, and hence only 3 scatter points in our three-dimensional scatter diagram, a plane can always be drawn through any three points in three-dimensional space (just as a straight line can always be drawn through any two points in 2-D). The consequence of this is that a plane of perfect fit will be drawn through these three points, yielding an R^2 of 1.00.

Thus the R^2 has increased from 0.8 to 1.00 simply because we have added another dimension to the graph, irrespective of whether the new variable has any role in explaining Y. The adjusted R-squared statistic adjusts for the number of variables in the equation.

vii) Analysis of Variance

To test the hypothesis that there is no linear relationship between X and Y, several equivalent statistics can be computed. When there is a single independent variable (Simple Regression), the hypothesis that the population $R^2 = 0$ is identical to the hypothesis that the population slope is 0. The test for $R^2 = 0$ can be obtained from the analysis of variance table: R^2 = explained sum of squares (also called the regression sum of squares) divided by the total sum of squares. We will now consider these terms in more detail.

The total observed variability in the dependent variable can be measured in terms of the *total* sum of squares, TSS. TSS is made up of the sum of two components, ESS (*explained* or *regression* sum of squares) and RSS (*residual* sum of squares):

$$TSS = ESS + RSS$$

This can be explained as follows: for a particular observation Y_i, the distance from Y_i to the mean of the Y's, Y^{bar}, can be divided into two parts,

$$Y_i - Y^{bar} = (Y_i - Y_i^{hat}) + (Y_i^{hat} - Y^{bar})$$

where Y_i^{hat} is the predicated value for Y at that point (ie given a particular X, Y_i^{hat} is the corresponding Y value determined by the OLS line). The distance from Y_i (the observed value) to Y_i^{hat} is called the *residual* from the regression. It is zero if the regression line passes through the point.

The second component $(Y_i^{hat} - Y^{bar})$ is the vertical distance from the regression point to the mean of the Y's. This distance is *explained* by the regression in that it represents the improvement in the estimate of the dependent variable achieved by the regression.

Now suppose we wish to gain some insight into how the *residuals* and *explained deviations* fair for the sample as a whole. We could sum $(Y_i - Y^{bar})$ and $(Y_i^{hat} - Y^{bar})$ for all i. However, negative deviations would cancel out positive deviations. The absolute values of the deviations could be used, but this poses particular problems when calculating other statistics based on the results. Hence, the most common method is to consider the *sum of squared deviations*. Thus we have:

$$\sum_{i=1}^{n}(Y_i - Y^{bar})^2 = \sum_{i=1}^{n}(Y_i - Y_i^{hat})^2 + \sum_{i=1}^{n}(Y_i^{hat} - Y^{bar})^2$$

Or as we had before,

$\sum_{i=1}^{n}(Y_i - Y^{bar})^2$ = TSS = the sum across the whole sample (from $i - 1$ to $i = n$) of the squared deviations of: the observed values (Y_i) from the mean value (Y_i^{bar}).

$\sum_{i=1}^{n}(Y_i^{hat} - Y^{bar})^2$ = ESS = the sum across the whole sample (from $i - 1$ to $i = n$) of the squared deviations of: the predicted values (Y_i^{hat}) from the mean value (Y^{bar}).

$$\sum_{i=1}^{n}(Y_i - Y_i^{\text{hat}})^2 = \text{RSS} =$$

the sum across the whole sample (from $i - 1$ to $i = n$) of the squared deviations of: the observed values (Y_i) from the predicted values (Y_i^{hat}).

The *mean square* for each entry is the sum of squares divided by the degrees of freedom (*df*). If the regression assumptions are met, the ratio of the *mean square regression* to the *mean square residual* is distributed as an F-distribution, with k and $n - k - 1$ degrees of freedom (where k is the number of parameters being estimated). F serves to test how well the regression model fits the data. If the probability associated with F is small, the hypothesis that $R^2 = 0$ is rejected. With just one regressor, the square root of the calculated F value is equivalent to the t statistic for the slope coefficient.

viii) Standard Error

In SPSS output, this is the standard error of the estimate (also called the standard error of the regression), which is calculated as the square root of the residual mean square. The predicted Y values Y^{hat} can be viewed as □+□x plus some error term, e_i equal to $Y_i - Y_i^{\text{hat}}$. The standard error of the regression is thus the estimated standard deviation of the error term. It is the standard deviation of the Y values about the estimated regression line and is often used as a summary measure of the *goodness of fit* of the estimated regression line. The lower standard error of the regression, the better *cet par*.

ix) *F*-Statistic

The F-statistic presented in the ANOVA table tests the null hypothesis that there is no linear relationship between the dependent and independent variables. That is, it tests the null hypothesis that all slope coefficients equal zero:

$$H_0: \beta_1 = \beta_2 = \beta_3 = ... = \beta_k = 0$$

It is thus a test of the *joint significance* of the regressors, as opposed to the t-statistics which test for the individual significance of each regressor. If the significance level of the F-statistic is less than 5%, then H_0 is rejected (see below).

x) Significance of *F*

This is also called the *Probability of F*, and measures the observed significance level of F. If this probability is small enough, the null by hypothesis that there is no linear relationship between dependent and independent variables is rejected. If Sig $F < 0.05$, then there is less than a 1 in 20 chance of making a Type I error (i.e. of rejecting the null of no relationship when in fact the null hypothesis is correct). If the chances of rejecting the null incorrectly are small, then we can confidently reject it.

xi) B

This is the OLS estimator for the slope coefficient of a particular regressor. It is BLUE and consistent if the Gauss-Markov conditions are fulfilled.

xii) SE B

That is, the standard error of B, the OLS estimator. This is the estimated standard deviation of the regression coefficient.

xiii) Beta

The Beta coefficient output from SPSS (sometimes called standardized regression coefficients), are the regression coefficients when all variables are expressed in standardized (Z-score) form. Transforming the independent variables to standardized form makes the coefficients more comparable since differences in the units of measurement are eliminated. However, the Beta coefficients do not in any absolute sense reflect the importance of the various independent variables since they depend on the other variables in the equation.

xiv) *T* or *t*

In regression analysis, the t value for a particular coefficient, *b*, is calculated as:

$$t = \text{coefficient / Standard Error of the coefficient}$$
$$= b / SE_b$$

It is used to test the null hypothesis that $b_k = 0$, where k is the kth coefficient. For example,

H_0: $\beta_1 = 0$
H_1: $\beta_1 \neq 0$

This is a two-tailed test because under the alternative hypothesis, β can be less or greater than zero. If the alternative hypothesis was formulated as: H_1: $\beta_1 > 0$, then we would have an upper-tail test, and if the alternative hypothesis was formulated as: H_1: $\beta_1 < 0$, then we would have a lower-tail test. The standard output from SPSS only offers the two-tailed significance level.

The rule to decide whether the null hypothesis is accepted or rejected goes as follows: *Reject H_0 if and only if the significance value associated with the t-test in SPSS is less than 0.05.*

xv) Sig t

That is, the significance of t, also called the probability of t. As noted above, the standard SPSS output presents only the two-tailed significance level of t. The smaller the Sig t, the more confidence we have that β, the coefficient, is significantly different from zero. If Sig t < 0.025, for example, then we can reject the H_0 knowing that there is less than a 1 in 40 chance of having rejected it incorrectly.

7.5 Conclusion

This chapter began with an examination of how to test for the existence of a relationship between two categorical variables. We employed two-way tables and a Chi-square test to help us verify whether two categorical variables are independent or contingent. We then went on to consider regression analysis as a means of examining possible relationships between a single continuous dependent variable and one or more independent variables. We looked at the interpretation of basic regression output and tried to summarise the vast array of output and terminology.

This chapter has also brought us to the end of our course in social and business statistics. We set ourselves a difficult challenge at the outset: to learn both introductory statistics and the widely used statistics package, SPSS. If you have worked carefully through the examples and exercises, you should by now have a good grasp of how to do applied statistics.

Some students graduate from a course in statistics feeling more determined than ever to avoid working with "children, animals or data" (a quote we referred to in the very first paragraph of Chapter 1). Hopefully this will not be true in your case. Hopefully learning statistics and SPSS in an integrated way, as we have attempted in this book, will leave you with sufficient confidence to make tentative steps towards doing your own analysis and even to delve deeper into the nether regions of SPSS. Even if your immediate research does not require statistical analysis, it will certainly be worth keeping-up your statistical and SPSS skills. Learning statistics is *not* like riding a bicycle – the knowledge will not stay with you unless you apply it. It's a case of *use it or lose it.*

We have made extensive use of macros in this book and although the mechanics of those macros have largely been in the background, I hope that the course will have provided you with a taster of how useful macros can be. Sites such as www.spsstools.net offer new routines, automated tasks, and thousands of extra facilities that greatly expand the versatility of the standard SPSS package. Having learnt the basics of SPSS syntax, you should now have sufficient knowledge to make use of some of these resources, and perhaps even make the first steps towards creating a few of your own.

Note also that SPSS comes supplied with lots of reference and learning materials, some of which are more useful than others. If you want to develop your knowledge of syntax (highly recommended – see the summary of advantages listed in Chapter 1) then a particularly useful document is the **spssbase.pdf** file, which should have come supplied with your SPSS software. Depending on how you have installed your version of SPSS, you will find a link to this file in the Help menu (click on Help and then select Command Syntax Reference and a PDF document of the same title should open automatically). If not, you should be able to find the file on the CD that you used to install the software. **spssbase.pdf** is the definitive guide to SPSS syntax, and is updated with each new version of SPSS. At the last count, it had nearly two thousand pages, but it is fairly easy to find your way around do to the hyperlinked index and bookmark system. If you are interested in learning how to write macros, you should note that there is an appendix at the end of the document that introduces the basic principles of macro-programming.

Anyhow, good luck with your future statistical research and please don't hesitate to pass on any suggestions you may have as to how the book could be improved (email g@geebeejey.co.uk).

Appendix 1 Macro Programs

This appendix provides a copy of the QUANTSCOMMANDS.SPS file available from the *Downloads* page of www.geebeejey.co.uk.

```
*========================================.
*Macros for "Inference and Statistics in SPSS", .
*by G. Pryce, GeeBeeJey Publishing.
* Version: 2nd Sept 2005.
*========================================.

*========================================.
* Copyright (c) 2005 Gwilym Pryce.
*========================================.

DEFINE pz_lt_zi (!POSITIONAL !ENCLOSE('(',')')).
GET FILE='C:\QUANTS\one.sav'.
compute Zi_Var = !1 .
COMPUTE PROB = CDFNORM(Zi_Var).
EXECUTE.
MATRIX.
GET PROB_VAR /VARIABLES = PROB.
GET Zi_Var /VARIABLES = Zi_Var.
COMPUTE Prob = PROB_VAR(1).
COMPUTE zi = Zi_Var(1).
COMPUTE ANSWER = {zi, PROB}.
PRINT ANSWER / FORMAT "F10.5" /Title = " Prob(z < zi) for a given zi " / CLABELS = zi, Prob.
END MATRIX.
!ENDDEFINE.

DEFINE pz_gt_zi (!POSITIONAL !ENCLOSE('(',')')).
GET FILE='C:\QUANTS\one.sav'.
compute Zi_Var = !1 .
COMPUTE PROB = 1 - CDFNORM(Zi_Var).
EXECUTE.
MATRIX.
GET PROB_VAR /VARIABLES = PROB.
GET Zi_Var /VARIABLES = Zi_Var.
COMPUTE Prob = PROB_VAR(1).
COMPUTE zi = Zi_Var(1).
COMPUTE ANSWER = {zi, PROB}.
PRINT ANSWER / FORMAT "F10.5" /Title = " Prob(z > zi) for a given zi " / CLABELS = zi, Prob.
END MATRIX.
!ENDDEFINE.

DEFINE pz_lg_zi (zil = !ENCLOSE('(',')')  / ziu =  !ENCLOSE('(',')')).
GET FILE='C:\QUANTS\one.sav'.
compute ZiL_Var = !zil .
compute ZiU_Var = !ziu .
EXECUTE.
COMPUTE PROBL = CDFNORM(ZiL_Var).
COMPUTE PROBU = 1 - CDFNORM(ZiU_Var).
COMPUTE PROBLG = PROBL + PROBU.
EXECUTE.
MATRIX.
GET PROB_VAR /VARIABLES = PROBLG.
GET ZiL_Var /VARIABLES = ZiL_Var.
GET ZiU_Var /VARIABLES = ZiU_Var.
COMPUTE Prob = PROB_VAR(1).
COMPUTE ziL = ZiL_Var(1).
COMPUTE ziU = ZiU_Var(1).
COMPUTE ANSWER = {ziL, ziU, PROB}.
PRINT ANSWER / FORMAT "F10.5" /Title = " Prob((z < ziL) OR (z > ziU)) for a given zi " / CLABELS = ziL, ziU, Prob.
END MATRIX.
!ENDDEFINE.
```

```
DEFINE pz_gl_zi (zil = !ENCLOSE ('(',')') / ziu = !ENCLOSE('(',')')).
GET FILE='C:\QUANTS\one.sav'.
compute ZiL_Var = !zil .
compute ZiU_Var = !ziu .
EXECUTE.
COMPUTE PROBL = CDFNORM(ZiL_Var).
COMPUTE PROBU = 1 - CDFNORM(ZiU_Var).
COMPUTE PROBLG = 1 - (PROBL + PROBU).
EXECUTE.
MATRIX.
GET PROB_VAR /VARIABLES = PROBLG.
GET ZiL_Var /VARIABLES = ZiL_Var.
GET ZiU_Var /VARIABLES = ZiU_Var.
COMPUTE Prob = PROB_VAR(1).
COMPUTE ziL = ZiL_Var(1).
COMPUTE ziU = ZiU_Var(1).
COMPUTE ANSWER = {ziL, ziU, PROB}.
PRINT ANSWER / FORMAT "F10.5" /Title = " Prob(ziL < z < ziU) for a given zi " / CLABELS = ziL, ziU, Prob.
END MATRIX.
!ENDDEFINE.

DEFINE zi_lt_zp (p = !ENCLOSE('(',')')).
GET FILE='C:\QUANTS\one.sav'.
COMPUTE Zi = PROBIT(!p).
EXECUTE.
MATRIX.
GET Zi_VAR /VARIABLES = Zi.
COMPUTE Zi = Zi_VAR(1).
COMPUTE PROB= {!p}.    /*Enter the given probability into the curly brackets*/
COMPUTE ANSWER = {Zi, PROB}.
PRINT ANSWER / FORMAT "F10.5" /Title = " Value of zi such that Prob(z < zi) = PROB when PROB is given" /
CLABELS = zi, PROB.
END MATRIX.
!ENDDEFINE.

DEFINE zi_gt_zp (p = !ENCLOSE('(',')')).
GET FILE='C:\QUANTS\one.sav'.
COMPUTE Zi = PROBIT(1-!p).
EXECUTE.
MATRIX.
GET Zi_VAR /VARIABLES = Zi.
COMPUTE Zi = Zi_VAR(1).
COMPUTE PROB= {!p}.    /*Enter the given probability into the curly brackets*/
COMPUTE ANSWER = {Zi, PROB}.
PRINT ANSWER / FORMAT "F10.5" /Title = " Value of zi such that Prob(z > zi) = PROB when PROB is given" /
CLABELS = zi, PROB.
END MATRIX.
!ENDDEFINE.


DEFINE zi_gl_zp (p = !ENCLOSE('(',')')).
GET FILE='C:\QUANTS\one.sav'.
COMPUTE PROB = !p.
COMPUTE PROBLG = 1 - !p.
COMPUTE PROBL = PROBLG / 2.
COMPUTE ZiL_Var = PROBIT(PROBL).
COMPUTE ZiU_Var = -1 * ZiL_Var .
EXECUTE.
MATRIX.
GET PROB_VAR /VARIABLES = PROB.
GET ZiL_Var /VARIABLES = ZiL_Var.
GET ZiU_Var /VARIABLES = ZiU_Var.
COMPUTE Prob = PROB_VAR(1).
COMPUTE ziL = ZiL_Var(1).
COMPUTE ziU = ZiU_Var(1).
COMPUTE ANSWER = {ziL, ziU, PROB}.
PRINT ANSWER / FORMAT "F10.5" /Title = " Value of zi such that Prob(-zi < z < zi)  = PROB, when PROB is given  " /
CLABELS = ziL, ziU, Prob.
END MATRIX.
!ENDDEFINE.
```

```
DEFINE CI_L1M (n = !ENCLOSE('(',')') /x_bar = !ENCLOSE('(',')') /s = !ENCLOSE('(',')') /c = !ENCLOSE('(',')')).
GET FILE='C:\QUANTS\one.sav'.
COMPUTE PROB = !c.
COMPUTE PROBLG = 1 - !c.
COMPUTE PROBL = PROBLG / 2.
COMPUTE ZiL = PROBIT(PROBL).
COMPUTE ZiU = -1 * ZiL .
EXECUTE.
MATRIX.
COMPUTE n       = {!n}.      /* Enter the sample size here (i.e. change the number in curly brackets)*/
COMPUTE x_bar   = {!x_bar}.  /* Enter the sample mean here*/
COMPUTE s       = {!s}.      /* Enter the sample standard deviation here*/
COMPUTE SE = s/SQRT(n).
GET ZiL /VARIABLES = ZiL.
COMPUTE ERR = -ZiL * SE.
COMPUTE LOWER = x_bar - err.
COMPUTE UPPER = x_bar + err.
COMPUTE ANSWER = {n, x_bar, ZiL, SE, err, Lower, Upper}.
PRINT ANSWER / FORMAT "F10.5" /Title = "Large sample confidence interval for the population mean" / CLABELS =
n, x_bar, ZiL, SE, err, Lower, Upper.
END MATRIX.
!ENDDEFINE.


DEFINE CI_S1M (n = !ENCLOSE('(',')') /x_bar = !ENCLOSE('(',')') /s = !ENCLOSE('(',')') /c = !ENCLOSE('(',')')).
GET FILE='C:\QUANTS\one.sav'.
COMPUTE df = !n - 1.
COMPUTE PROB = !c.
COMPUTE PROBLG = 1 - !c.
COMPUTE PROBL = PROBLG / 2.
COMPUTE TiL = IDF.T(PROBL, df).
COMPUTE TiU = -1 * TiL .
EXECUTE.
MATRIX.
COMPUTE n       = {!n}.      /* Enter the sample size here (i.e. change the number in curly brackets)*/
COMPUTE x_bar   = {!x_bar}.  /* Enter the sample mean here*/
COMPUTE s       = {!s}.      /* Enter the sample standard deviation here*/
COMPUTE SE = s/SQRT(n).
GET TiL /VARIABLES = TiL.
GET df /VARIABLES = df.
COMPUTE ERR = -TiL * SE.
COMPUTE LOWER = x_bar - err.
COMPUTE UPPER = x_bar + err.
COMPUTE ANSWER = {n, x_bar, TiL, SE, err, Lower, Upper}.
PRINT ANSWER / FORMAT "F10.5" /Title = "Small sample confidence interval for the population mean" / CLABELS =
n, x_bar, TiL, SE, err, Lower, Upper.
END MATRIX.
!ENDDEFINE.


DEFINE CI_S2Mp (n1 = !ENCLOSE('(',')') /n2 = !ENCLOSE('(',')') /x_bar1 = !ENCLOSE('(',')') /x_bar2 =
!ENCLOSE('(',')') /s1 = !ENCLOSE('(',')') /s2 = !ENCLOSE('(',')') /c = !ENCLOSE('(',')')).
GET FILE='C:\QUANTS\one.sav'.
COMPUTE df = !n1 + !n2 - 2.
COMPUTE PROB = !c.
COMPUTE PROBLG = 1 - !c.
COMPUTE PROBL = PROBLG / 2.
COMPUTE TiL = IDF.T(PROBL, df).
COMPUTE TiU = -1 * TiL .
EXECUTE.
MATRIX.
GET df / variables = df.      /* Enter the df here (i.e. change the number in curly brackets)*/
COMPUTE x_bar1    = {!x_bar1}.  /* Enter the sample mean here*/
COMPUTE x_bar2    = {!x_bar2}.  /* Enter the sample mean here*/
COMPUTE sp = SQRT(( (!n1 - 1)* !s1**2 + (!n2 - 1) * !s2**2 ) / (!n1 + !n2 - 2) ).
COMPUTE SE = sp*(SQRT((1/!n1) + (1/!n2))).
GET TiL /VARIABLES = TiL.
GET df /VARIABLES = df.
COMPUTE ERR = -TiL * SE.
COMPUTE SAMPDIFF = x_bar1 - x_bar2.
COMPUTE LOWER = SAMPDIFF - err.
COMPUTE UPPER = SAMPDIFF + err.
COMPUTE ANSWER = {SAMPDIFF, SP, TiL, SE, err, Lower, Upper}.
PRINT ANSWER / FORMAT "F10.5" /Title = "CI for the difference between 2 population means (pooled variance)" /
CLABELS = SAMPDIFF, SP, TiL, SE, err, Lower, Upper.
END MATRIX.
!ENDDEFINE.
```

```
DEFINE CI_S2Md (n1 = !ENCLOSE('(',')') /n2 = !ENCLOSE('(',')') /x_bar1 = !ENCLOSE('(',')') /x_bar2 = !ENCLOSE('(',')') /s1 = !ENCLOSE('(',')') /s2 = !ENCLOSE ('(',')') /c = !ENCLOSE('(',')')).
GET FILE='C:\QUANTS\one.sav'.
COMPUTE df = min((!n1 -1), (!n2 - 1)).
COMPUTE PROB = !c.
COMPUTE PROBLG = 1 - !c.
COMPUTE PROBL = PROBLG / 2.
COMPUTE TiL = IDF.T(PROBL, df).
COMPUTE TiU = -1 * TiL .
EXECUTE.
MATRIX.
GET df / variables = df.        /* Enter the df here (i.e. change the number in curly brackets)*/
COMPUTE x_bar1    =  {!x_bar1}.  /* Enter the sample mean here*/
COMPUTE x_bar2    =  {!x_bar2}.  /* Enter the sample mean here*/
COMPUTE SE = SQRT((!s1**2/!n1) + (!s2**2/!n2)).
GET TiL /VARIABLES = TiL.
GET df /VARIABLES = df.
COMPUTE ERR = -TiL * SE.
COMPUTE SAMPDIFF = x_bar1 - x_bar2.
COMPUTE LOWER = SAMPDIFF - err.
COMPUTE UPPER = SAMPDIFF + err.
COMPUTE ANSWER = {SAMPDIFF, TiL, SE, err, Lower, Upper}.
PRINT ANSWER / FORMAT "F10.5" /Title = "CI for the difference between 2 population means (different variances)" / CLABELS = SAMPDIFF, TiL, SE, err, Lower, Upper.
END MATRIX.
!ENDDEFINE.
```

```
DEFINE CI_L1P (n = !ENCLOSE ('(',')') /x = !ENCLOSE('(',')') /c = !ENCLOSE('(',')')).
GET FILE='C:\QUANTS\one.sav'.
COMPUTE PROB = !c.
COMPUTE PROBLG = 1 - !c.
COMPUTE PROBL = PROBLG / 2.
COMPUTE ZiL = PROBIT(PROBL).
COMPUTE ZiU = -1 * ZiL .
EXECUTE.
MATRIX.
COMPUTE n = !n.        /* Enter the sample size here */
COMPUTE x = !x.        /* Enter the number of "successes" or particular outcomes here */
COMPUTE CONFID = !c.  /* Enter the desired confidence level here */
COMPUTE pTrad = x/n.              /* the traditional estimate of the pop. proportion used in CI estimation */
COMPUTE pWlsn = (x+2)/(n + 4).  /* the Wilson estimate */
GET zstar /VARIABLES = ZiL.
COMPUTE SE_Trad = SQRT((pTrad*(1-pTrad))/n).
COMPUTE SE_Wlsn = SQRT((pWlsn*(1-pWlsn))/(n+4)).
COMPUTE eTrad = -zstar * SE_Trad.
COMPUTE eWlsn = -zstar * SE_Wlsn.
COMPUTE LOW_Trad = pTrad - eTrad.
COMPUTE LOW_Wlsn = pWlsn - eWlsn.
COMPUTE UP_Trad = pTrad + eTrad.
COMPUTE UP_Wlsn = pWlsn + eWlsn.
COMPUTE ANSWER = {pTrad, zstar, se_trad, etrad, low_trad, up_trad}.
PRINT ANSWER / FORMAT "F10.6" /Title = "Traditional Large sample CI for one proportion" / CLABELS = ptrad, zstar, se_trad, etrad, low_trad, up_trad.
COMPUTE ANSWER = {pWlsn, zstar, se_wlsn, ewlsn, low_wlsn, up_wlsn}.
PRINT ANSWER / FORMAT "F10.6" /Title = "Wilson Large sample CI for one proportion" / CLABELS = pwlsn, zstar, se_wlsn, ewlsn, low_wlsn, up_wlsn.
END MATRIX.
!ENDDEFINE.
```

```
DEFINE N_L1M (e = !ENCLOSE('(',')') /c = !ENCLOSE('(',')') /s = !ENCLOSE('(',')')).
GET FILE='C:\QUANTS\one.sav'.
COMPUTE PROB = !c.
COMPUTE E = !E.
COMPUTE PROBLG = 1 - !c.
COMPUTE PROBL = PROBLG / 2.
COMPUTE ZiL_Var = PROBIT(PROBL).
COMPUTE ZiU_Var = -1 * ZiL_Var .
COMPUTE N = (ZiL_Var**2) * (!s**2) / (!e**2).
EXECUTE.
MATRIX.
GET PROB_VAR /VARIABLES = PROB.
GET N / VARIABLES = N.
GET E / VARIABLES = E.
GET ZiL_Var /VARIABLES = ZiL_Var.
GET ZiU_Var /VARIABLES = ZiU_Var.
COMPUTE Prob = PROB_VAR(1).
COMPUTE ziL = ZiL_Var(1).
COMPUTE ziU = ZiU_Var(1).
COMPUTE ANSWER = {e, PROB, ziL, ziU, N}.
PRINT ANSWER / FORMAT "F10.5" /Title = "n_hat = estimated sample size needed to achieve an error of size e given
c" / CLABELS = e, c, ziL, ziU, n_hat.
END MATRIX.
!ENDDEFINE.


DEFINE H_L1M (n = !ENCLOSE('(',')') / x_bar = !ENCLOSE('(',')') / m = !ENCLOSE('(',')') / s = !ENCLOSE('(',')') ).
GET FILE='C:\QUANTS\one.sav'.
COMPUTE x_bar = !x_bar.
COMPUTE m = !m.
COMPUTE s = !s.
COMPUTE n = !n.
COMPUTE zi = (!x_bar - !m) / (!s /sqrt(!n)) .
EXECUTE.
* This calculates the Large sample Significance Test for a Single Population mean.
MATRIX.
GET ZI / VARIABLES = zi.
GET X_BAR / VARIABLES = X_BAR.
GET N / VARIABLES = N.
GET S / VARIABLES = S.
COMPUTE SE = S / (SQRT(N)).
COMPUTE SIGz_2TL = 2 * (1 - CDFNORM(ABS(Zi))).
COMPUTE SIGz_LTL = CDFNORM(Zi).
COMPUTE SIGz_UTL = 1 - CDFNORM(Zi).
COMPUTE ANSWER = {n, x_bar, SE, zi, SIGz_2TL, SIGz_LTL, SIGz_UTL}.
PRINT ANSWER / FORMAT "F10.5" /Title = "Large sample sig. test for one mean" / CLABELS = n, x_bar, SE, zi,
SIGz_2TL, SIGz_LTL, SIGz_UTL.
END MATRIX.
!ENDDEFINE.


DEFINE H_S1M (n = !ENCLOSE('(',')') / x_bar = !ENCLOSE('(',')') / m = !ENCLOSE('(',')') / s = !ENCLOSE('(',')')).
GET FILE='C:\QUANTS\one.sav'.
COMPUTE x_bar = !x_bar.
COMPUTE m = !m.
COMPUTE s = !s.
COMPUTE n = !n.
COMPUTE ti = (!x_bar - !m) / (!s /sqrt(!n)) .
EXECUTE.
MATRIX.
GET TI / VARIABLES = ti.
GET X_BAR / VARIABLES = X_BAR.
GET N / VARIABLES = N.
GET S / VARIABLES = S.
COMPUTE SE = S / (SQRT(N)).
COMPUTE SIGt_2TL = 2 * (1 - TCDF(ABS(ti), n-1)).
COMPUTE SIGt_LTL = TCDF(ti, n-1).
COMPUTE SIGt_UTL = 1 - TCDF(ti, n-1).
COMPUTE ANSWER = {n, x_bar, SE, ti, SIGt_2TL, SIGt_LTL, SIGt_UTL}.
PRINT ANSWER / FORMAT "F10.5" / /Title = "Small sample sig. test for one mean" / CLABELS = n, x_bar, SE, ti,
SIGt_2TL, SIGt_LTL, SIGt_UTL.
END MATRIX.
!ENDDEFINE.
```

```
DEFINE H_S2Mp (n1 = !ENCLOSE('(',')') / n2 = !ENCLOSE('(',')') / x_bar1 = !ENCLOSE('(',')') / x_bar2 = !ENCLOSE('(',')') / s1 = !ENCLOSE('(',')') / s2 = !ENCLOSE('(',')') ).
GET FILE='C:\QUANTS\one.sav'.
MATRIX.
COMPUTE n1 = {!n1}. /* Enter the first sample size here */
COMPUTE n2 = {!n2}. /* Enter the second sample size here */
COMPUTE x_bar1 = {!x_bar1}. /* Enter the mean of sample 1 here */
COMPUTE x_bar2 = {!x_bar2}. /* Enter the mean of sample 2 here */
COMPUTE s1 = {!s1}. /* Enter the first standard deviation here*/
COMPUTE s2 = {!s2}. /* Enter the  second standard deviation here*/
COMPUTE sp = SQRT(((n1-1)*s1**2+(n2-1)*s2**2)/(n1 + n2 -2)).
COMPUTE x1b_x2b = x_bar1 - x_bar2.
COMPUTE SE = sp * SQRT((1/n1)+(1/n2)).
COMPUTE ti = (x_bar1 - x_bar2) /SE.
COMPUTE df = n1 + n2 -2.
COMPUTE SIGt_2TL = 2 * (1 - TCDF(ABS(ti), df)).
COMPUTE SIGt_LTL = TCDF(ti, df).
COMPUTE SIGt_UTL = 1 - TCDF(ti, df).
COMPUTE ANSWER = {df, x1b_x2b, SE, ti, SIGt_2TL, SIGt_LTL, SIGt_UTL}.
PRINT ANSWER / FORMAT "F10.5" /Title = "Equal vars Indep samples t-test for equal means (H0 pop1ave = pop2ave)" / CLABELS = df, x1b_x2b, SE, ti, SIGt_2TL, SIGt_LTL, SIGt_UTL.
END MATRIX.
!ENDDEFINE.
```

```
DEFINE H_S2Md (n1 = !ENCLOSE('(',')') / n2 = !ENCLOSE('(',')') / x_bar1 = !ENCLOSE('(',')') / x_bar2 = !ENCLOSE('(',')') / s1 = !ENCLOSE('(',')') / s2 = !ENCLOSE('(',')') ).
GET FILE='C:\QUANTS\one.sav'.
COMPUTE n1 = !n1.
COMPUTE n2 = !n2.
COMPUTE x_bar1 = !x_bar1.
COMPUTE x_bar2 = !x_bar2.
COMPUTE s1 = !s1.
COMPUTE s2 = !s2.
COMPUTE SE = SQRT((s1**2/n1)+(s2**2/n2)).
COMPUTE x1b_x2b = x_bar1 - x_bar2.
COMPUTE ti = (x_bar1 - x_bar2) /SE.
COMPUTE df1 = n1 -1.
COMPUTE df2 = n2 - 2.
COMPUTE df = MIN(df1, df2).
COMPUTE SIGt_2TL = 2 * (1 - CDF.T(ABS(ti), df)).
COMPUTE SIGt_LTL = CDF.T(ti, df).
COMPUTE SIGt_UTL = 1 - CDF.T(ti, df).
EXECUTE.
MATRIX.
GET TI / VARIABLES = ti.
GET x1b_x2b / VARIABLES = x1b_x2b .
GET df / VARIABLES = df.
GET SE / VARIABLES = SE.
GET SIGt_2TL / VARIABLES = SIGt_2TL.
GET SIGt_LTL / VARIABLES = SIGt_LTL.
GET SIGt_UTL / VARIABLES = SIGt_UTL.
COMPUTE ANSWER = {df, x1b_x2b, SE, ti, SIGt_2TL, SIGt_LTL, SIGt_UTL}.
PRINT ANSWER / FORMAT "F10.6" /Title = "Uneq vars Indep samples t-test for equality of means (H0 pop1ave = pop2ave)" / CLABELS = df, x1b_x2b, SE, ti, SIGt_2TL, SIGt_LTL, SIGt_UTL.
END MATRIX.
!ENDDEFINE.
```

```
DEFINE H_S2VF (n1 = !ENCLOSE('(',')') / n2 = !ENCLOSE('(',')') / s1 = !ENCLOSE('(',')') / s2 = !ENCLOSE('(',')') ).
GET FILE='C:\QUANTS\one.sav'.
COMPUTE n1 = !n1.
COMPUTE n2 = !n2.
COMPUTE s1 = !s1.
COMPUTE s2 = !s2.
EXECUTE.
DO IF (s1 GE s2) .
COMPUTE V_nmrtor = s1 * s1.
COMPUTE V_dnmtor = s2 * s2.
COMPUTE n_nmrtor = n1 - 1.
COMPUTE n_dnmtor = n2 - 1.
ELSE IF (s1 LT s2) .
COMPUTE V_nmrtor = s2 * s2.
COMPUTE V_dnmtor = s1* s1.
COMPUTE n_nmrtor = n2 -1.
COMPUTE n_dnmtor = n1 - 1.
END IF.
COMPUTE Fc = V_nmrtor / V_dnmtor.
COMPUTE SIGF_UTL = 1 - CDF.F(Fc, n_nmrtor, n_dnmtor).
EXECUTE.
MATRIX.
GET V_nmrtor / VARIABLES = V_nmrtor .
GET V_dnmtor / VARIABLES =  V_dnmtor .
GET n_nmrtor  / VARIABLES = n_nmrtor  .
GET n_dnmtor  / VARIABLES = n_dnmtor  .
GET Fc / VARIABLES = Fc .
GET SIGF_UTL / VARIABLES = SIGF_UTL .
COMPUTE ANSWER = {V_nmrtor, V_dnmtor, n_nmrtor, n_dnmtor, Fc, SIGF_UTL}.
PRINT ANSWER / FORMAT "F10.5" /Title = "F-Test for equality of variance (H0 V_nmrtor = V_dnmtor)" / CLABELS =
V_nmrtor, V_dnmtor, df_nmrtor, df_dnmtor, Fc, SIGF_UTL.
END MATRIX.
!ENDDEFINE.
```

```
DEFINE H_L1P (n = !ENCLOSE('(',')') / x = !ENCLOSE('(',')') / pi = !ENCLOSE('(',')') ).
GET FILE='C:\QUANTS\one.sav'.
MATRIX.
COMPUTE n = {!n}.  /* Enter the sample size here */
COMPUTE x = {!x}.   /* Enter the number of "successes" or particular outcomes here */
COMPUTE pi = {!pi}.  /* Enter the hypothesised value for the population proportion /*
COMPUTE p = x/n.
COMPUTE s2 = pi*(1-pi).
COMPUTE SE_pi = SQRT(s2/n).
COMPUTE z = (p - pi) /SE_pi.
COMPUTE SIGz_2TL = 2 * (1 - CDFNORM(ABS(Z))).
COMPUTE SIGz_LTL = CDFNORM(Z).
COMPUTE SIGz_UTL = 1 - CDFNORM(Z).
COMPUTE ANSWER = {n, p, SE_pi, z, SIGz_2TL, SIGz_LTL, SIGz_UTL}.
PRINT ANSWER / FORMAT "F10.5" /Title = "Large sample sig. test for one proportion" / CLABELS = n, p, SE_pi, z,
SIGz_2TL, SIGz_LTL, SIGz_UTL.
END MATRIX.
!ENDDEFINE.
```

```
DEFINE H_L2P (n1 = !ENCLOSE('(',')') / n2 = !ENCLOSE('(',')') / x1 = !ENCLOSE('(',')') / x2 = !ENCLOSE('(',')')).
GET FILE='C:\QUANTS\one.sav'.
MATRIX.
COMPUTE n1 = {!n1}.  /* Enter the first sample size here */
COMPUTE n2 = {!n2}.  /* Enter the second sample size here */
COMPUTE x1 = {!x1}.  /* Enter the number of "successes" or particular outcomes for sample 1 here */
COMPUTE x2 = {!x2}. /* Enter the number of "successes" or particular outcomes for sample 2 here */
COMPUTE p1 = x1/n1.
COMPUTE p2 = x2/n2.
COMPUTE phat = (x1 + x2) / (n1 + n2).
COMPUTE SE_phat = SQRT(phat * (1 - phat) * ((1/n1) + (1/n2))).
COMPUTE z = (p1 - p2) /SE_phat.
COMPUTE SIGz_2TL = 2 * (1 - CDFNORM(ABS(z))).
COMPUTE SIGz_LTL = CDFNORM(Z).
COMPUTE SIGz_UTL = 1 - CDFNORM(Z).
COMPUTE ANSWER = {p1, p2, SE_phat, z, SIGz_2TL, SIGz_LTL, SIGz_UTL}.
PRINT ANSWER / FORMAT "F10.5" /Title = "Large sample sig. test for two proportions" / CLABELS = p1, p2, SE, z,
SIGz_2TL, SIGz_LTL, SIGz_UTL.
END MATRIX.
!ENDDEFINE.
```

```
DEFINE CLT (variable = !ENCLOSE('(',')') /nsample = !ENCLOSE('(',')') /Npop = !ENCLOSE('(',')') /reps =
!ENCLOSE('(',')') ).
!DO !L = 1 !TO !reps.
- TITLE !reps Repeated Samples of size !nsample .
- temporary.
- sample !nsample from !Npop.
- MATRIX.
- GET VARIABLE / VARIABLES = !variable.
- COMPUTE N = NROW(VARIABLE).
- COMPUTE I = MAKE(n,1,1).
- COMPUTE X_BAR = (1/N)*(TRANSPOS(I) * VARIABLE).
- SAVE {X_BAR} / OUTFILE =!CONCAT('CLT__', !variable, '_sample', !L, '.sav') /VARIABLES = X_BAR.
- END MATRIX.
!DOEND.
GET FILE= !CONCAT('CLT__', !variable, '_sample', '1.sav').
!DO !J = 2 !TO !reps.
- ADD FILES /FILE=*
/FILE=!CONCAT('CLT__', !variable, '_sample', !J, '.sav').
- EXECUTE.
!DOEND.
SAVE / OUTFILE =!CONCAT('CLT__n', !nsample, !variable, '_sample', 'ALL', !reps, '.sav') .
TITLE !reps Repeated Samples of size !nsample .
GRAPH /HISTOGRAM=X_BAR /TITLE= 'Histogram of Sample Means from Repeated Samples'.
TITLE !reps Repeated Samples of size !nsample .
DESCRIPTIVES VARIABLES=X_BAR /STATISTICS=MEAN STDDEV MIN MAX .
!ENDDEFINE.
```

Appendix 2: Installation Instructions

This appendix provides a copy of the installation instructions text-file available from the *Downloads* page of www.geebeejey.co.uk.

*=====================================.
* Installation Instructions for
* SPSS MACROS for Basic Inference.
* Version: 16th Sept2005
*=====================================.

You need 4 files to fully install and run the macros:

one.sav
QUANTSCOMMANDS.SPS
QUANTSMACROCALL.SPS
QUANTSCOMMANDSUMMARY

Instructions for installing these files are given below.

*--.
*STEP 1. CREATE A FOLDER ON YOUR HARD DISK CALLED: C:\QUANTS\
*--.

You need to create a folder called "QUANTS" in the root
directory of your C: drive.

You can create this folder using Windows Explorer or My Computer
or some other similar program.

We shall assume below that you have managed to create this new folder,
so that it can be referenced exactly as:

C:\QUANTS\

If you are unable to create this folder, see note at the end of this document.

*--.
*STEP 2. COPY THE FILES INTO THE C:\QUANTS FOLDER:
*--.

Assuming you have been able to create the C:\QUANTS\ folder,
you should now download the 4 files listed above into that folder.

These files are available from the Downloads page of www.geebeejey.co.uk.

These four files are explained below:

one.sav
*--------.
This is simply an SPSS data file with just one observation in the
first cell equal to 1.
Most of the macros open this file before attempting any calculations
because SPSS requires a valid data file to be open before any computations
can be run.

Note that the macros will tell SPSS to open this file without saving any
existing data file you have open, so you should SAVE AND CLOSE ANY DATA FILE
BEFORE RUNNING THE MACROS.

QUANTSCOMMANDS.SPS
*-----------------.
This is the file with all the macros in (macros are mini computer programs
that enhance the facilities SPSS in some way). This file
needs to run every time you open SPSS otherwise none of the commands
will work. It can either be opened manually (by going to the file
menu, opening the QUANTSCOMMANDS.SPS syntax file, selecting all and running
all), or (preferably) by running the following QUANTSMACROCALL.SPS file
(see below).

QUANTSMACROCALL.SPS
*-----------------.
This is the "macro call" file and simply has one line in it (copied below)
to tell SPSS to run the QUANTSCOMMANDS.SPS file:

INCLUDE FILE = 'C:\QUANTS\QUANTSCOMMANDS.sps'.

Note that it assumes that you've placed the QUANTSCOMMANDS.SPS file in a folder called "C:\QUANTS\" which will need to be created in Windows Explorer or My Computer as noted above.

*QUANTSCOMMANDSUMMARY
*-------------------.

The third file is not essential but you might find it useful as a check that everything is working OK. It includes a summary of all the commands which you can use to test that all the macros are installed correctly.

*---.
*STEP 3. RUN THE QUANTSMACROCALL.SPS FILE EVERY TIME YOU OPEN UP SPSS.
*---.

Every time you open up SPSS you need to run the QUANTSMACROCALL.SPS file.

You only need to run the file once during any one SPSS session (once the macros are loaded into SPSS's memory, they remain there until you close SPSS).

You can either run the QUANTSMACROCALL.SPS file by opening it each time and selecting the running the syntax, or you can simply type and run the following,

INCLUDE FILE = 'C:\QUANTS\QUANTSCOMMANDS.sps'.

A third alternative is to open the QUANTSCOMMANDS.SPS file itself, select a particular macro (or all the macros, if you prefer), run it, and close the QUANTSCOMMANDS.SPS file.

A fourth, and preferred, alternative, is to customise the SPSS Menu bar as explained below.

*---.
*STEP 4. CUSTOMISE THE SPSS MENU BAR.
*---.

If you customise the SPSS menu bar it will make it a lot easier to run the macro call. Each window in SPSS -- the Data window, the Syntax window, and the Output window -- has its own menu bar, and each can be customised. Here's how to customise the Syntax menu bar:

(a) Open SPSS. Go to "Utilities", and select "Menu Editor" (this option is called "Edit menu" in earlier versions of SPSS).

(b) In the "Apply to:" box of the Menu Editor, select "Syntax".

(c) Now scroll down the list of Menu items in the left box of the Menu Editor, select "(End of Menu)" and click on the "Insert Menu" button on the right. Then type "&Macros" and press <Enter> on your keyboard to create a new Menu item.

(d) Click on the plus sign to the left of your new Macros menu item, click on "(End of Macros Menu)" and click on the "Insert Item" button on the right. Then type "&Inference" and press <Enter> on your keyboard to create a new Menu item.

(e) Under File Type in the centre box, click on "Syntax".

(f) Now select the QUANTSMACROCALL.SPS file as the file you want to run by clicking on the "Browse" button, go to the C:\QUANTS folder and select "QUANTSMACROCALL.SPS". Then click OK.

You have now added a new item to the menu bar of the syntax window. To run the macros, all you need to do is to open up a syntax file, click on "Macros", and select "Inference". The "macro call" will run, and all the macro commands should be available to you.

For example, if you open a new syntax file and type and run the following line,

```
pz_lt_zi      (-2.897) .
```

SPSS should calculate the probability that z is less than -2.897. The results should be posted to your output viewer in the following form:

```
Run MATRIX procedure:
Prob(z < zi) for a given zi
      zi      Prob
  -2.89700    .00188
```

*--.
*STEP 4. (OPTIONAL) OPEN AND RUN THE QUANTSCOMMANDSUMMARY.SPS FILE.
*--.

If you have correctly followed the above instructions, all the macro commands should run.

It's a good idea to check that you have installed everything correctly.

You can do this by opening the QUANTSCOMMANDSUMMARY syntax file, highlighting of all the sample commands and then run them. If you get any error messages, go through the above steps again. If you get stuck, email g@geebeejey.co.uk for advice.

*--.
WHAT TO DO IF YOU CANNOT CREATE THE C:\QUANTS\ FOLDER.
*--.

If you cannot place the QUANTS folder on your C: drive as suggested, but you can put it on another drive, you must edit the QUANTSCOMMANDS.SPS and QUANTSMACROCALL.SPS files accordingly (simply replace all references to "C:\QUANTS" with the folder name and location you have chosen). Both these files are just standard SPSS syntax files so you can open and edit them in SPSS. We recommend that you use search-and-replace to make the changes.

If you cannot create a QUANTS folder anywhere on your computer (for example, if you are using a lab-based PC), you can still use the macros, but you will need to open and run the macro file QUANTSCOMMANDS.SPS each time you open SPSS. You will also need to prevent the macros from telling SPSS to open the 'C:\QUANTS\one.sav' file. This is easy enough to do. Simply enter an asterisk before the line in each of the macros that says GET FILE='C:\QUANTS\one.sav'. For example, you would edit the pz_lt_zi macro so that it looks like this (only thing that has changed is the start of line two):

```
DEFINE pz_lt_zi (!POSITIONAL !ENCLOSE('(',')')).
*GET FILE='C:\QUANTS\one.sav'.
compute Zi_Var = !1 .
COMPUTE PROB = CDFNORM(Zi_Var).
EXECUTE.
MATRIX.
GET PROB_VAR /VARIABLES = PROB.
GET Zi_Var /VARIABLES = Zi_Var.
COMPUTE Prob = PROB_VAR(1).
COMPUTE zi = Zi_Var(1).
COMPUTE ANSWER = {zi, PROB}.
PRINT ANSWER / FORMAT "F10.5" /Title = " Prob(z < zi) for a given zi " / CLABELS = zi, Prob.
END MATRIX.
!ENDDEFINE.
```

Then save your edited QUANTSCOMMANDS.SPS under a new name and remember where you've saved it so that you can use it next time. (To use it, simply open it, highlight all the macro commands, and run them. The commands will then be available for you to use, provided you have a data file open with at least one cell of data).

If you get stuck, email g@geebeejey.co.uk for advice.

Appendix 3: Macro Command Summary

This appendix provides a copy of the QUANTSCOMMANDSUMMARY.SPS syntax file available from the *Downloads* page of www.geebeejey.co.uk.

```
*==============================================================================.
* SELECT AND RUNNING COMMAND LINES.
*==============================================================================.
*Note that you should only select lines with command text on it (not the headings or any lines beginning with " * ").
*So, to run a command, simply edit the figures in brackets according to the problem you are trying to solve and select the line using the mouse (or Shift+arrow keys),
*and then click the arrow on the toolbar (or press "Ctrl+R").
*If you want to run several commands in one go, remove all headings first  or any lines beginning with " * ". For example, the following set of commands lists all the examples included in this .
*document.  If you select them all as one block and then run, they should all run:.

pz_lt_zi     (-2.897) .
pz_gt_zi     (-2.897) .
pz_lg_zi     zil=(-2)     ziu=(2).
pz_gl_zi     zil=(-2)     ziu=(2).
zi_lt_zp     p=(0.005).
zi_gt_zp     p=(0.005).
zi_gl_zp     p=(0.95) .
CI_L1M     n=(45)      x_bar=(22.2)   s=(7) c=(0.95).
CI_S1M     n=(15)      x_bar=(22.2)   s=(7) c=(0.95).
CI_S2Mp  n1=(10)      n2=(12)        x_bar1=(100)   x_bar2=(94)   s1=(30)   s2=(31)   c=(.95).
CI_S2Md  n1=(10)      n2=(12)        x_bar1=(100)   x_bar2=(94)   s1=(30)   s2=(31)   c=(.95).
CI_L1P     n=(4040)  x=(2048)       c=(.99).

N_L1M     e=(2)       c=(.95)        s=(37).

H_L1M     n=(107)    x_bar=(10.92)   m=(11)          s=(0.28).
H_S1M    n=(107)    x_bar=(10.92)   m=(11)          s=(0.28).
H_S2Mp  n1=(22)    n2=(27)          x_bar1=(33.4)   x_bar2=(40.1)  s1=(22.4)  s2=(22).
H_S2Md  n1=(22)    n2=(27)          x_bar1=(33.4)   x_bar2=(40.1)  s1=(22.4)  s2=(42).
H_L1P     n=(102)    x=(70)           pi=(0.78).
H_L2P     n1=(22)    n2=(19)          x1=(7)          x2=(9) .
H_S2VF  n1=(39)    n2=(42)          s1=(40198)      s2=(46125).

*==============================================================================.
* CALCULATING Z SCORES.
*==============================================================================.
*pz_lt_zi  Calculates the probability that z is less than zi.
*eg.
pz_lt_zi (-1.897) .

*pz_gt_zi Calculates the probability that z is greater than zi.
*eg.
pz_gt_zi (1.3897) .

*pz_lg_zi Calculates the probability that z is less than ziL or greater than ziU.
*eg.
pz_lg_zi zil=(-2) ziu=(2).

*pz_gl_zi Calculates the probability that z is greater than ziL AND less than ziU.
*eg.
pz_gl_zi zil=(-2) ziu=(2).

*zi_lt_zp  Calculates the value of zi such that Prob(z < zi) = PROB for a given PROB.
*eg.
zi_lt_zp p = (0.005).

*zi_gt_zp Calculates the value of zi such that Prob(z > zi) = PROB for a given PROB.
*e.g.
zi_gt_zp p = (0.005).

*zi_gl_zp Calculates the value of zi such that Prob(-zi < z < zi)  = PROB, when PROB is given .
*e.g.
zi_gl_zp p=(0.95) .
```

```
*==================================================================================.
* CONFIDENCE INTERVALS AND SAMPLE SIZE DETERMINATION.
*==================================================================================.
*CI_L1M            Large sample CI for one mean (M&M pp.417-424) .
*eg.
CI_L1M n=(45) x_bar=(22.2) s=(7) c=(0.95).

*CI_S1M            Small sample CI for one mean (M&M p.494) .
*eg.
CI_S1M n=(15) x_bar=(22.2) s=(7) c=(0.95).

*CI_S2Mp           Small Independent Samples CI for differences between 2 means (pooled variance M&M p.538) .
*              (NB see the H8_S2VF command below to test whether the variances are the same or different).
*e.g.
CI_S2Mp  n1=(10)  n2=(12)  x_bar1=(100)  x_bar2=(94)  s1=(30)  s2=(31)  c=(.95).

*CI_S2Md           Small Independent Samples CI for differences between 2 means (different variances M&M p.532) .
*              (NB see the H8_S2VF command below to test whether the variances are the same or different).
*e.g.
CI_S2Md   n1=(10)  n2=(12)  x_bar1=(100)  x_bar2=(94)  s1=(30)  s2=(31)  c=(.95).


*CI_SMP Traditional & Wilson Large sample CI for a Single Proportion (M&M p. 572ff) .
*e.g.
CI_L1P   n=(4040)  x=(2048)  c=(.99).

*N_L1M  Sample size for desired margin or error of size, e, for the mean for a given confidence interval, c, and
standard deviation, s (M&M p.425).
*eg.
N_L1M  e=(2) c=(.95) s=(37).

*==================================================================================.
* HYPOTHESIS TESTS.
*==================================================================================.
*H_L1M  Large sample significance test on one mean (M&M pp. 444-447)
*eg.
H_L1M    n=(107)  x_bar=(10.92)   m=(11)   s=(0.28).

*H_S1M  Small sample significance test on one mean (M&M pp. 496-501)
*eg.
H_S1M  n=(107)  x_bar=(10.92)  m=(11)   s=(0.28).

*H_S2Mp Small Independent Samples significance test for equality of 2 means (pooled variance M&M pp.537-542)
*              (NB see the H8_S2VF command below to test whether the variances are the same or different).
*eg.
H_S2Mp    n1=(22)  n2=(27)  x_bar1=(33.4)  x_bar2=(40.1)  s1=(22.4)  s2=(22).

*H_S2Md Small Independent Samples significance test for equality of 2 means (different variances M&M pp.529-532)
*              (NB see the H8_S2VF command below to test whether the variances are the same or different).
*eg.
H_S2Md    n1=(22)  n2=(27)  x_bar1=(33.4)  x_bar2=(40.1)  s1=(22.4)  s2=(42).

*H_L1P   Large Sample significance test on one proportion (M&M pp. 575-577)
*eg.
H_L1P    n=(102)   x=(70)    pi=(0.78).

*H_L1P   Large Sample significance test on one proportion (M&M pp. 575-577)
*eg.
H_L1P    n=(22)   x=(7)   pi=(0.4).

*H_L2P   Large Samples significance test on two proportions (M&M pp. 591-592)
*eg.
H_L2P    n1=(22)    n2=(19) x1=(7)  x2=(9) .

*H_S2VF Simple Small sample F-test on equality of two variances (M&M p.554; see Levene's test in SPSS for more
sophisticated test of homogenous variances).
*eg.
H_S2VF   n1=(39)  n2=(42)  s1=(40198)  s2=(46125).
```

Appendix 4: Statistical Tables

Table A: Standard Normal Probabilities

Table B: *t*-Distribution Critical Values

Table A: Standard Normal Probabilities

Each entry in the body of the table is the area under the standard normal curve to the left of *z*.

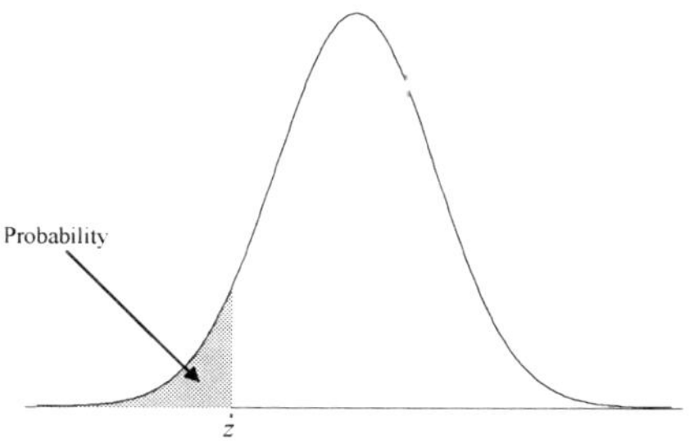

z	.00	.01	.02	.03	.04	.05	.06	.07	.08	.09
-3.40	.0003	.0003	.0003	.0003	.0003	.0003	.0003	.0003	.0003	.0002
-3.30	.0005	.0005	.0005	.0004	.0004	.0004	.0004	.0004	.0004	.0003
-3.20	.0007	.0007	.0006	.0006	.0006	.0006	.0006	.0005	.0005	.0005
-3.10	.0010	.0009	.0009	.0009	.0008	.0008	.0008	.0008	.0007	.0007
-3.00	.0013	.0013	.0013	.0012	.0012	.0011	.0011	.0011	.0010	.0010
-2.90	.0019	.0018	.0018	.0017	.0016	.0016	.0015	.0015	.0014	.0014
-2.80	.0026	.0025	.0024	.0023	.0023	.0022	.0021	.0021	.0020	.0019
-2.70	.0035	.0034	.0033	.0032	.0031	.0030	.0029	.0028	.0027	.0026
-2.60	.0047	.0045	.0044	.0043	.0041	.0040	.0039	.0038	.0037	.0036
-2.50	.0062	.0060	.0059	.0057	.0055	.0054	.0052	.0051	.0049	.0048
-2.40	.0082	.0080	.0078	.0075	.0073	.0071	.0069	.0068	.0066	.0064
-2.30	.0107	.0104	.0102	.0099	.0096	.0094	.0091	.0089	.0087	.0084
-2.20	.0139	.0136	.0132	.0129	.0125	.0122	.0119	.0116	.0113	.0110
-2.10	.0179	.0174	.0170	.0166	.0162	.0158	.0154	.0150	.0146	.0143
-2.00	.0228	.0222	.0217	.0212	.0207	.0202	.0197	.0192	.0188	.0183
-1.90	.0287	.0281	.0274	.0268	.0262	.0256	.0250	.0244	.0239	.0233
-1.80	.0359	.0351	.0344	.0336	.0329	.0322	.0314	.0307	.0301	.0294
-1.70	.0446	.0436	.0427	.0418	.0409	.0401	.0392	.0384	.0375	.0367
-1.60	.0548	.0537	.0526	.0516	.0505	.0495	.0485	.0475	.0465	.0455
-1.50	.0668	.0655	.0643	.0630	.0618	.0606	.0594	.0582	.0571	.0559
-1.40	.0808	.0793	.0778	.0764	.0749	.0735	.0721	.0708	.0694	.0681
-1.30	.0968	.0951	.0934	.0918	.0901	.0885	.0869	.0853	.0838	.0823
-1.20	.1151	.1131	.1112	.1093	.1075	.1056	.1038	.1020	.1003	.0985
-1.10	.1357	.1335	.1314	.1292	.1271	.1251	.1230	.1210	.1190	.1170
-1.00	.1587	.1562	.1539	.1515	.1492	.1469	.1446	.1423	.1401	.1379
-.90	.1841	.1814	.1788	.1762	.1736	.1711	.1685	.1660	.1635	.1611
-.80	.2119	.2090	.2061	.2033	.2005	.1977	.1949	.1922	.1894	.1867
-.70	.2420	.2389	.2358	.2327	.2296	.2266	.2236	.2206	.2177	.2148
-.60	.2743	.2709	.2676	.2643	.2611	.2578	.2546	.2514	.2483	.2451
-.50	.3085	.3050	.3015	.2981	.2946	.2912	.2877	.2843	.2810	.2776
-.40	.3446	.3409	.3372	.3336	.3300	.3264	.3228	.3192	.3156	.3121
-.30	.3821	.3783	.3745	.3707	.3669	.3632	.3594	.3557	.3520	.3483
-.20	.4207	.4168	.4129	.4090	.4052	.4013	.3974	.3936	.3897	.3859
-.10	.4602	.4562	.4522	.4483	.4443	.4404	.4364	.4325	.4286	.4247
0.0	.5000	.4960	.4920	.4880	.4840	.4801	.4761	.4721	.4681	.4641

Table B: *t*-Distribution Critical Values

Each entry in the body of the table is the critical value, t_c, associated with area in the lower-tail of the *t*-distribution.

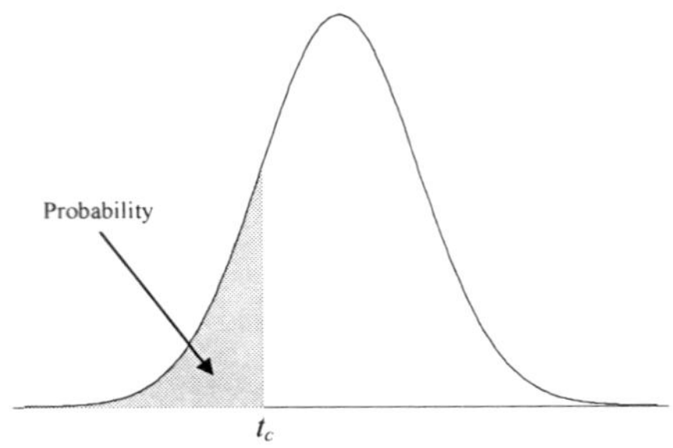

df	Lower-Tail Probability											
	0.250	0.200	0.150	0.100	0.050	0.025	0.020	0.010	0.005	0.0025	0.001	0.0005
1	-1.000	-1.376	-1.963	-3.078	-6.314	-12.706	-15.895	-31.821	-63.657	-127.321	-318.309	-636.619
2	-0.816	-1.061	-1.386	-1.886	-2.920	-4.303	-4.849	-6.965	-9.925	-14.089	-22.327	-31.599
3	-0.765	-0.978	-1.250	-1.638	-2.353	-3.182	-3.482	-4.541	-5.841	-7.453	-10.215	-12.924
4	-0.741	-0.941	-1.190	-1.533	-2.132	-2.776	-2.999	-3.747	-4.604	-5.598	-7.173	-8.610
5	-0.727	-0.920	-1.156	-1.476	-2.015	-2.571	-2.757	-3.365	-4.032	-4.773	-5.893	-6.869
6	-0.718	-0.906	-1.134	-1.440	-1.943	-2.447	-2.612	-3.143	-3.707	-4.317	-5.208	-5.959
7	-0.711	-0.896	-1.119	-1.415	-1.895	-2.365	-2.517	-2.998	-3.499	-4.029	-4.785	-5.408
8	-0.706	-0.889	-1.108	-1.397	-1.860	-2.306	-2.449	-2.896	-3.355	-3.833	-4.501	-5.041
9	-0.703	-0.883	-1.100	-1.383	-1.833	-2.262	-2.398	-2.821	-3.250	-3.690	-4.297	-4.781
10	-0.700	-0.879	-1.093	-1.372	-1.812	-2.228	-2.359	-2.764	-3.169	-3.581	-4.144	-4.587
11	-0.697	-0.876	-1.088	-1.363	-1.796	-2.201	-2.328	-2.718	-3.106	-3.497	-4.025	-4.437
12	-0.695	-0.873	-1.083	-1.356	-1.782	-2.179	-2.303	-2.681	-3.055	-3.428	-3.930	-4.318
13	-0.694	-0.870	-1.079	-1.350	-1.771	-2.160	-2.282	-2.650	-3.012	-3.372	-3.852	-4.221
14	-0.692	-0.868	-1.076	-1.345	-1.761	-2.145	-2.264	-2.624	-2.977	-3.326	-3.787	-4.140
15	-0.691	-0.866	-1.074	-1.341	-1.753	-2.131	-2.249	-2.602	-2.947	-3.286	-3.733	-4.073
16	-0.690	-0.865	-1.071	-1.337	-1.746	-2.120	-2.235	-2.583	-2.921	-3.252	-3.686	-4.015
17	-0.689	-0.863	-1.069	-1.333	-1.740	-2.110	-2.224	-2.567	-2.898	-3.222	-3.646	-3.965
18	-0.688	-0.862	-1.067	-1.330	-1.734	-2.101	-2.214	-2.552	-2.878	-3.197	-3.610	-3.922
19	-0.688	-0.861	-1.066	-1.328	-1.729	-2.093	-2.205	-2.539	-2.861	-3.174	-3.579	-3.883
20	-0.687	-0.860	-1.064	-1.325	-1.725	-2.086	-2.197	-2.528	-2.845	-3.153	-3.552	-3.850
21	-0.686	-0.859	-1.063	-1.323	-1.721	-2.080	-2.189	-2.518	-2.831	-3.135	-3.527	-3.819
22	-0.686	-0.858	-1.061	-1.321	-1.717	-2.074	-2.183	-2.508	-2.819	-3.119	-3.505	-3.792
23	-0.685	-0.858	-1.060	-1.319	-1.714	-2.069	-2.177	-2.500	-2.807	-3.104	-3.485	-3.768
24	-0.685	-0.857	-1.059	-1.318	-1.711	-2.064	-2.172	-2.492	-2.797	-3.091	-3.467	-3.745
25	-0.684	-0.856	-1.058	-1.316	-1.708	-2.060	-2.167	-2.485	-2.787	-3.078	-3.450	-3.725
26	-0.684	-0.856	-1.058	-1.315	-1.706	-2.056	-2.162	-2.479	-2.779	-3.067	-3.435	-3.707
27	-0.684	-0.855	-1.057	-1.314	-1.703	-2.052	-2.158	-2.473	-2.771	-3.057	-3.421	-3.690
28	-0.683	-0.855	-1.056	-1.313	-1.701	-2.048	-2.154	-2.467	-2.763	-3.047	-3.408	-3.674
29	-0.683	-0.854	-1.055	-1.311	-1.699	-2.045	-2.150	-2.462	-2.756	-3.038	-3.396	-3.659
30	-0.683	-0.854	-1.055	-1.310	-1.697	-2.042	-2.147	-2.457	-2.750	-3.030	-3.385	-3.646
40	-0.681	-0.851	-1.050	-1.303	-1.684	-2.021	-2.123	-2.423	-2.704	-2.971	-3.307	-3.551
50	-0.679	-0.849	-1.047	-1.299	-1.676	-2.009	-2.109	-2.403	-2.678	-2.937	-3.261	-3.496
60	-0.679	-0.848	-1.045	-1.296	-1.671	-2.000	-2.099	-2.390	-2.660	-2.915	-3.232	-3.460
80	-0.678	-0.846	-1.043	-1.292	-1.664	-1.990	-2.088	-2.374	-2.639	-2.887	-3.195	-3.416
100	-0.677	-0.845	-1.042	-1.290	-1.660	-1.984	-2.081	-2.364	-2.626	-2.871	-3.174	-3.390
1,000	-0.675	-0.842	-1.037	-1.282	-1.646	-1.962	-2.056	-2.330	-2.581	-2.813	-3.098	-3.300
z^*	-0.674	-0.842	-1.036	-1.282	-1.645	-1.960	-2.054	-2.326	-2.576	-2.807	-3.090	-3.291

Lightning Source UK Ltd.
Milton Keynes UK
08 October 2009

144677UK00001B/14/P

9 780955 143304